Waking Up In
ICELAND

Printed in the United Kingdom by MPG Books Ltd, Bodmin, Cornwall

Published by Sanctuary Publishing Limited, Sanctuary House, 45–53 Sinclair Road,
London W14 0NS, United Kingdom

www.sanctuarypublishing.com

ISBN: 1-86074-460-5

Waking Up In
ICELAND

Paul Sullivan

Sanctuary

About The Author

Paul Sullivan has been writing about music, travel and culture for the last five years. His reviews, articles and photographs have appeared in a range of respected newspapers, magazines and Internet publications such as *The Independent*, *The Wire*, *Dazed And Confused*, *Sleazenation*, *Muzik*, *DJ*, *XLR8R*, *7*, *Dotmusic*, *Amazon*, *iDJ*, *Hip-Hop Connection*, *Knowledge*, *Touch*, *Urb* and *BPM*. Sullivan's writing and photography work have taken him all over the world, covering music scenes and cultural movements in places such as South Africa, Cuba, Brazil, Southeast Asia, North America, New Zealand, Australia and Europe. He currently lives and works from London, though his insatiable wanderlust and passion for exploring new cultures and music prevents him from staying in one spot for too long.

Contents

Acknowledgements   6

1   Airwaves   7
2   Voices From The Past   25
3   Way Out West   39
4   Vikings   55
5   Rimur   71
6   Poetry In Motion   80
7   Asatru   93
8   Hidden People   109
9   Landmannalaugur   120
10 Rock 'n' Roll Revolution   131
11 Sveitaball   148
12 Megas   159
13 Rokk I Reykjavík   168
14 Punk International   182
15 On The Music Map   191
16 Pop Stars   203
17 Pop In Reykjavík   215
18 Thule   227
19 All You Need Is The Fantasy   238
20 Independent People   253
21 The Future   268

Appendix 1: Sounds, Tastes, Places   279
Appendix 2: Hotels, Getting There, Getting Around   286
Bibliography   290
Index   292

Acknowledgements

Thanks first of all to the musicians of Iceland who generously gave me their time, their honesty and their insights, and to all the other excellent people I met who made my visit so memorable. Extra special thanks to Ian Bradley at Iceland Air, Sigrún Sigurdardóttir at the Tourist Office, Einar Örn Benediktsson, Hilmar Örn Hilmarsson, Johann Johansson and Viddi Hakar Gislason, all of whom went out of their way to assist me in the writing of this book. My eternal gratitude also goes out to Julie Drazen, Stuart Fagg, Christina Hester, Matthew Jennings, Nik Metcalf and Alice Pryke – thank you all for your invaluable feedback and support.

1 Airwaves

No matter how many times I saw the aurora borealis – or as they are commonly known, the 'northern lights' – they never got boring. I thought that seeing them night after night might dull their impact, but incredibly they just kept on hitting the spot. Frankly, I felt I deserved the continuous thrill they gave. For my first few weeks in Iceland I had put in some serious neck craning, desperate to experience first hand the majestic beauty I had witnessed so many times in photographs. For a long time, the sky responded to my eagerness with its normal star-strewn blankness.

Then, just when I wasn't looking out for them, they turned up. One late September evening I happened to glance out of my apartment window and – 'QUICK! THERE THEY ARE!' Frantically pulling on every remnant of spare clothing I could find to combat the freezing night – jumper, hat, coat, gloves, boots, more jumpers – I struggled outside to the balcony to get a better view of my first ever celestial light show.

It was stunning. Everything I had hoped for and more. The lights cavorted around with the grace and fluidity of a choreographed ballet troupe, morphing from thick, vertical streaks that dangled over Reykjavík like ghostly fingers, into vast veils that billowed and bucked alluringly like a giant green flag flapping in a cosmic wind. I braved the cold for more than an hour to watch their breathtaking performance, staying until they eventually retreated into the infinite blackness of the night. I was so entranced that I didn't think about getting my camera. I didn't want to miss any of the show.

I needn't have worried. That performance was a mere dress rehearsal. The lights were in town for a while: 'Playing Nightly Until Further Notice'. For almost two weeks they showed up each evening, just as the cold azure of the day slowly ebonised into night. Commendably, they never played the same show twice. Some evenings they would shimmy seductively, others they would boogie frenetically. Whatever grooves they decided to dig, they never missed a step.

One night in October, the lights went into 'Moulin Rouge' mode, their green tendrils forming grand, theatrical arcs that cancaned across the sky, then coalescing again in dizzying spools. It was a total trip. That same night was the inauguration of the 2002 edition of Airwaves, Reykjavík's annual music event. The lights, like the town below them, were putting some extra dip in their hip and a little more glide in their stride. For a couple of weeks I had been absorbing the buzz around town as bands started to prepare themselves for the festival: recording demos, rehearsing in cafés and restaurants and generally building up an atmosphere of expectancy. Finally, the big night had arrived.

I knew enough about the aurora borealis by now to know that if they were out, the weather was cold. Hunkering down inside an overcoat large enough to provide shelter for stray fishing vessels, I prepared to hit the mean streets of Reykjavík. In fact 'mean streets' is a somewhat inappropriate phrase. Thanks to a criminally low crime rate, the only thing 'mean' about the streets in Iceland is the cruel glacial wind that sometimes whips through them at hyper-speed, robbing passers-by of scarves, hats and, on occasion, their dignity. 'Clean streets' might be a more apt phrase.

Contrary to popular belief, Iceland did not get its unwelcoming name because it's completely covered in thick layers of snow and ice: that's Greenland. The titular confusion can be laid squarely at the sandalled feet of the Vikings who settled both countries. The theory – or at least one of them – goes that the first Viking settlers in Iceland were on the run from a tyrannical Norwegian king called Harold Fairhair. They wanted to make their new home sound uninviting to anyone who might have been thinking about following them – especially, presumably, the king himself. It didn't work. More

Vikings came in droves to settle as sheep-farmers and use the country as a convenient base for their raids around Europe. It's a wonder that the Vikings who named the place didn't realise that their fellow Vikings wouldn't have been stupid enough to fall for it. Still, ten out of ten for trying.

Greenland, on the other hand, got given its somewhat optimistic name to try and persuade people to migrate there after being 'discovered' a few years after Iceland. That didn't work either. A small Viking settlement did exist there though for a few hundred years but then disappeared, leaving the place to be run by the native Inuits. No one knows why the Vikings disappeared from Greenland, or where they went, but it certainly took them a while to realise they had been duped.

Though not as close to the Arctic Circle as Greenland, Iceland can still get cold – bitterly so in winter. Its location in the middle of the chilly North Atlantic means it doesn't get much in the way of tropical warmth. A slight compensatory factor for downtown Reykjavík – known colloquially as '101' after its postcode – is that it's incredibly compact. If things become really arctic, you can get to most destinations by means of a short, sharp sprint. A trip to the single state-run liquor store in town, for example, can be done in under a minute with the right shoes and a favourable wind. However, if the winds are travelling against you at speeds greater than those at which you are trying to move forwards, you will be pushed rudely backwards. In these conditions, it's best to stay at home and order pizza.

101 is the pulsing heart of Reykjavík, the area that contains the city's picture-postcard charm. The cute, colourful houses, pretty lake and mellow harbour that adorn postcards and tourist brochures around the world are all here, and can all be taken in during a leisurely afternoon stroll. The organisers of the Airwaves festival had decided to spread their event out across various venues in 101. None of them were more than a five-minute walk from each other. I pulled my bobble hat hard over my ears to show the weather I meant business and struck out for Vidalin, a cosy joint just off the square at the bottom of Adalstræti. Before I got there, I was arrested mid-stride by

an aggressive burst of rock guitar issuing forth from what looked like the local post office. I was used to bands converting everyday spaces – cafés, restaurants, record shops – into temporary concert venues, but a post office? This gave a whole new twist to the term 'post-rock'. An investigation was essential.

I found the entrance around the corner, at the side of the building, but the doors were firmly closed. A few feet along the wall a crowd of adolescents stood around spitting and smoking cigarettes. Behind them was a set of open doors. Music throbbed in time with my steps as I bounced up a staircase. The violent, staccato blasts of feedback and distortion, driven home by fierce, tribal drums and vocals – which may or may not have been human – got louder as I ascended. When I reached the third and final floor, a supermarket-strength fluorescent bulb lit up a scene that resembled a London punk party *circa* 1975: crucifix earrings, spiky belts, studded necklaces, leather jackets covered in correction fluid and at least one Mohican flashed in front of my eyes as I filed swiftly past and into a thankfully darker room from which the music was emanating.

A hundred or so people were gathered around a sweating four-piece, whose collective eyes were all closed as hands, feet and mouths worked hard to create the bloodthirsty soundscape. T-shirts testified to the tastes of the audience: Iron Maiden, Slipknot, Metallica. To the left of the speakers, several kids in wheelchairs nodded solemnly to the wash of ferocious rhythms and accompanying guitar wails. I walked closer to investigate, almost stepping directly into a maelstrom of thrashing bodies, which I hadn't noticed until I was almost on top of it. Boys and, worryingly enough, one or two *petites* girls, were launching themselves at each other with gusto. They pogo'd vertically up and down, jumped on backs, shoved one another hard and played air guitar passionately while their long, greasy hair swung in arcs through the smoky air. The elongated, casually clad singer of the band (who was indeed human) seemed to be focusing hard on forcing his lungs out of his mouth. The microphone was almost being swallowed in the process.

As I watched, a topless man with blonde dreadlocks stage-dived bravely from a two foot-tall speaker, almost landing on top of the singer.

I wouldn't regard myself as a religious man usually, but I felt this was a sign from God that I should retreat to the back of the room, where a man dressed in leather, spikes and chains looked, under the circumstances, to be much safer company. He handed me some anarchist literature and showed me some of the CDs he was selling. 'Who's the band?'

'Snafu,' he replied with a knowing grin. 'Fucking great, aren't they?' I nodded grimly. Out of duty, I stayed for a couple more songs, bought a CD adorned with interesting artwork and then slipped out unnoticed into the dark night.

Such was my introduction to Airwaves. In typical Iceland style, the festival was started pretty much accidentally in 1999, when Gus Gus, Quarashi and Sigur Ros, three of Iceland's hottest pop acts, were brought together for a concert. The gig took place in a warehouse during a windstorm, and has subsequently been mythologised in Icelandic musical history (mainly by the promoters of Airwaves). The show has now evolved into a three-day event, which attracts a plethora of international visitors. Journalists armed with dictaphones, photographers armed with cameras, record-label execs armed with chequebooks and music fans armed with enthusiasm pour into Iceland's diminutive capital, eager to check out some of Europe's most innovative and 'underground' sounds.

Since Björk and The Sugarcubes burst onto the international arena back in the '80s, Iceland has had a reputation for consistently coming up with the musical goods. It's no exaggeration to say that music has played a major role in putting the country firmly on the world map. This isolated island, roughly the same size as Cuba with one-fortieth of the population, has managed to produce a steady flow of young bands over the last 15–20 years – Sigur Ros, Múm, Gus Gus, Lhooq, Apparat Organ Quartet, Trabant, The Leaves, The Funerals – which have charmed music fans worldwide with high calibre and often quite leftfield sounds. Airwaves has finally provided a window through which the world can witness the country's prodigious musical output live. Judging from previous reactions to the event, there was every reason to believe that my first view through that window would be as consistently impressive as the northern lights.

Rejoining my original route to Vidalin, I passed through the square at the bottom of Adalstræti, where in the daytime I had often watched Icelandic teenagers suck cigarettes, push hot dogs into their faces and fall off skateboards – sometimes all at once. This square is where the Viking settlers kept their hay over 1,000 years ago. Faint green traces of the lights decorated the sky above me but their main show was over; they were just hanging around for an encore.

Unfortunately there didn't seem to be much of an audience. The streets were conspicuously devoid of people. I looked in the windows of a couple of restaurants as I walked. They seemed quite busy, full of diners glancing nonchalantly at me as I glanced nonchalantly back at them. Everything felt a little low key for the opening hour of a lauded music festival, but then again, when was Reykjavík ever high key? If anyone ever decided to hold a competition for Mellowest European Capital Ever, Reykjavík probably wouldn't even get around to entering.

That said, Iceland is allegedly an industrious nation. Underneath the calm, still lake that most visitors encounter, thousands of feet paddle madly to make this mini-society tick over. With only 300,000 people and a whole country to run, there isn't a great deal of spare time. Resources are stretched and every man, woman and animal counts. Especially the animals, since farming and fishing are what make up a large percentage of the economy. Icelanders have to push themselves to meet diverse challenges and, on average, tend to work many more hours than most nations. At least, that's what the Icelanders told me.

I finally arrived at Vidalin, but, from the look of the sizeable crowd outside, so had the rest of Europe. I could have waited, but the queue looked solid and it would mean missing other bands elsewhere. I crossed back over the square and pressed on up to Laugavegur towards Grand Rokk. Laugavegur is a narrow, protracted road littered with an assortment of hairdressers, record shops, fashion stores, funky boutiques, delis, cafés, restaurants, bars, tattooists, supermarkets, bakeries and other routine businesses. It's the closest Reykjavík has to a high street.

By day, Laugavegur is usually bustling with people exploring what is ostensibly a shopper's paradise. At night it is transformed into a raucous booze strip, as the cafés magically transform into bars, and restaurants clear tables to create dance floors. Whatever time of day you stroll – or teeter – along Laugavegur, you can guarantee a steady stream of four-wheel drives rolling slowly along the road. These large, impressive vehicles are built for tackling Iceland's rugged mountains, glaciers and lava fields but are more often used to return a video or pick up a takeaway. They are popular status symbols in Iceland, overt signs of an ever-modernising and increasingly affluent society.

Grand Rokk was neither modern nor affluent. It was austere and charmless, an overgrown pub complete with a boozy clientele and a slightly dodgy sound system. It has become popular as a live venue presumably because the options aren't too numerous. Reykjavík is a capital city with six municipalities, but that doesn't detract from the fact there are only 170,000 official residents living in the Greater Reykjavík area. This is equal in size to towns like Luton in the UK or Salt Lake City in the USA. Add to this the fact that the capital's urbanisation process only began earlier this century and it comes as no surprise that it has developed just the right amount of facilities to keep everything going.

I had often heard it said that Iceland has everything that bigger countries have, but only one of them. There is apparently no such thing as a tautology in Iceland. After spending time in big, sprawling cities with row upon row of shops and stores trading the same goods and services over and over again under barely differing guises, I found it infinitely refreshing to be in a place where not much is superfluous. The best illustration of the city's scaled-down yet perfectly sufficient services is the fact that there is just the one McDonald's in the downtown area, although this could well have more to do with the nation's endearing obsession with hot dogs than any kind of resistance to multinationals.

Icelanders are a pragmatic people and tend to make the best of what they have. Inside Grand Rokk, Iceland's best-known independent label, Smekkleysa ('Bad Taste') were making good use of its copious space to throw a 15th anniversary party. The label was famously started by The Sugarcubes as an outlet for music, poetry, literature, artwork and pretty much anything else the bunch of creative mavericks decided to release into the public sphere. The fact that it was founded 16 years ago, rather than 15, didn't seem to bother anyone. Why let a little thing like accuracy get in the way of a good party?

The atmosphere in Grand Rokk was relaxed. People milled casually around, waiting patiently for the first act, an experimental soundsculptor and noisescape artist named Bibbi Curver. Bibbi has been releasing music through Smekkleysa for over a decade via a vast array of projects mostly with either a hard rock or conceptual edge. He has progressed from rock bands, via an intriguing flirtation with '50s surf rock, to a one-man show that consisted of him playing guitar and wearing a wedding dress. He is now one of the most popular producers in Reykjavík, lending his Midas touch to a range of bands from metal extremists Minus and Klink, electronic pop acts Maus and Heida, sleaze-rock band Singapore Sling and former Sugarcube Einar Örn Benediktsson.

For tonight's performance, Bibbi was impeccably bedecked in a black suit and busying himself with a trio of turntables and a mixing desk. To his right, a large screen played video footage of the 'Cubes. He placed some of his old rock records on the turntables. Each record had a sticker strategically placed on it which made it jump back to form an irregular rhythm loop. He got three records going at once to make some complex polyrhythms, which he then fed through the desk, adding echo and reverb to create eerie, dubby soundscapes. It was the sound of the musical envelope being pushed.

After his performance, I tracked Bibbi as far as the bar and asked him about Iceland's music scene. 'It's quite unique,' he said brightly, not seeming in the least bit surprised at the question. 'The activity here is high compared to the amount of people we have in the country. Not only that, but a high percentage of the bands are trying to do something genuine, which is a legacy of the punk-rock scene that happened here in the '80s. It has to be a good thing for a producer to be able to work with people that have this mind-set of making something special.'

Bibbi was chatty and immediately likeable. Icelanders can be a frosty bunch sometimes, at least until you take time out to talk to them properly. Then they usually become warm and friendly, and would genuinely do anything for you. Add a few drinks into the equation and you can't shut them up. Bibbi was sober, but genuinely outgoing. I asked him what the advantages of being a producer in Iceland were.

'Intimacy and working with really good music,' he said. 'Bands here know they probably won't make the cost, let alone profit from their albums, so they just want to make a record they can be proud of. The result is often more interesting and more genuine than you might get from artists that rely on music as an income. Also, because there are so few of us, there is less fighting over the bands that you want to produce. I think we are all sharing the scene in a quite brotherly way right now.'

And the disadvantages?

'The disadvantages are that the market is really small. Because of this there is less money around, which means more interesting music but cheaper or worse equipment in studios and less time for projects. The digital revolution in musical equipment over the last five years has helped a lot, but there has never been a real professional level of music production in Iceland. Mastering a record was almost unheard of in Iceland until the 1990s. Producers here have lacked the equipment and experience that people in other countries had, but the fact is, the various musical fields here are relatively unploughed, which gives us a chance to make our own marks. The other good thing about this lack of recording culture, of course, is that I never had to be a tea boy.'

Back outside, life on Reykjavík's clean streets was picking up. The lights had dissipated completely but a full, luminescent moon hovered prettily above Hallgrímskirkja, the tall, rocket-shaped church that dominates Reykjavík's skyline from all angles. I walked back down Laugavegur, past groups of Icelandic girls in their traditional winter uniforms – mini-skirts, high heels, tiny tops, small jackets, large goosebumps – and a few young men who were swaying from side to side as they walked. It could have been Liverpool in December.

Though I had been in Iceland some weeks by now, I was still failing miserably to pronounce any Icelandic words. Icelanders speak almost the same tongue that their Viking ancestors spoke 1,000 years ago. This is akin to an Englishman trying to talk like Chaucer. The other post-Viking Scandinavian languages – Finnish, Swedish, Danish and Norwegian – have all evolved into more modern forms, but Iceland's isolation has meant much of the original culture has remained pure.

From a visitor's point of view, you must therefore be prepared to look and sound quite stupid when attempting to say something in Icelandic. For a start, there are letters that simply don't exist in the English alphabet – ð, for example, which is pronounced like the *th* in 'thin'. Then there's æ, which is pronounced like the *i* in 'mile', and Þ, which is pronounced like the *th* in 'that'. Aside from these, there are a multitude of accented vowels, plus the discomforting fact that normal-looking letters can be pronounced differently. What you thought were innocent *a*s for example can sound like the 'ou' in 'house'; 'hv' can sound like the 'qu' in 'quick'; *p*s are sometimes the same as in English, but when placed before an *s*, *k* or *t* sound more like an *f*.

The language seems to defy all the linguistic rules we habitually know, particularly the art of balancing vowels and consonants out to form open and manageable words. In Iceland they have as much regard for this as the manufacturers of car registration plates, pushing as many consonants together as possible and dropping vowels in randomly over the top. On the rare occasions when I had tried to say something apart from *takk* ('thank you'), it had resulted in the person I was talking to either nodding off or chuckling softly to themselves. Fortunately, most Icelanders are sympathetic enough to have learned English, as well as one or two other Scandinavian languages.

I arrived on a road called Tryggvagata and headed for Spotlight, a stylish bar that ordinarily serves as one of Reykjavík's principal gay/lesbian hang outs. For Airwaves, the place had been appropriated by Iceland's premier electronic music imprint, Thule Musik. Thule was an old name for Iceland, used and documented by travellers from Europe before it was settled. It is also the name of a type of beer in Iceland, as is Viking: yet more cultural heritage poking through the modern veneer. The dim neon lighting in Spotlight had turned people into shadows. Most of these adumbrations were seated around tables, receiving an aural massage from two sombre youths who called themselves Einoma. Their music was anything but sombre, however, as they tweaked laptops to produce lush, gently flowing electronic ambience. This was music for cerebration, not celebration.

Thule started out a few years ago as a club-based music label, releasing strong-arm minimal techno and house music. It has since explored other electronic musical realms – ambient, experimental, downtempo and pop – and is a more exciting and diverse label for it. Lurking in Spotlight's neon shadows I discovered Biogen, one of Thule's more experimental collaborators. Biogen has been nicknamed the 'Icelandic Aphex Twin' due to his challenging, whimsical and leftfield approach to music production. With his bulging blue eyes, long ZZ Over-The-Top-style beard and scruffy, baggy clothing, he resembles some kind of ancient wizard.

The comparison with Aphex Twin, as is to be expected, is an over-simplification and largely unjustified. The producers are certainly connected through their use of the digital domain to create intriguing and convoluted think-pieces, but the Cornwall-born veteran Richard D James has been honing his art for much longer and has taken bigger, more confident strides. Biogen's sounds are generally less abrasive and less fussy than James's, though he has a similar penchant for exploring macabre contrasts and eccentric dream worlds. James has also found an immensely bigger audience, especially since Biogen seems to prefer putting most of his music out on self-recorded CD-Rs instead of through a proper label.

Like his music, Biogen is complex, abstract and deftly surreal. I once tried to ask him some questions by email. I heard nothing back for a few weeks and then a while later a reply popped into my inbox. Biogen had chopped up my questions into words, phrases and letters that made absolutely no sense and sent them back to me. I spent days trying to see if there was some kind of code to it all before realising he had simply attacked them randomly. I had finally nailed him down to a face-to-face meeting in the wonderful Mokka Café, the oldest coffee venue in Reykjavík and the best place to dine on waffles and jam. Biogen arrived looking like he hadn't slept all night. 'I didn't sleep all night,' he explained whilst lighting a fresh cigarette from the remains of another and blowing a nebulous cloud of blue smoke towards me.

He proceeded to describe in a manic and elliptical fashion how he came to produce the music he does, going into discursive theories on art, computer chips and hidden worlds. 'My mind-space is full of weird states,' he concluded at the end of an exhaustive but entertaining hour. 'If you try to describe these states too much they lose their specialness. It's all in the mind of the beholder. The best approach is to not take it too seriously, and if you think you're going mad, slice your head off.' This was as animated an introduction to Reykjavík's underground as I could hope to get.

I tried Vidalin again in an attempt to catch one of Airwaves' most hyped bands, The Funerals. As the name suggests, they are not the happiest sounding act in the world, but their genius for updating blues/country music into a raw and more crapulous context makes you want to head for the bottle and divide your time squarely between laughing and crying. Alas, a live experience was to elude me, as a crowd once again protected the small doorway. Not even space for a press pundit.

Defeated once more, I sought refuge back at Grand Rokk, where the crowds had multiplied to sardine levels to watch a decidedly raw punk quartet. The lead singer flopped around cathartically while a very young guitarist next to him plucked at his bass feverishly. Who were these guys? A man with extremely long arms dressed coolly in a three-piece suit and trilby hat told me that the bassist was Sindri, Björk's son from her first marriage with Thor Eldon. This wasn't so much of a surprise. Björk's stepfather was a musician. So was Thor. Her sister is also a singer. Her brother dabbles in bands. There was every chance the tradition was going to be passed on. It just added more fuel to my growing conviction that anyone under the age of 40 in Iceland was, or had been, involved in music in some way.

It was approaching midnight and the crowds were becoming belligerent, though it wasn't hitting total bacchanalia just yet. I took a deep breath and pushed my way forward to get a better look at the band, lodging myself into the jostling crowd and trying, unsuccessfully, to dodge the waves of cigarette smoke and lager sprays that were washing over me. I walked into the lurching, amorphous mass until I became so lodged I couldn't even move my arms up or down – I was in a straight jacket made up of other people. I could just about see the heads of the band through the gaps in the crowd.

After a few minutes I could smell burning. Then I saw smoke, which looked like it was trailing up from my t-shirt. Jumping back, I inspected with mild horror the circular hole that someone's cigarette had burned into my clothing. Two men standing directly in front of me both glanced around when I hopped back. They were both holding cigarettes. I held out my ruined garment in front of me like Exhibit A. It was still smouldering around the edges. In perfect synchronisation, they both tipped their pint glasses forward and poured a twin stream of lager onto my top. The fire went out but I now had a wet shirt as well as a burnt one. The two gentlemen nodded sincerely in acknowledgement of the appreciation they imagined I was about to give them for their efforts and turned around to watch the band.

Though I had never suffered from any mild cases of arson in a nightclub before, I knew that going out in Reykjavík could be a perilous experience. The nightlife here is notorious all over the world, which is justified because it usually turns up some kind of alcohol-related surprise. The most common excuse for this is that Icelanders are still learning how to drink. Alcohol was heavily regulated here up until 1989. A total prohibition was announced in Iceland in 1912, which was partially broken by Spain, who demanded after World War I that Iceland buy a certain quantity of wine each year in return for purchasing the country's fish. Since the economy was dependent on selling fish to survive, the government could hardly refuse.

In 1935, the sale of spirits was permitted in restaurants and a few select stores, but anything stronger than weak beer was still prohibited. The government then began producing hard spirits and allowed them to be sold in bars alongside the weak beer. The inevitable happened: in order to make their beer stronger, punters mixed it with spirits and called it *bjorliki* – literally 'like beer'. Bjorliki became a favourite national tipple for some years. When it was banned in 1985, mock funerals broke out all over the country.

Up until 1989, strong beer had to be smuggled in from abroad or brewed at home for many years, which was obviously a hassle. In 1974, almost 20 per cent of the population were abstainers. In a total population of around 280,000, that was a lot of people not drinking. It wasn't until 1 March 1989 – a day known as Beer Day – that Icelanders could legally buy beer with alcohol content greater than 2.2 per cent. But even though the prohibition has effectively been lifted, alcohol is still heavily state-controlled, with only one store licensed to sell the stuff outside of bars and restaurants. This medium-sized but generally well-stocked store is on Austurstræti; it resembles a Duty Free shop.

The last 13 years, so it is said, have thus been spent making up for lost time. On Friday and Saturday nights, Reykjavík becomes, generally speaking, a raging mass of booze, flesh, fun – and puke. It's not a place for the weak-hearted, but tourists travel for hundreds of miles to get in on the action. The traditional weekend drinking ritual, brought about mainly by the high price of alcohol in Iceland (£3–£5/$5.50–$7.50/€5–€7 for a pint of beer or a glass of wine), is to get 'warmed up' (leathered) at home before hitting the bars. It is rare to see a crowded venue in Reykjavík before midnight. By 2am, however, most places are jammed with people ready to party.

The first place I ever experienced Reykjavík's notorious revelry levels was in a tiny bar just off Laugavegur. After more or less fighting my way in, I was thrown into a scene that veered dangerously close to insanity. People were swinging from the stairwell and dancing on every available surface: tables, chairs, cigarette machines, the bar and other people's shoulders. At least two people were pouring beer over each other's heads and cackling maniacally. It wasn't unlike the mosh pit at a Slayer concert. Indeed, rock music was rife. Fists punched the air to a range of music that included Bon Jovi, Black Sabbath and Survivor's 'The Eye Of The Tiger'.

I had unwittingly discovered Kaffibarrin, the place where Blur's Damon Albarn once famously passed out on the bar two nights running. On the third day he decided he liked the place so much he brought a share in it. This explains why there is a London Underground sign hung prominently on the wall outside and is at least part of the reason why the bar is one of the hippest in town.

The next day I had returned to Kaffibarrin to meet the bar's owner, the film director Baltasar Kormakur. Another aspect of the bar's appeal, aside from its wild parties, stems from its role in the movie *101 Reykjavík*, which Kormakur directed. While music has soundtracked Iceland's newly found place-to-be status over the last 20 years or so, there wasn't any real visual representation of the country until this film was released in 2000 and became a celebrated international art-house classic.

As the title suggests, the movie is set principally in the downtown area of Reykjavík. It depicts a dyspeptic 20-something called Hlynur who floats through life on a cloud of nihilism, not giving much of a damn about anything except Internet porn, remaining steadfastly unemployed and reacting numbly to life's major events. A dark but comedic tale, the themes in the movie are universal rather than local, but its title, characters and occasional shots of glaciers and teeming nightlife have provided the world with the first real insight into Iceland's groovier side.

At two in the afternoon, Barrin was much less libidinous. The absence of cavorting bodies and smoky fug revealed smart wooden furnishings, frugally decorated walls and a pleasing, cosmopolitan ambience. Squashed into one corner of the room when I arrived were a group of young men sporting the traditional

Reykjavík it's-half-past-four-in-the-afternoon-and-I-look-like-I've-just-rolled-out-of-bed-but-it-doesn't-really-matter-because-I'm-an-artist look whilst frolicking animatedly with a video camera. A man with a black leather jacket and a harrowed expression contemplated a newspaper while his cigarette released lazy curls of smoke up to the ceiling. It all felt vaguely bohemian.

In Iceland everyone calls everyone else by his or her first name, since most second names are composed of the individual's father's name with the suffix *dóttir* (daughter) or *son* (son). Hence Vidar Jonsson is Vidar, the son of Jon. Björk Gudmundsdóttir is the daughter of Gudmund. Baltasar's last name, Kormakur, is an exception due to his mixed Italian/French/Catalan/Icelandic roots. These roots also made him immediately recognisable. Leaning casually against the bar, his swarthy complexion and long, black hair tied back into a ponytail, made him stand out like a tanned thumb against the backdrop of paler patrons. We went through into the dimly lit and deserted back room, where I asked Baltasar if he was born in Reykjavík.

'Not born,' he said, 'but I have spent the last 15 years of my life around here. I lived in a suburb called Kópavogur for ten years and then moved here to 101 about five years ago. I started working in the theatre and doing some acting work in films and then bought the bar after it had been running for one or two years. It was going bankrupt so I changed the style of it and it started to become a bit of an artist hang out. One day I came in and there was an author sitting at the bar. He told me he had written a book but wasn't sure what to call it. I told him to give it to me and that I'd read it and see if I could think of a title. He gave me this large pile of paper and I came back the day after and told him he could name it whatever he liked, but I wanted to buy the rights to film it.'

How much of the movie did Baltasar think was representative of real life in Reykjavík? 'I didn't intend for there to be a lot of Reykjavík in the movie,' he answered, 'and I don't think that it really originally had so much to do with Iceland. The reason I did it was more because I wanted to get at the relationships inside the story rather than make something "Icelandic". If I was going to make a hip Reykjavík film, I would probably choose four young people and the story would revolve around some sexual problem or whatever. But because it was shot here in 101 and because the bar ended up in the book, it did become quite a good representation in some respects. It was accidental, really, but then that's often the way things work.

'I don't think Björk made music to make Iceland a cool place, you know? It just comes naturally from being a part of this, from the energy that is generated by being here. It's nothing objective. The movie is about just one layer of Icelandic society. It's about the artists, the slackers, the barflies, all living in their cool little houses. It's about the funky side of Reykjavík, which does exist. It's about the sexuality and how everything is a little bit fucked up at times.'

It was interesting that Baltasar talked about sexuality as a typical issue for Icelanders. Iceland has a permissive society when it comes to such matters, especially sex outside of marriage. It was all but encouraged a few years ago, when the government offered incentives for couples to have babies in a bid to boost the population. It's not quite as open as Greenland, however, where it is still customary to wife-swap and for a man to offer a guest his wife for the evening as a gift.

The Airwaves brochure had included some comments on dating in Iceland, pointing out that it simply doesn't happen. The reason is simple: dating is about getting to know someone. In Iceland, most people know each other already, so you don't have to waste time finding out about what school someone went to, who their parents are, who they know, etc. In Iceland, the brochure suggested, people just get straight to the nitty-gritty.

'When I shot the film in 1999, Iceland was already a trendy place,' continued Baltasar. 'That process had started with Björk, really. I'm sure the tourist office would like to credit themselves for it, but it really wasn't them. It was the music that was being made here. Icelandic people had been making music for a long time but suddenly there was a possibility of exporting that music, and that gave young people hope that, even though we live in this remote country, we can create something that can travel and have an impact outside. This was a big inspiration and has continued up until the present day. Although I knew this, I wasn't fully aware of how cool people thought Reykjavík was until after the film, mainly because I didn't really start travelling regularly until after I'd made it.'

Despite having given countless interviews about his movie, Baltasar's dark eyes were still dancing when he talked about it. So engrossed was he in our conversation that he failed to notice the pretty girl that dutifully appeared at his side to take our order. I asked for a latté. Baltasar just carried on talking. 'I think the movie also feels more Icelandic simply because Icelanders are very universal,' he said. 'I chose to portray the main character as someone very Icelandic in his style of dress and his overall look. People that come in here really do wear these big coats and have that slacker look. Gus Gus are in here all the time and one of them has that kind of look. This is very Icelandic but at the same time very international. The really cool thing is that young people in other countries often leave for bigger cities elsewhere, but in Reykjavík they prefer to stay and make their own hotpot. This makes it a very vibrant place to be. It really is a wild party here at weekends. The urge to go out and get drunk and go crazy is in the blood of people here and it's an urge that's been with us from the Viking times. If anything, what happens in the bar in the film is very understated.'

Having witnessed the place at its most boisterous, I could hardly argue with that.

2 Voices From The Past

'This is the big thing,' said Gudrun Gudmundsdóttir, drawing in her breath to give her next statement a palpable sense of drama. 'Iceland never really had any musical instruments. People say that Old Icelandic music is rubbish or that it didn't exist, but no one has really had the opportunity to research it. I have, and in truth our lack of instruments has actually made our music develop in a very different way to the rest of Europe. It has made it, in a way, more unique.'

I was talking to Gudrun in the upper-level coffee shop of Mal Og Menning, Iceland's biggest bookstore, located on Laugavegur. The café had a suitably bookish atmosphere. Its few tables were occupied by quiet, slightly repressed types and some light jazz tinkled away insouciantly in the background. Gudrun was sitting opposite me, a young 20-something with long, straight hair and a sweet demeanour. After studying musicology and history at university, she was now researching Icelandic music from the Reformation, in 1550, up until 1850.

I had wanted to find out more about the roots of Iceland's contemporary scene, to discover the origins of all the talent and diversity I had seen at Airwaves. Everyone in Iceland seemed to be a musician – or an artist, a filmmaker, a poet or a novelist – and there had to be a reason behind it.

When Gudrun made her statement, I was gobsmacked. I found myself trying to imagine a European country with no musical instruments. The idea of large, opulent orchestras and flamboyant operas in a place as remote and rural as Iceland did seem a little incongruous, but even so... 'We had one or two types of basic fiddle, called the langspil and the fiddla, but nothing else,' Gudrun explained. 'We tried to import some organs and other instruments here but the weather was so cold they got ruined. In my research I have found evidence for three or four organs that existed but they all got wasted in the snow and the rain. The oldest one is from the 14th century, but all of them are usually only mentioned once in the sources and then never again. They obviously didn't have a long lifetime.

'Iceland got its first proper organ in 1840, which was the first one in the Dome Church, downtown, and we got our first organist at the same time. Up until that point, people just used their voices, and since there was no instrument to lead the melody or anything, we sang the songs however we wanted. This gave us the freedom to develop our own distinctive melodies, which gave rise to a peculiar style of group singing. Instead of everyone singing harmoniously, everyone just kind of did his or her own thing in congregations.'

Groups of people standing around singing their own indiscriminate melodies sounded like it may have been an acquired taste. 'Reports from visitors to Iceland during the 17th, 18th and 19th centuries complain that the singing was awful,' confirmed Gudrun, 'but I think this kind of reaction was exaggerated and probably caused by the fact that the visitors were usually quite wealthy and came from bigger cities. They were often used to the harmonic singing in big churches, which came with full musical accompaniment. Compared to that kind of richness, the Icelanders *did* sound bad, but probably no worse than in the smaller villages in England or Norway, for example. Many of the songs are also very Icelandic in that the melody was very heavy and sad and the lyrics were often quite morose. People were praying to God to make their lives lighter and saying things like, "If I die tonight, let me die without pain."'

Not the chirpiest lyrics in the world, but they simply reflected the times. Today, Iceland is a prosperous nation – one of the wealthiest in the world, in fact – but it has had to endure some serious darkness to get to that point. Iceland was under foreign rule from 1262 until its independence in 1944. It was ruled by Norway initially, but when the

Norwegians formed a union with Denmark in 1380, the Danes took control of both Greenland and Iceland.

Christianity arrived in Iceland around the year 1000. Up until the Reformation, the country enjoyed relative economic, religious and political freedom. Icelanders could pretty much behave as they wanted, as long as they abided by a few ground rules. The Catholic Church held most of the power in the country, but the farmers still had a lot of say and flexed their muscles when they had to, such as when they drowned the unpopular Danish bishop Jon Gerrekson in a bag. After the Danish King introduced the Reformation, the colonial screw was tightened. Jon Arason, the last Icelandic Catholic bishop was the last person to try and drive out the reformers: he was stopped in his tracks by the old-fashioned trick of removing his head from his shoulders with a sharp axe.

Unimpeded, between 1602 and 1787 the Danes placed a trade monopoly on Iceland that proved cruelly oppressive. By 1660 almost all Icelandic trade was in the hands of a few Danish merchants, and the country was divided into districts which weren't allowed to sell fish or any other goods to each other. People were more or less forced to hand over their goods for prices set by the Danish. They were effectively robbed of their food and profits.

These repressive trade measures were only part of the country's troubles however. In the 1600s a climate drop had already made it difficult for Icelanders to grow crops or even fish in the frozen seas. In 1707 a smallpox epidemic broke out, decimating a quarter of the population. In the 1750s yet another climate change froze the fishing grounds again and killed much of the country's livestock, causing a famine. Then, in 1784–5, a volcanic explosion covered the country in lava and scattered poisonous ash all over the country. This created another period of starvation, which became known as the Mist Famine, after the toxic haze that subsequently arose. Iceland lost 9,000 people – 20 per cent of the total population.

The Danish government's reaction to this series of catastrophes was initially one of negligence, followed by the slightly unrealistic suggestion that the entire population move to the West Jutlands in

Denmark, where the land was more receptive to farming. The Icelanders stood firm and opposed the idea. Europe then fell into turmoil during the Napoleonic Wars. Some historians allege that the precursor of these wars – the French Revolution of 1789 – was sparked off by the mist of the Icelandic volcano explosion, which travelled as far as France, causing the country to have a bad harvest, thus exacerbating the hunger and discontent of the peasants.

Whatever the truth behind this theory, the Icelanders certainly suffered as a result of the wars. Shipments of vital resources – coal, iron, timber and grain – failed to arrive, and people were forced to eat such culinary indelicacies as seaweed, leather, roots and lichen to survive. Many more died. This long, harsh sequence of events perhaps makes the melancholic nature of the Icelandic melodies and lyrics at this time somewhat understandable.

For her research, Gudrun has been going through old manuscripts in the National Library of Iceland, the University Library and the Árni Magnússon museum, looking for any scraps of old music that might be preserved in them. Gudrun's valuable work follows on from other collections of traditional folk songs, the most important of which was written by the priest Bjarni Thorsteinsson in 1906.

Bjarni had been as thorough as he could, said Gudrun, but his research was made over 100 years ago. Most of the institutions that Gudrun had access to hadn't been set up at that time. Until a few decades ago, the manuscripts were all kept in Denmark. Bjarni did travel there, but with the basic research facilities he had, couldn't find many manuscripts containing music. Most of the music in Bjarni's important and highly influential book was collected by travelling around Iceland and writing down the songs that he heard. Since many of those songs had developed in such a particular way and didn't adhere to any conventional musical scales, it was difficult for him to notate them accurately. 'He changed some of the tunes slightly because he wanted people to like them more,' said Gudrun, 'but this actually changed the special nuances that make some of these songs distinctly Icelandic.'

Thanks to the increased availability of the manuscripts and her remarkable diligence, Gudrun has now found a staggering 120 containing music, and she hasn't finished yet. The fact that the songs developed in a unique way in Iceland suggested that there may have been something like an Icelandic 'sound'. 'You could say that, yes,' agreed Gudrun. 'The main style that developed uniquely here is known as *fimmundar söngur*, or what is known as "fifth song" in English. *Fimmundar* means "five" in Icelandic, and the style is so called because the melody is sung five notes apart, obviously with more than one person.

'It was actually forbidden in some parts of Europe for a while but because us Icelanders were so isolated from what was happening, we didn't know and we just carried on using it. Then it developed in its own way. The same thing goes for many of the other rules that were followed in Europe. We did not know them and so our music developed without following them. I don't know why we liked it so much, as it is very strange sounding, but it's what we could call a very Icelandic sound. It has a darkness and strangeness that can also be heard in the ancient *rimur*, which is a kind of chanted poetry, and even in the sound of modern artists such as Sigur Ros or even Björk. It has a very special atmosphere, even if it takes a little effort to enjoy it sometimes.'

Gudrun explained that the reason why Bjarni had collected the old folk tunes was that, by the late 1800s, Icelandic people were starting to become more interested in the instrument-led songs that were coming in from Denmark and other European countries. After a while the old songs were seen as embarrassing as the new imported tunes became *de rigueur*. In her research she has found newspaper editorials that rubbished the old songs while encouraging the move to modern European music. In the next column, the newspaper would then slyly advertise the imported sheet music that went with the tunes.

At the end of our conversation, I asked Gudrun more about the fiddla and the langspil. She told me that they still existed, mainly in museums, but there were a few men alive today who could still play them. 'One of them,' she said, 'is called Diddi Fiddla.'

Diddi Fiddla lives in Vatnsendahverfi, a pretty lakeside area just outside Breiðholt, one of Reykjavík's six municipalities. At times it's easy to slip into the idea that Reykjavík is all about 101, but life does go on in other areas, even if there's not much to attract tourists. Judging from the stories people had told me about growing up in the Reykjavík 'burbs, things ranged between quite nice, dull and crap. Kira Kira, one of the members of the avant-garde collective Kitchen Motors, reminisced on her growing up in Breiðholt to me one day. 'It was quite difficult for me,' she said. 'I got beaten up and picked on quite a lot and the school I went to, Fellaskóli, was renowned for its wall-writing, wallet-stealing, vandalising, and teasing pranksters who ganged up on people and hurt them for their amusement. I was 12 when I moved out of the city to Gardur, after I got fed up with mean kids. By then, ten-year-olds were smoking, drinking, fucking and beating the living daylights out of kids who were walking alone somewhere, none of which I had any interest in being involved with. I enjoyed writing and drawing on walls, but other than that I'd have nothing to do with their activities, and after I moved, I never went back. A lot of good musicians come from Breiðholt, though!' she added cheerfully.

Diddi wasn't born in Breiðholt, but he is a good musician. He is also one of the most prominent experts on Iceland's folk music. The instructions he gave me to his house when I called him had seemed clear enough on the phone, but half an hour after our scheduled appointment I was still roaming around the area looking for his house with no access to a telephone. Breiðholt is built on a hill, and I had wasted some time admiring the views over Reykjavík.

I decided I had better try and get some help. I followed a trail of roads around a fairly charmless residential sector before swallowing my pride and entering a supermarket. Supermarkets are not the sexiest of establishments at the best of times, but Icelandic supermarkets are a complete turn-off. The striplights seem harsher, the uniforms less inspiring and the general atmosphere more nauseating. That's just the overall aesthetic. In terms of content, things get worse. Thanks to a largely uncultivatable landscape, Iceland is not one of the world leaders in local crop produce. Spring onions, potatoes and carrots do not tend to thrive in lava. What is grown inside the country is nurtured in geothermally heated greenhouses. The concomitant reliance on imports drives prices sky-high.

My first ever excursion to the 10–11 supermarket in Reykjavík was a mild disaster. Naively, I went looking for that most exotic of fruits, the avocado. After finding the small and miserable-looking fruit-and-vegetable section, I discovered a selection of what looked like large green prunes. After a double-take, some squinting and a spot of light petting, I checked with an attendant, who appeared to be either intensely taciturn – which Icelanders sometimes are – or mute. He confirmed, via rigorous up-and-down head movements, that they were indeed avocados. Each one cost approximately the same amount of money as a hair dryer.

On the upside, the staff at Icelandic supermarkets are generally helpful, even if the younger ones have the same aversion to shampoo, spot cream and social prowess as their counterparts all over the world. I asked if anyone knew Sigurdur Jonsson, Diddi Fiddla's real name. The spotty, greasy-haired young man at the counter and the middle-aged lady he was serving both shot me a sympathetic look. They said nothing. 'Diddi Fiddla?' I tried.

The lady's eyes brightened. 'Yow, yow, yow,' she cooed. 'He lives close by. How well do you know Breiðholt?' I put on my best lost-little-puppy look.

She put her bag of hysterically overpriced goods on the floor and mysteriously produced a telephone directory from nowhere. In the back were maps of Greater Reykjavík. She began to flick rapidly through the pages with the kind of familiarity that only a middle-aged lady could possibly have with a telephone directory. 'We are here,' she said, poking a finger towards the middle of a page. She then flipped the page over, twice, at high speed. 'And he is here.' It meant *nada* to me. I stared at her blankly. She flipped into hyper-velocity local-giving-directions-to-tourist mode: 'Right here...couple lefts...hill...another right...left...come lake...house grass roof...can't miss it.'

Splendid. I followed what I could comprehend of her directions and eventually the rows of concrete housing blocks gave way to a scattering of pretty houses that wound down onto a large frozen lake. This place was infinitely more charming than Breiðholt, but all the houses seemed to have grass roofs. Which one was Diddi's? I was an hour late by now so I couldn't waste any more time. The only sign of human life I could see was a man mending a roof in the distance. As I approached, he spotted me coming. I waved and shouted, 'Diddi Fiddla?' He silently pointed to a house just at the end of the road, near the lake. People around here really didn't like talking. I waved my appreciation and five minutes later I was knocking on Diddi's large wooden front door.

I expected him to perhaps be angry with me for being late, but he didn't seem to even notice. He came outside with his wife, who gave me a cheery hello before driving off in a four-wheel drive. Diddi ushered me into an anteroom littered with computers, recording equipment and a ton of musical paraphernalia. A large, old-looking mixing desk dominated the centre of the room. 'It's from the English record label Pye,' said Diddi patting it as if it were a pet dog. 'It's the desk that Pink Floyd used to mix *Dark Side Of The Moon*.' We stepped through into a much larger room. A slightly disjointed array of antique furniture gave the place a homely feel, enhanced by a large piano that squatted in the corner. Rows of books made the shelves on the walls bow gently. Three large windows around the room flooded it with natural light; through one of them I spied a cluster of ducks running around in a fenced-off section of garden.

Diddi had built much of this place himself, adapting it from two or three small buildings that he had bought five years ago. He hadn't quite finished it yet, but he gave me a tour of the other two parts that were still under construction. A dead goose hung limply from one of the rudimentary walls. 'It tried to take on my brother-in-law's car the other day,' explained Diddi. It had obviously come second. We returned to the ornate living room where I noticed a flask sitting on a large wooden table. Every Icelandic home has one of these flasks; they seem to fuel the nation. Settling into a chair at the table, Diddi lit up a cigarette, poured us both a coffee from the flask and we started to talk. He looked relaxed in what could well have been his favourite armchair.

The light from the window behind him illuminated his snow-white hair and his glasses dangled from their leather cord around his neck, lending him a professorial air. He started to tell me about his life, starting with how he almost lost it to the indiscriminate fury of an Icelandic volcano.

'Myself and my wife moved to Heimaey, in the Westman Islands, in 1972 to teach,' he began. 'I was working as a music teacher and a conductor, and my wife was a primary-school teacher. One day, I noticed on my way to the school that the fleet at the harbour had their engines running, but they hadn't left because they were waiting for the strong wind to die down. There was a break at school between 10am until 10:20am usually, but because of the storm the children were kept inside. Later that day I went downtown again to buy some liqueurs, as I had some friends coming round to help us celebrate our decision to stay in the Westman Islands for two or three years. We were going to save and buy a house there.

'As I was walking down the road I noticed there was now no wind at all. This was strange as there are only three days a year when the Westman Islands have no wind. There were lots of little birds on the ground too, the kind you never see in the Islands. There were hundreds of them and when I approached them, instead of flying, they just parted and hopped out of the way. I realised something strange was happening but couldn't tell what. That same evening there were some seriously heavy northern lights, the heaviest I've ever seen, and then at 1:55am the eruption started. Our place was downtown, close to the harbour. The first I heard of the action was a woman shouting outside our house, trying to get the attention of her daughter, who lived upstairs. I opened the door and let the woman in, and when I looked out of the door I heard a loud bang and saw some fire shoot up. It looked very close, and my first thought was that a volcano was erupting in the village. Then I saw a second explosion and then a third, and then I realised that it was wide and that it might spread across the harbour. I presumed the fleet had gone, as it had been ready to leave when I had been past the harbour in the daytime, and the wind had dropped in the afternoon.

'The only way you could get access to the island if the harbour was blocked was by small boats as planes can't go near erupted areas in case the motors stop. I called my mother in Reykjavík and asked her to arrange ships and helicopters to come here. I told her we were in a lot of danger and to call the emergency services, to do whatever she could. She said, "My dear son, can I speak to your wife?" She thought I was going mad; she didn't believe me! My wife had to come to the phone and told her I was telling the truth, so she then called the Icelandic police and explained what was happening. The guy said, "My dear lady, according to my news report, everything is okay. Please go to bed." He didn't believe her! She got another number for National Security and fortunately they weren't allowed to ignore any emergency calls. They rang the police in the Westman Islands and got it confirmed and then everything got going. She then called the local police again and they apologised for not believing them. My mother was the first one to call them.

'Everyone was woken up then as the police drove around with their sirens blasting. People went out to the street and luckily the fleet was still in the harbour. Only one ship had left, and the explosion had not yet reached there. Everyone just ran for the boats to get out. The last thing I did was to look around the apartment for things to take. The money we had been counting to see how much we had for our house was on the table. There was a lot of it but there was nothing I could do with money at that point so I just left it. I thought food would be more useful than money so I grabbed a frozen leg of lamb and some cheese and my wife took the child and off we went down to the harbour. There was no time to think about anything except getting out.'

I had read about the Heimaey eruption. It was the last such eruption to have occurred in Iceland and was remarkable for the fact that the rescue operation was a 100 per cent success. Thanks to the fast and skilful reactions of the emergency services and fortuitous factors such as the fleet being in the harbour, the weather being calm enough to enable planes and boats to land, and the eruption not cutting off the harbour, all 5,000 residents were ferried or flown to safety. By the time the lava had stopped flowing, some months later, 20 per cent of Heimaey was under lava and ash and the fissure that had opened measured 1.6km (1 mile) long.

The explosion also created the island of Surtsey, named after the character in Norse mythology who sets fire to the earth after a great battle between the gods and the giants. Surtsey is accessible only to marine biologists, who are using it to study the development of life on a new island. Iceland was formed in a similar way a few million years ago. As North and South America have moved steadily away from Europe and Africa, the Atlantic Ocean has been formed as well as a tear along the centre of the Earth. Magma from deep inside this gap swells and forms a ridge from the Arctic to the Antarctic. Iceland is the result of this magma rising above the surface of the ocean. This process is ongoing and is what creates Iceland's hot springs, geysers and mud pools. It is also what generates the sometimes stomach-churning smell of rotten eggs (sulphur) when you turn the hot water tap on, since Iceland has harnessed the heat from its natural resources below the ground.

Happily, Diddi had managed to persuade a policeman to break in and get his cash back the day after he left. He found himself in Reykjavík again after this tumultuous event. His father had worked for the Icelandic Symphony Orchestra for years and was also a member of a jazz band that played concert-hall gigs most week nights. Diddi had started playing the violin at an early age and also enjoyed a spell with the orchestra at the tender age of 15. Before he moved to Heimaey he had been writing for strings and producing for pop bands, even joining in as a member of one of Iceland's best-known hippy bands, Nattura, in the '70s. One of the principal reasons Diddi had moved to the Westman Islands in 1972, though, was to get off the band circuit on which he was increasingly finding himself travelling. He had seen his father gigging five nights a week and didn't want to end up with that kind of lifestyle. In 1971, a rogue fire in a concert hall had destroyed a lot of his musical equipment. The owner wasn't insured. Diddi decided he would use the experience to change direction in his life.

When he returned from the Islands, he began teaching and playing classical music, working with the National Theatre and acting as a freelance producer. He set up his own company, Studio Stemma, in 1980 and after that began exploring Iceland's folk music. 'My interest in folk started when I was 12,' said Diddi, pouring us some more coffee. The light outside had dimmed considerably by now and we were talking in twilight. The curtains were open and I could see house-lights winking romantically in the encroaching blackness. The room looked cosier and Diddi more relaxed than ever. He was on a roll. 'My mother used to sing for us children when we were young,' he continued. 'She knew loads of folk songs and they grabbed me at an early age. When I was 15 I was playing guitar with a friend of mine who was singing folk music and we started to play some standards and also some Icelandic stuff. I began looking into the history of music in Iceland and discovered this instrument here...'

He reached down underneath the table and pulled up a slightly worn leather case. Placing the case on the table, he clicked the locks open to reveal a long, rectangular instrument that tapered off at one end and had three strings running across its length. Next to it was a bow. 'This is the langspil,' imparted Diddi. 'It has been known in Iceland since 1700 or so. It was imported from Norway and is from the family of instruments called the dulcimer, which you can find in every country. A distinction with the Icelandic version, though, is that Icelanders have always played it with a bow, which doesn't happen anywhere else. The reason for that is that when it arrived here in Iceland the only local instrument was this...' He pulled up another case onto the table and opened it to show a similar instrument, though this one had a bridge under the strings and different decorations.

'This is the fiddla, and the bow moved from being used with this fiddla to the langspil when it arrived. There aren't any fiddlas around any more, apart from two in the National Museum. I had to make this one myself. One of the versions in the museum is a bastard from 1800. It's not an original because for some reason the person who made it has adapted it a little to the style of the new violins at the time. Mine comes from a drawing that was found of one in 1840. Bjarni Thorsteinsson had been asking for information about the fiddla for his book of folk songs as he had heard of them but never seen one. Someone made him an instrument based on memory from around 1840 and that instrument is the second one to be found in the National Museum; that's what I based my fiddla on. There is also another drawing from 1840 that shows the instrument in the same way. It didn't work when I first made it and it took us a while to work out that the artist had forgotten to include the bridge. We know that bridges were used on the instrument as one was dug up from Greenland a few years ago, made from tooth.'

Diddi played the fiddla for me. Placing his hand not above the two strings, as I had expected, but below them, he drew the bow across and played a sorrowful, haunting tune which sounded a tad Arabic. It was striking, though, even played on this rudimentary instrument. The simple construction of the fiddla made it a difficult instrument to play. There was no fretboard or tuning keys, but it could obviously produce great music if you knew how to work it. 'This is one of the most beautiful songs I've ever heard,' said Diddi after the performance. 'It's among the oldest Icelandic songs that exists and is called "Lilja". No one really knows how it was composed. A cousin of mine was writing a big lexicon of Icelandic music and I asked him about the tune. He told me that it's not in any known mode, not major or minor like church music. His theory was that someone made a mistake when copying it down from one manuscript to another and mixed up the sharps and flats. I love the song, though, even if it is a bastard.'

Diddi has spent the last decade or so playing Icelandic folk songs to the rest of the world, along with Njal Sigurdsson from the Ministry of Culture and one or two other musicians and artists. The team's repertoire includes the *fimmundar söngur* (also known as *kvint*-song), which Gudrun had told me about, as well as examples of old *rimur* ('sung poetry') and folk melodies including tunes like 'Lilja' which have been found in the manuscripts and also some Icelandic religious music. I wondered why the langspil was no longer in use.

'The instrument arrived in Iceland around 1700,' came the reply. 'In the 1850s there was a book published to help people learn songs that were played with the langspil. The text was written down and the letters for the tone to play. It was in the same way that guitar chords are put into a text today. There were instructions on how to build a langspil in this book, but because of the printing technique at that time, all the schematics were wrong. The author in fact advised people not to use the schematics, but to measure each fret from a tablet he wrote. Many people did use the schematics, though, and the resulting instruments were terribly out of tune. The respect for the langspil went down a lot.

'We also lost a lot of our music culture because of the ban on dancing here in Iceland,' said Diddi. 'Before our last Catholic bishop was killed in 1550 and we transformed to Lutheranism, both the Pope and the Danish King forbade any kind of dancing. It was also banned in other Scandinavian countries, but in these other countries people could gather together in villages to sing and dance when there were no priests or authorities around. Iceland had no villages, just farms, and there was quite a distance between them so people did not get together unless it was a baptism, a marriage or a funeral. This meant that there was always a priest around so people could not dance or sing songs that were not religious. The only way to pass songs on to the next generation was by singing them to people at the farms when there was no priest around. This is why so much old Icelandic music is based on the voice.'

3 Way Out West

One afternoon, when a fierce wind was making my entire apartment wobble, I listened to a CD called *Raddir*. *Raddir* is the Icelandic word for 'voices'. The cover of the album, which was released by Smekkleysa, bore a simple, slightly abstracted vision of the countryside – white clouds, green grass, grey sky – which was unmistakably Icelandic in its pastoral gloominess. The album was a collection of songs sung by farmers, housewives, fishermen and carpenters, many of them born in the previous century. They sang songs that had been passed down from generation to generation, including some from Bjarni Thorsteinsson's songbook.

The singers had been recorded between 1903 and 1971 by various cultural conservationists armed with wax cylinders, phonographs and, later, cassette recorders. Bjarni had tried to notate the songs as best he could, but as Gudrun noted, there were obstacles to how accurate he could be. With the advent of recording technology at the turn of the century, those obstacles were removed and people travelled around Iceland recording songs before they were lost to history.

Raddir had been compiled from these recordings: voices singing poems, hymns, lullabies, drinking songs and nursery rhymes. I relaxed on my sofa and closed my eyes as the voices, many recorded on rudimentary technology, crackled through the speakers. They sounded isolated without musical accompaniment, but also very human, real and incredibly close. After a few songs I was lost in this strange world that had caught me up from a bygone era. I wouldn't have been surprised if I had opened my eyes and found a living room full of rural

Icelanders sitting and standing around in traditional costume, weaving wool or mending fishing nets while they waited for their turn to sing.

Many of the performers on *Raddir* are now dead, but a few are still alive. I managed to track down the singer of the last song on the album, a short, sweet lullaby. Her name was Asa Ketilsdóttir and she lived in Ísafjörður, the largest town in the Westfjords, the block of land that extends out from the northwest corner of Iceland like a giant lobster trying to pinch Greenland's icy butt. The fjords themselves are famously rugged. They account for more than half of Iceland's coastline yet are one of the most sparsely populated areas in the country. This has a lot to do with the fact that they're a stone's throw from the Arctic Circle and have a reputation for some of the worst weather conditions in Iceland. The residents are necessarily resilient.

For centuries, the Westfjords were about farming, but in the 20th century motorised fishing vessels discovered large amounts of fish off the coast and people moved in to help with the processing of these new-found riches. Villages subsequently sprang up and flourished, but due to the declining fishing industry over the last few decades, the communities have begun to seep south to Reykjavík in search of new employment and new lives.

The tricky part was getting to meet Asa. I could take a plane there but I wanted to see some of the scenery, which was supposed to be impressive. And I couldn't hire a car as I had no driving licence. Fortunately I had a friend, Julie, visiting from out of town, who did have a driving licence. I asked if she would like to take on the coveted role of author's chauffeur. To my delight she agreed, but we had to check out the condition of the roads. This was the month of October and they were often closed around this time. The roads in Iceland can get very dangerous in winter, especially in the colder north of the country, where we wanted to go.

The tourist board in Akureyri, Iceland's 'capital of the north' and its second biggest town (population 15,000), informed us that the roads were still open: 'They are a little icy here in the north as it has been snowing for a few weeks, but if you drive carefully and use a car with winter wheels, you should be okay.' I thanked the lady for her help and called Asa's son, Thordur, as his English was better than his mother's. Most people speak English fluently in Reykjavík, but in the countryside it's not as commonplace. Thor agreed to meet us part of the way, at a guesthouse near a small town called Hólmavík. It was run by a friend of theirs and we could also spend the night there.

I didn't realise until we started leaving town how claustrophobic even a pretty and natural little town like Reykjavík could become. I had been there for several weeks and it felt surprisingly refreshing to be getting out for a couple of days. The brooding dignity of the landscape didn't take long to impress itself upon us as we followed a route that took us around the base of Esja.

Esja is Reykjavík's most visible mountain. She can be seen from many spots, including the harbour and all the way along Laugavegur, and serves as a constant reminder of the closeness of nature. She changes colour constantly, which locals attribute to her mood swings. She also seems to change size on occasion, sometimes appearing large and looming, other times distant and defenceless. I had noticed before we set off that she had been glowing brightly and had looked most feminine in her effulgent state. Up close, though, she possessed a masculine cragginess which diminished the admittedly romanticised view I held of her.

As we drove, the first winter snowflakes of the south landed on the car. It looked pretty but I also hoped it wouldn't get any worse and cause us driving problems ahead. The further onto the country's main ring-road we got, the more rural the views became. The familiar mix of mountains and barren fields of lava caused by the country's regularly exploding topography were punctuated with isolated farmhouses, the occasional water silo and little clusters of forests.

I had been told by many smirking Icelanders that the most beautiful thing about their forests is that, if you get lost in one, you needn't worry – just stand up. Now I understood. Once upon a time, around the time of the Settlement, Iceland had been covered in lush forest, but the axe-heavy ways of the Vikings, a series of harsh climatic spells and grass-munching livestock all helped to reduce the country to its present deforested state. Squat horses and fat, cloud-like sheep were right now grazing away in front of the mountains, nibbling at what little vegetation there was. Both these animals are a source of national pride. The isolated nature of the country has prevented cross breeding, ensuring their purity. Icelandic wool and dairy products are hence prosperous commodities, while the horses, descendants of the animals that carried the Viking settlers across the rough and riven terrain, have a unique gait and shape.

People visit Iceland just to experience the annual round-up of these animals, called the *rettir*. The *rettir* is a huge celebration. When the animals are born they are kept on the farms for a while and then released to roam free into the highlands. A few months later, farmers head out to round the animals up and herd them back to their homes. The animals charge dramatically across mountain tracks and lava fields in their thousands, and when the animals and farmers are all safely back home a large party ensues with the mandatory elements of booze, food and song.

Source of national pride they may be, but next to the vastness of the mountains and fields the animals looked insignificant. Iceland's powerful scenery has a tendency to humble pretty much everything around it. As we drove, I reflected on how admirable it was that such a small community of settlers had managed to survive all these centuries in such a remote and unyielding place. Not just survived, but learned to live and work with the incredible, endless rawness, and developed a fine and worldly culture from it, too.

The weather suddenly changed. The snow and oppressive gloom was replaced by bright sunshine and blue skies, as if someone had simply lifted one canvas backdrop and replaced it with another while we blinked. We chuckled in disbelief. The weather in Iceland is famously capricious. It is not unusual to experience all four seasons in the space of a day, or even a few hours. In the summer, the sun shines all night long, and in deepest, darkest winter it hardly comes out at all, especially in the Westfjords, where total darkness occurs for approximately four months of the year. This adds to the extreme nature of the country and helps explain why the weather is such a continual talking point for Icelanders.

Splashes of light were now streaming through the clouds like descending angels or, for those with a more secular imagination, UFO beams. The brightness helped Esja regain some of her femininity. The further north we drove, the scenery became streaked with a sparkling white rime, which made a change from the usual splashes of green moss and lichen. Snow began to bounce from the windscreen once again. I noticed that the lakes we were passing were frozen solid; grass tufts were fighting their way through blankets of frost on roofs and the chocolate-brown mountains looked like they had been sprinkled generously with icing sugar.

Our speed dropped to 60kph (35mph) as we turned off the main road and started the narrow trail around the fjords. I felt my mouth shape itself involuntarily into a grin as my eyes beheld scenes directly out of a fairy tale. The scenery opened right up so we could see for miles and miles across the scarred, snow-covered fjords that rose steeply from the water. Salmon streaks of sunset coloured the sky and the subtle tones of the sea changed from deep blue to purple as it stretched outwards to the horizon. The clear, unpolluted air made the visibility extra sharp. This was nature, wild and remote and deliriously devoid of human impact. It felt like we had reached the end of the world.

We drove slowly to better absorb this indescribable natural beauty. Eventually we started to encounter dots of human settlement. Impeccably constructed red churches clashed handsomely against the pure-white backgrounds. Tiny groups of houses teetered on the tips of narrow promontories that edged bravely out to sea. Sheep grazed next to the sea mere feet away from the car. It took me a while to accept the fact that the sheep were pretty much paddling in the water. I had only ever seen them in fields before. It looked like they were on holiday.

We lost ourselves to our surroundings, stopping the car intermittently to take pictures and drink everything in. The air tasted deliciously clean, if a little cold. Before we knew it, the light started to fade and the scenery took on a silvery glow. We decided to drive on. Already the roads were getting icier – a combination of our driving towards the Arctic Circle and the sun starting to retreat across the horizon. The roads were also becoming quite steep, and we noticed that they didn't have any barriers. Julie slowed the car down to a crawl. She was becoming understandably nervous as the car was starting to slip when she hit the brakes.

The reflectors on the road flashed like flames as our headlights picked them out one by one. There were no signs of human life, no houses for miles in any direction. If a car toppled over the edge here, it might never be found. The danger inherent in Iceland's remoteness crept up on us like a bad dream. We wound on slowly, and Julie got more and more distressed at having to drive in these conditions. But we had come so far it would be equally dangerous to turn back. We couldn't just stop, either; it was far too cold to sleep in the car.

Sometimes only a few inches of icy road separated the car from steep drops down to an even icier sea. Although we were going slowly, we had to keep dabbing the brakes to stop our speed from gaining down hills. The brakes began to slip more and more and I began to curse myself for wasting time taking photographs and admiring the views. Our admiration for the scenery was now turning into fear of it. We drove over the crest of a steep hill and I felt Julie touch the brakes slightly. The wheel slid; we had hit ice.

The whole vehicle started to glide towards the right-hand side of the road. I watched in disbelief as the edge came ineluctably closer. We were hardly going forward at all, just sideways. Julie was in a state of shock and didn't know what to do. I didn't either. She didn't want to hit the brakes again in case it pulled us more into the skid and over the edge, but we were just a foot or two away from the edge and the car wasn't going to stop on it's own. There was no choice. Blood started to pound in my ears. I realised that, even if I wanted to try and jump at this stage, the only place I could throw myself would be down the cliff that was looming sickeningly near. I felt powerless.

Then Julie slammed her foot on the brakes and the car stopped dead. Miraculously, the wheels had gripped tarmac. We were no more than 5cm (2in) from a drop of around 20m (20 yards) – centimetres from potential death. Julie was breathing hard and close to tears. She pulled up the handbrake and jumped out the car. I was too dumbstruck to move. The reality of what had almost just happened refused to sink in. I just stared at the drop to my right hand side. Julie got back in and snapped me out of my stupor. She had been crying.

For a while we just sat there, in the middle of the cold, isolated road. Nothing moved outside. It was silent. I realised the folly of the journey. I had recklessly endangered my own life and that of a friend. I couldn't help feeling that the landscape had almost charmed us into our danger, lured us in like a siren. The two sides of Iceland's natural habitat, its beauty and its violence, had been driven home – hard.

Neither of us wanted to start the car again but we had no choice. We rolled the vehicle back into the centre of the road and rolled it down the hill a little with the engine turned off. After a minute or so we plucked up the courage to get back in and drive. I prayed to myself silently. I could tell Julie was praying, too. Around a few more bends, we finally saw some house-lights, although it was hard to tell exactly how far away they were. By the time we were pulling into the driveway of our destination, 20 minutes or so later, night had descended on us completely.

I told Jon, the owner of our guesthouse, about our near-death experience. He didn't say much. 'Does it happen a lot?' I asked.

'Not really,' he said, 'only four or five a year or something like that.'

Our massive experience felt immediately smaller. Jon asked us if we wanted to eat at the guesthouse, pointing out that we didn't have any choice since the one other option, a restaurant in Hólmavík, was closed. We wouldn't have driven anyway. Twenty minutes later, his wife appeared with a steaming-hot fish pie.

If anything can help make the memory of a near-fatal experience recede, it's steaming-hot fish pie. An hour after almost plummeting to our deaths in the icy sea, we were slouched on a sofa watching Icelandic TV, feet up on the coffee table, waiting for Asa and Thordur to appear. They arrived around 9pm. Thordur came in first, pumping my hand heartily.

His mother stepped in behind him, looking slightly bashful. I had been expecting her somehow to look representative of another era in Iceland, perhaps in the way she dressed or spoke, but she looked as modern as any other lady of her age I had seen. In fact, she reminded me slightly of my own grandmother. She was smartly dressed in a blouse and cardigan and a long pleated skirt, and possessed a disarmingly sweet smile.

Mother and son sat next to each other on the sofa while I made some coffee and asked Thordur about his job – or, as it turned out, his jobs. He has several of them, ranging from sheep farming to driving the school bus and being the local postman. I was beginning to realise how much Iceland's traditional farming and fishing enterprises had been hit in recent years. It seemed everyone who lived anywhere outside Reykjavík and maybe Akureyri was struggling to resist the pull to the capital. Due to the decline in the agricultural industries that have traditionally fuelled the countryside, many rural dwellers had been forced to seek alternative methods of income if they wished to remain where they were.

The guesthouse we were in represented Iceland's changing times. Jon had never been a farmer and wasn't one now. He had moved from Reykjavík to live in the country and had bought the farmhouse not for agricultural purposes but to make money from renting it out. While the locals in the countryside have to move out as they can't afford to stay, the monied people in the city – as well as wealthy foreigners – were taking over their houses and putting them to different uses. This was seemingly the final stage in Iceland's modernisation. Reykjavík was now a modern urban centre, and the countryside – the last vanguard of Iceland's traditional culture – was also set to change. Since the economy was still dependent on agriculture, I felt the transition would be a precarious process, to say the least.

I returned to the front room with the coffee. Flicking off the TV with the remote control, I asked Asa how she came to start singing traditional Icelandic songs. 'It was a family tradition,' she explained. 'My father always chanted a lot of the old songs and what we call *rimur*, long epic rhymes which are kind of sung poetry. I learned all this at the same time as I was learning to talk. That was my father's way of teaching me how to speak. He was also fond of *Thules*, long poems that are similar to the *rimur* but are more about just putting words together in an abstract way and don't mean as much. My father learned how to chant from his grandmother, so it missed a generation, just as it has missed a generation after me.' She looked at Thordur, who shrugged amiably. 'None of my own children picked up on it,' she said, 'but I am now teaching Thordur's daughter, so hopefully it will continue through her. All the generations lived together on our farm when I was growing up, and even though we have our own places now we still live very close to each other, so it's easy to keep up these traditions in a way.'

This sounded a little like the scenarios I had read in *Independent People*, the book by the late, great Icelandic writer and Nobel Prize-winner Halldór Laxness. I had been told that if I wanted to know *anything* about Iceland or its people, I had to read his work, in particular *Independent People*. So many people insisted that I eventually succumbed. I was greatly rewarded. Laxness has an epic style and an eye for describing people and nature that is on a par with celebrated literary legends like George Eliot, Thomas Hardy and James Joyce. I enjoyed the book as much as I had enjoyed work by any of these authors, if not more. It was surely a mark of Iceland's isolation – rather than any lack of prowess of Laxness' part – that he wasn't better known abroad.

Independent People is set at the turn of the century and centres around a farmer named Bjartur. A big, strong and intensely proud man, Bjartur has worked all his life for a landowner and finally gets the opportunity to buy his own sheep farm. He then becomes obsessed with the idea of independence. The farm he buys is cursed by a monster that dwells under the earth, yet Bjartur isn't the type to bow down to such things and he ignores it. In fact, his sole *raison d'être* is to ignore all threats – real or imagined – from ghosts, whimsical wool and mutton dealers, his family or the modern co-operative of farmers that eventually forms around him. Through his stupefying intransigence and blind idealism, he manages to lose almost everyone that he has ever loved or that has loved him.

Despite its concerns with parochial life, the book's dimensions are deceptively huge. It is meant as a metaphor for Icelandic agrarian society. Hence every conceivable emotion is conjured up through life on this poor, insular little farmhouse. There are moments of touching human tenderness, heartbreaking descriptions of wretched poverty and ignorance, black humour and a lot of warnings about the dangers and cruelty inherent in bloody-minded pride. The book gave me an insight into life in Iceland less than a hundred years ago. After reading it, I looked at the country with a whole new perspective.

In the book, Bjartur regards nature as a living, breathing entity. He believes in – indeed, fights with – supernatural powers. And to make the hard day-to-day life and labour on the farm a little bit lighter, he makes rhymes, both on his own and for his family. I was curious as to how similar or dissimilar Asa's life had been when she was growing up. Did her family also sing songs to get them through a hard day's work on the farms? 'During my youth we would sing during the day as we worked and sometimes when we had finished work,' she confirmed. 'Then we would come together after dinner to recite poems and read stories together. The house I grew up in was an old traditional Icelandic house with no electricity and no radio. The farm was a little old-fashioned, but it wasn't slavery or anything like the poor lives described in *Independent People*. Some people in Iceland really had lives like that, but we had time to enjoy ourselves.

'I started working when I was six, looking after the children and running errands, but it wasn't a very hard life. It was very natural and normal to help out. My grandparents had to work much harder than we did. My father was born in 1896 and when he was 12 he started to write a diary, which I still have. Judging by his entries it was a lot tougher then than during my childhood. He was very accurate about the events he recorded, so the diary is a good insight into those times. Each time he went into the next village, for example – which wasn't very often at all – he recorded what he bought there, how much sugar he got for how much money and that kind of thing. He also recorded what the weather was like each day and wrote some of his own poetry, too. The rhymes he used to write were for entertainment, mostly.' Asa pointed to the television. 'It was our version of that. My father also sang them to make the time go quicker as we worked. Sometimes they would be amusing and sometimes serious. There were a lot of stories and fairy tales going on as well as the rhymes, adventures about outlaws, about ghosts, and also true stories about past events and stuff about neighbours, too. I made a lot of drawings about these stories and rhymes, and it was because of his influence that I started writing my own poems and stories.'

Talking to Asa, the realisation slowly dawned on me that Iceland's primarily vocal musical heritage was also inextricably linked to the poetry and literature for which Icelanders are more famous. Asa said that she enjoyed singing but that many of the old songs were really about the words and the rhymes. 'Poems for me are like true friends that you can count on,' she said. 'I really feel that you can rely on poetry to get you through life. In a very short and compact system of words, you can get all kinds of feeling and emotions across. I can find myself in the poems because I can put myself into them. It's the oldest tradition in Iceland, really, so it is important to every Icelander. Even people who aren't able to put a poem together get quite a lot out of reading them. There is a similarity of emotion which bonds people together.

'Unfortunately this has been lost a little bit in the last few years. When the influences from abroad came into Iceland, people were more and more attracted to the new melodies and wanted to forget about the old traditions. My mother used to sing them, but she started to turn and say it sounded like the cows singing. In 1968, when a man and woman came to our farm to record us, my mother was afraid that she would be made a fool of for singing, so she refused to do it, even though she knew a lot of songs. At that time, people were singing rhymes and lullabies from the older generation, and I was very young compared to a lot of the other people performing. I did it just because I enjoy performing them, and also because I am proud of them, too. I am proud that Icelanders have these things and hopefully by continuing to perform them I can keep them alive.'

When Asa and Thordur had left, I stayed up to ponder our conversation. The image I had of Iceland was increasingly dualistic. The image from the outside was of a country packed to the rafters with young, creative types who make exceptionally innovative music, drive large, expensive cars around unique landscapes and spend far too much of their income on groceries, but the more traditional side of the culture – which I had discovered through music and poetry – seemed hidden from view.

The feeling was that much of Iceland's traditional culture has been forgotten in the rush for modernisation. Although it wasn't a secret to Icelanders, much of the musical and cultural heritage was buried so deep that it was invisible to people peering in from the outside. I got the feeling that it was seen as a little embarrassing. Asa, and people like her, were valuable keys to a time that some in Iceland would rather forget about but which contained invaluable riches. Sticking up for something that everyone else seems to be against takes guts. Asa was a brave lady and was instrumental in keeping a whole culture alive.

The next morning, we woke up feeling renewed. We were glad to be alive. The previous day's experience hadn't quite dissipated, but we felt a lot more positive about having to drive again. The views looked inspiring once again and, to our immense relief, there didn't seem to be so much ice on the roads. After a hearty breakfast, courtesy of the guesthouse, we drove on to Skagaströnd, a tiny fishing village an hour or two away from the fjords. We wound our way back around to the main ring road, moving slowly and passing no more than two or three cars along the way. Skagaströnd wasn't in our guidebook so we stopped off at a service station to get some fuel and check out some directions.

Iceland's service stations have roughly the same romantic appeal as the country's supermarkets. They are large, sterile places that sell snacks, burgers, cakes and coffee, and provide pretty much the only services along Iceland's remote roads. I stepped inside to find a few people sitting around watching an episode of *Neighbours* on a TV set bracketed to a wall. I marvelled at the fact that even this North Atlantic outpost has not been spared from Australia's most ubiquitous cultural export. It must have been a good episode as no one stared when we walked in. This was highly unusual for Icelanders, who are more often than not trying to work out if you are some kind of distant relation. Harold Bishop stammered away in the background as I grabbed two coffees and some directions.

We were heading for Skagaströnd to meet Iceland's only 100 per cent *bona fide* cowboy, Hallbjörn Hjartason. Back in Reykjavík, I had visited the Icelandic filmmaker Friðrik Thor Friðriksson and been given a pile of his movies to check out. One of them was called *Icelandic Cowboys*. It documented Iceland's first country-and-western festival, which Hallbjörn had organised. The event was an historic moment in the country's music and cultural history. The movie showed Hallbjörn performing his hip-swivelling, ten-gallon-hat-tipping, guitar-twanging live show in front of a large crowd of Icelanders who sang and barn-danced along with him. The next day, the film showed everyone participating in organised events like horse riding, bull lassoing and can shooting.

The notion of a living, breathing cowboy living in a remote fishing village in Iceland is undeniably amusing. Indeed, Hallbjörn and his western ways were initially met with laughter and even some derision. But that was a long time ago. Since he first started to champion the music in the '60s, he has hosted almost ten successful country-music festivals in Skagaströnd, (the biggest of which, last year, pulled in a stunning 10,000 people), started his own Texan restaurant (Kantrybaer, meaning 'Country Bar') and established his own country-music radio station. By sticking to his guns, he is now a hugely successful entrepreneur and doesn't have to catch fish each day as most of his fellow Skagaströnders do.

Skagaströnd wasn't in the guidebook, but it should have been. While not exactly a bustling megalopolis, it is a pretty seaside village, slightly worn at the edges but every bit as colourful as downtown Reykjavík with its painted houses and bright murals splashed onto the sides of buildings. Being isolated at the northernmost end of an already remote country was obviously not an obstacle to cheerful creativity for the residents of Skagaströnd. We found Hallbjörn's house directly opposite his Kantrybaer, the only restaurant in town. We parked the car and crunched through the snow to his front door, which he opened and stood before us, a slightly tubby, white-haired Icelandic cowboy with a neat black shirt, well-pressed black trousers and a grin that extended from one ear to the other.

He put his cowboy boots on and motioned for us to follow him across to the restaurant, where, he explained in broken English, there was someone around who could translate. The translator turned out to be the chef, Gunnar, also the boyfriend of Hallbjörn's daughter. Both our hosts made us feel extremely welcome, taking our coats and sitting us down at one of the restaurant's wooden tables. The restaurant had country-style dining booths along one wall and a large wooden bar along the back. Behind the bar were two swing doors that led to the kitchen and a service hatch through which hot French fries and tasty Creole burgers could be passed. The place was adorned with pictures of Hallbjörn taken at differing stages of his long career as a cowboy.

Gunnar brought back two bottles of beer for us. They had specially made 'Kantrybaer' labels stuck on them. Hallbjörn pointed at them and smiled proudly. He wasn't missing out on any potential marketing tricks. I asked him how he had managed to lose his head over country music. 'I think I must have been a cowboy in a former life,' he laughed. 'Everyone asks me that question, but I never really know what to say. It's just my life. I love it and I always have. I first got introduced to the music when I was working at the Keflavík air base in Reykjavík in 1965. I worked there for around three years in the kitchen. The base was owned by the Americans who were located here during the war. They had their own radio station that played all American music, mainly rock 'n' roll, but a lot of country music too.

'I just loved country music from when I first heard it. It was nice and light and really caught me in the right spot. I liked Johnny Cash, Jim Reeves and all that kind of stuff and started to join rock 'n' roll bands. We used to play to the soldiers at the base. Everyone carried on doing rock 'n' roll, but I was the first one to do country music. I started to copy the American style but adapted the format of blues, folk and country music to our Icelandic way of life. I moved back here to Skagaströnd in the late '60s and then started to play all over the country.

'I recorded my first record in 1975, which is that one there.' He pointed at a large poster of himself. He was in his mid 20s and cut a dashing figure. 'That one next to it is album number two. I kept making albums and selling them myself. Everyone thought I was crazy at first but I kept doing it and eventually they started to enjoy it. With the money from the LPs I set up the restaurant here. It used to be in another building, but that burned down, so we rebuilt this one a few years ago.'

I told Hallbjörn I had seen the documentary and asked him about the festival. 'I put on the first festival in 1984 just because someone suggested it to me. I thought, "Why not?" It took place just a few hundred metres from here and it went absolutely crazy. The festival has been held nine times so far. There was a break for a few years after the first one, but since then we've had eight of them in a row, always on the first weekend of August. Everyone comes and sets up tents. We don't bring famous artists, as they want too much money. We just bring local musicians and have a good party. Skagaströnd is packed from Thursday to Tuesday because it's a bank-holiday weekend.'

Hallbjörn's radio station is located upstairs from the restaurant. He invited us up to take a look. Outside were various uniforms that Hallbjörn had worn throughout the years, placed inside glass cases and hung ostentatiously on the wall. The station was fairly roomy and professional looking set up with CDs arranged in neat spirals around some surprisingly modern equipment. A side room was stacked with vinyl, mostly arranged on shelving but some scattered loosely around on surfaces and on the walls. Elvis, Tina Turner and Donna Summer smiled cheesily at me from different spots around the room. 'All the vinyl was donated to me after my last place burned down and took my collection with it,' explained Hallbjörn. 'Everyone came and gave me records and I have ever since been trying to find time to put them all in alphabetical order.' The distinctive voice of Tammy Wynette came flowing through the speakers, advising us to 'Stand By Your Man'. Hallbjörn was standing next to me. We looked at each other and edged a couple of inches apart. 'The show I put out is all country music,' he explained. 'It's pre-recorded a couple of days a week and I host it live the rest of the time. The station is transmitted to the local area and is the only one dedicated to country music in Iceland.' I had heard that Hallbjörn has a curious habit of always personally thanking the artist whose record he is playing. The whole set-up smacked of dreams being realised.

I asked Hallbjörn if he'd ever fulfilled the ultimate cowboy dream, visiting Nashville. 'I recorded an album there,' he beamed. 'I went there for three days and spent a fortune. The record flopped. I swore I would never do it again, but I think now I would again if the opportunity came up. I didn't meet anyone famous, as there was no time. We went to Graceland for a day, recorded the LP in three days and then came home again.'

I asked if there were any more dreams an Icelandic cowboy could have. 'Yes,' he asserted. 'My next dream is to put up a country-and-western garden. It will be a small amusement park with maybe 10 or 20 small houses that people can rent and stay in when they come to Iceland. I will make this dream too. Maybe it will take time but I will do it.'

Gunnar nodded at me as Hallbjörn shuffled back down the stairs. 'He will,' he said. 'He'll do it.'

4 Vikings

Vikings settled Iceland between AD 870 and AD 930. Some of them were allegedly fleeing Harold Fairhair, while others were fuelled by nothing more than that restless spirit for adventure with which the Vikings seemed blessed. The Vikings emanated principally from Sweden, Denmark and Norway and were, by all accounts, a generally calm people who enjoyed a bit of pastoral living.

Something, and no one seems to be sure exactly what, must have rattled the collective cage of the Vikings around AD 750. From then until around 1050 (the time between these dates is known as the Viking Era), a large proportion of them decided to build longships from iron and wood and start raiding and pillaging their way around the world. They swarmed as far as their distinctive single square sails would carry them, which happened to be everywhere from Greenland and America to Greece, France, Germany and Britain, and even a brief jaunt to Baghdad.

The first documented Viking raid was in AD 793 on the famous monastery of Lindisfarne, in the east of England. This kicked off a spate of hostilities in Western Europe, principally between the Scandinavians, British and French. Danes settled in England early on, primarily in the north and northeast regions. A man named Ubbi and his two excellently titled brothers, Halfdan the Wide-Reaching and Ivor the Boneless, captured York in AD 866. The English and the Vikings carried on scrapping for years. By AD 878 the latter controlled much of the north of Britain, where a huge amount of Norse culture is still visible today, particularly in place names, almost 1,500 of which have Nordic origins, and everyday language. Three English weekday names are derived from the three main Norse gods: Wednesday is taken from 'Odin's Day', Thursday from 'Thor's Day' and Friday from 'Freyr's Day'. Without the Norse influence on the English language, we would also be without words like *rotten*, *skull*, *sky* and *freckle*, amongst numerous others.

The Vikings seemed to get a kick out of harassing Ireland. Attacks on the island were common from AD 795, with the invaders finally settling in 840 and founding Dublin in 841. Vikings also settled the Faroe Islands in the early part of the 800s, so it was only a matter of time before they also discovered nearby Iceland. They certainly weren't the first people to know about the country, either; a number of travellers had already passed through the country and noted it in their travelogues. In fact, when the Vikings first landed in Iceland to settle, there were already a few monks hanging around who had sailed over from Ireland, presumably for a bit of peace and quiet. Their sedate existence came abruptly to an end when the new visitors arrived. The monks ran bravely away.

Because of the various outposts that the Vikings occupied around the British Isles, the first settlers in Iceland were a mix of Nordic and Gaelic peoples, the latter introduced from Ireland, Scotland and the Scottish Isles. As such, Iceland enjoyed some pretty cosmopolitan beginnings. The strong Gaelic influence also explains the flurry of redheads and brunettes to be found around town.

The man credited as Iceland's first settler is Ingolfur Arnason, a statue of whom can be found atop a small hillock in front of the Ministry of Culture, in downtown Reykjavík. The statue stares out towards the harbour, where Ingolfur landed in 874. The story goes that he arrived from Norway with his foster brother Hjlorleifur, ready for a spot of ransacking. Hjlorleifur stopped off in Ireland on the way to pick up some slaves and the brothers were separated. They landed on separate promontories in Iceland which still bear their respective names today.

Hjlorleifur didn't manage to get overly settled in his new country, however; he was murdered by his own slaves, who took the women and rushed off west to some islands. These islands were ever after known as the Westman Islands, the very same ones that Diddi Fiddla resided on for a while. With Christian concepts like forgiveness and turning the other cheek not yet a part of the Viking world-view, Ingolfur hunted down the slaves like dogs and annihilated them. Before he did this, though, he threw the pillars of his high seat overboard and claimed that he would settle wherever they washed up. Ingolfur named the place Reykjavík, which means 'Smoky Bay'. He allegedly mistook the volcanic steam for smoke, although it's doubtful that snappy Viking phrases for things like subterranean geothermal activity existed, in any case.

By AD 930, a commonwealth was formed in Iceland known as the Althing. It was the first time a political assembly had been set up for a whole nation rather than just separate communities or areas within a nation and is often referred to as the first democratic parliament in the world. From the summer of AD 930 onwards, the chieftains that ruled different parts of Iceland met with other powerful men for two weeks at the plains of Thingvellir, 80km (50 miles) outside Reykjavík. A Law Speaker proclaimed the laws of the land from a natural promontory, which they named the Law Rock. At Thingvellir, and subsequently at other courts that were set up around the country, people met to make new laws, air grievances, settle feuds and discuss the issues of the day.

Thingvellir is still one of Iceland's most poignant places to visit. It's a vast, outdoor area that extends across a large part of Iceland. The place where the actual assemblies took place and a few miles around it have now been proclaimed a national park. The main area where the assemblies were held is a dramatic volcanic ridge created naturally from explosions and earthquakes. These were caused by the tearing apart of the two tectonic plates of Europe and America, which continue to be rent asunder a few more inches each year. The rift is now several kilometres wide, so there's not much hope of straddling both continents, but the landscape is certainly all the more dramatic for its presence.

When Iceland finally shrugged off seven centuries of colonial rule in 1944, Thingvellir was the obvious place to officially declare independence. It was a wet and cloudy day, but still a fifth of the population turned out for the momentous occasion. Many of them brought tents with them to camp there, just as their ancestors had at the dawn of the commonwealth. Due to the temporary accommodations of the settlers at Thingvellir, the site has no archaeological ruins or physical remains. It stands more or less the same as it was 1,000 years before.

I first travelled to Thingvellir as part of the Golden Circle tour. Most of Iceland's settled areas are on the coast, since the interior is uninhabitable, and are connected via a large ring-road that stretches around the entire country. The Golden Circle tour travels on this road and visits Iceland's 'Big Three' landmarks in the South: Thingvellir, the volcanic hot spring Geysir (from which all other hot springs take their name) and the mighty waterfall Gullfoss.

It was a deplorable day when I boarded the bus all blurry-eyed at 8am one morning. Raindrops hammered incessantly against the window, creating soporific polyrhythms that colluded with the hot air from the coach's heating system to send me into a state of mild catatonia. I fought the urge to fall asleep completely, but within ten minutes of setting off, the two American gents in front of me were snoring away peacefully. Our guide, a well-built German lady, cut through the wooziness with a loud, crackling and very formal 'hello everybody', delivered through the bus's PA system. Everyone seemed too dozy to answer. I watched the landscape roll by out of the wet window as she continued our itinerary for the day. We would be having lunch here, a coffee stop there, we would get 20 minutes for each attraction and so on and so forth. Oh, and if we were late, the bus would simply go and leave us there. It reminded me why I had spent the last few years avoiding package tours wherever possible.

As we drove past some rocks, I noticed there was a little red door painted on the front of one. 'The doors on the rocks are for the elves,' explained the guide. Eh? *Elves*? Did someone just say *elves*? No one showed any signs of being perturbed. I didn't want to start firing questions like an impetuous schoolboy and embarrass myself. Instead, I adopted a poker-faced expression that suggested I wasn't surprised in the slightest about the mention of elves and secretly vowed to find out more.

Our first stop was for a quick look around Eden. The misleading names given to Greenland and Iceland were nothing compared to this place. It had been called after the biblical garden of paradise due to the fact it contained some garden plants that had been grown in geothermal greenhouses, but the plants were stuck at the back of a horrible little mini-mall undoubtedly invented by Beelzebub himself. Japanese businessmen played on fruit machines and Space Invaders while a store offered tacky postcards and gifts and a café sold sandwiches containing unrecognisable ingredients.

I was hungry and the next stop wasn't for an hour or so. I had to risk it. The café attendant spoke only Icelandic and the descriptions of the food were all helpfully in Icelandic, too. I bought the smallest and least threatening-looking option and took a bite. It was the first time I have ever had to spit food out of my mouth in a public place. I accompanied the experience with an involuntary groan. There are many reasons to come to Iceland, but the food is not one of them. To top it off, I walked outside to find the bus pulling away. I gave chase and managed to get it to stop just before it turned onto the main road. I had only been a minute or two over our scheduled time. I looked askance at the guide as the doors hissed closed behind me but she regarded with me a hard stare that suggested I might like to just die right there on the spot. I shuffled off sulkily to the back.

The next stop was touted as Geysir, but in fact it was Strokkur. Geysir, which could once shoot sprays up to 100m (110 yards) high, had been rendered impotent by all the soap flakes poured into it in a misguided effort to make it erupt more regularly. Now it just gurgles dementedly, like a drugged patient. Soapless Strokkur, though, located just a few metres along, goes off every five or ten minutes without fail. It's a delightful experience to watch this large bubbling pool, a few metres across, start swelling like a huge balloon and send a huge gush of water several metres up into the air. The novelty wore off after 20 minutes or so, but it illustrated the immense power that lies beneath this volcanic island.

The weather was still grim as we approached the dramatic Gullfoss, our next destination. Gullfoss is Iceland's most famous waterfall, based in the mighty River Hvita. The water falls with a formidable rush into a long, narrow canyon, forming a fine mist at the point of contact. There is even a spot of vegetation around here, enabled by the moisture created by the mist. At one point, this glorious attraction was going to be sold to foreign investors, who were going to harness it for electricity and charge for entrance. They changed their minds when the daughter of the farmer who owned the land threatened to drown herself if the deal went ahead. The roar of the waterfall along the valley was another deeply impressive display of the raw power of Iceland's nature.

Half an hour later we were at Thingvellir and being reminded of our 20-minute time allocation. I had read about the place already in *Njal's Saga*, one of Iceland's most cherished literary works. The book, said to be part fact and part fiction, was written sometime in the 13th century and is a sprawling tale of feuding Icelandic families in the early days of the Settlement. It's an epic tale that allegedly contains the answers to all of life's problems. The families involved in the ongoing dispute came to Thingvellir on occasion to put their cases to the Law Speakers. I stood on the Law Rock and gazed out at the watery plains. I could see why it had been chosen as a meeting point for the nation. There was a sense of majesty still in the place which seemed perfectly in keeping with the noble causes of law and community.

Njal's Saga exposed the fact that the emphasis of the law was placed on honour and bravery in early Viking societies. If the Law Speaker decided that someone was guilty of a crime, he could outlaw the individual. (Outlawry amounted, more or less, to being hunted down and killed.) The law also condoned murder in cases where an assailant had committed a sexual assault against someone's wife, mother, daughter, sister, foster-mother or foster-daughter. *Njal's Saga* illustrated exactly how the beefs of the day could turn into bloody and protracted wars as one murder begat another in an endless series of battles that stretched on through generations and escalated until whole families were wiped out.

The style of the *Saga* was incredibly matter-of-fact, given its aggressive and epic content – the anonymous author (many saga writers didn't put their names to their works) declined to judge events or comment when a man smashed an axe into another man's skull, and so forth. An overriding feeling of fatalism pervaded the tale, that whatever happened to you was meant to be so there wasn't much point in wallowing around in self-pity. The heroes were just as likely to turn to comedy as sentimentality in their dying hour, and the sagas contain many scenes worthy of a Monty Python sketch. In one such scene, an unlucky man is run through with a sword. He looks down at the blade and comments memorably on how 'these kinds of sword are all the rage these days'. The overall terse style of the sagas is thought to have inspired the similarly hard-boiled style of modern writers such as John Steinbeck and Ernest Hemingway.

The word *saga* means 'story' and also 'history'. Most of the Icelandic sagas were written in the 13th and 14th centuries, initially by scholars but afterwards by anyone who had the means and desire to record some of the events that had occurred over previous centuries or wanted to write tales of current events. Icelanders became prolific writers almost as soon as Christianity had introduced the Latin alphabet, which they added to their own basic system of runes. The rest of the Norse world adopted Christianity and the alphabet, too, but the literature styles began to change form in mainland Europe and were affected by monarchs and the Church.

Due to its isolation, Iceland had no pressure from kings or priests and people there took to writing with an almost feverish devotion, continuing to write in the traditional heathen way. They wrote genealogies, historical accounts, tales of the old kings of Scandinavia before Iceland's Settlement, descriptions of the actual Settlement, stories about the Viking expansions to Greenland and North America and about family feuds in Iceland and Scandinavia. They also wrote *Eddas*, which recorded the pagan mythology of the Vikings through prose and poetry.

Many of these tales are astonishingly detailed, and while some of those details contradict each other or have been proven to be more fantastical than factual, many others have been corroborated by archaeological evidence. Without the Icelandic sagas, little would be known about the life and history of the Vikings or of the countries they settled and lived in.

Thanks to the sagas and to the subsequent emphasis on literature and poetry in Iceland, it is often described as a literary nation. Every Icelander, it is said, has a novel or a book of poetry in them just waiting to be written, and judging by the vast amount of locally produced literature, there would seem to be more than a grain of truth in the statement. Icelanders read and publish more books *per capita* than any other nation in the world. That literature touches the people of Iceland deeply is also evident in their respect for words and also for writers. Halldór Laxness, in particular, is a fine example. Laxness is regarded inside and outside of Iceland as a master of 20th-century fiction. He was a prolific novelist, essayist and poet (as well as a keen pianist), and his work often touches on themes close to the hearts of Icelanders. He is the only Icelander to have won a Nobel Prize, awarded to him in 1955 for his 'vivid, epic power, which has renewed the great narrative art of Iceland'.

Terry Gunnell, the head of the Folklore Department at Reykjavík University, revealed to me the extent to which Laxness is venerated in Iceland. Terry taught English for several years before he entered the Folklore Department. When I went along to his office one day for a chat, he noted that Icelanders on the whole are not prone to idolisation. He told me of a test he had run amongst his students to see how they would react to certain people suddenly appearing in their living rooms. When he mentioned the president of Iceland, no one batted an eyelid. When he said the Queen of England, there was still no sign of being overly impressed. No one flinched at the mention of Björk. But when Terry called Laxness's name, there was a palpable sense of awe and respect.

Laxness passed away in 1998, but I had the good fortune to meet his grandson. Also called Halldór Laxness, he is 17 years old and one of the most talented rappers on the Icelandic hip-hop scene. I had seen him perform at a freestyle jam in Gaukur Á Stöng, one of Reykjavík's premier live venues. A chubby, baby-faced young man, he stepped on stage with the cocky bravado typical of teenagers the world over. Many of the other MCs during the evening had presented an aggressive battle style, but Halldór combined humorous indifference with a calm, collected delivery. I couldn't understand his lyrics, but I could see plainly that he had the audience eating out of his hands. He came second, but he had by far the biggest personality of the evening. I met him the next day during his school lunch break.

'I beat that guy last year,' he smirked when I mentioned the previous night's performance. 'But the winner of this year's competition got a really nice trophy and everything. Last year I won but I only got a plastic one.' Halldór explained to me that he has been rapping for two years and is enjoying the recent vogue for rhyming in Icelandic since he always found English a little bit difficult. I asked him what his crew was called. He told me the name, which sounded very much like the name of the hot-dog stall in town. 'It is,' he admitted bashfully. 'It means "town's finest". It started as a joke but we ended up keeping it.' When I chuckled, Halldór held me fast with a mock-injured expression. 'Don't make me kick your ass, man,' he joked.

'So, Halldór, did your grandfather have any influence on you wanting to put the Icelandic language to good use?' I asked.

'No,' he replied, 'but I get a lot of pressure from the media and from Icelandic journalists who want to believe I do. A lot of them are snobs. I just deny any sign of influence; I think it's the best way. Every interview I do ends with, "So are you going to write a book?" I always say no, but I do like writing stories and sending them to my friends. I haven't read all of my grandfather's work, but I have gone through a lot of it. I lived next door to him when I was growing up and he was a very dear man. He achieved something that no one else in Iceland did, and he was also very funny. He did things in a certain way that he knew would amuse people. He was a good parent, though, and quite strict. He wasn't a clown; he was sophisticated. I wouldn't say his writing has inspired me, but his existence has.'

The elder Laxness had seen himself simply as continuing the work of his ancestors. In his acceptance speech for the Nobel Prize, he gave acknowledgement to the saga writers, who 'succeeded in creating not only a literary language which is among the most beautiful and subtlest there is, but a separate literary genre'. One morning, after a typically belligerent Friday night, during which the inebriated howls of Iceland's modern-day Vikings had sailed across the rooftops, I went to the Árni Magnússon Institute, where most of the country's ancient manuscripts are stored.

Stepping out of my apartment, I was impressed at how clean the streets looked. I had imagined them to be full of broken bottles, pavement pizzas and the occasional still-snoozing body, but they had magically recomposed themselves. It looked as if a spry night wind had whipped through them with the rapidity and efficiency of electricity around a circuit-board. It was a Saturday morning but it felt more like a Sunday afternoon. The charming tinkle of church bells as I walked towards the Institute enhanced the atmosphere of mellow geniality. I felt like I was strolling through a large village, which Reykjavík ostensibly is. Three hundred years ago, its population was a meagre 60, including the people who lived at the nearby farms. Without them, it was 21. Forty years before that, Reykjavík was literally just a farm, albeit a large one with its own church.

This explains perhaps why the place still feels so relaxed and low key. The burdens of most European cities simply don't exist here. There's no sense of urban entropy, no being packed into tight spaces with hundreds of people you don't know, no fighting your way through shops, no hour-long queues for exhibitions or museums. Iceland is also unencumbered by imposing architecture. There are no skyscrapers, voluminous palaces or grandiose castles. In fact, apart from a smattering of statues, public buildings and museums, Reykjavík has few real landmarks to speak of. The most important building in the city, the Parliament House, built in 1830, is so small it seems almost apologetic. Iceland's history lies not so much in buildings and monuments as in books.

Árni Magnússon had a museum named after him for a reason. He was an Icelander, born in the west of the country in 1663. He attended university in Copenhagen and the Danish government employed him in a rush of literary inspiration to come to Iceland and bring back all the manuscripts he could carry. Árni did so, with a diligence that bordered on obsession. He took them all back to Denmark, where they were safe for a while until 1728, when the Great Fire of Copenhagen ravaged a great deal of the city, including the University, where the manuscripts were kept. Fortunately many were salvaged and were eventually returned to Iceland following independence from Denmark.

In the Institute, I found myself beholding a spread of glass cabinets that contained manuscripts preserved from the Middle Ages. The slightly tattered tomes were laid open in their cases, revealing painstakingly neat and impressively ornate texts. The horror an author of the day must have felt if he made a mistake after spending hours and hours on one of these works of art was unimaginable. The writing of these books must have been a saga in itself, especially since they didn't have the luxury of paper. Until then, authors used vellum – tanned calfskin – which necessitated a time-consuming and complicated procedure of wetting, drying, stretching, turning, more wetting, more drying and leaving the material for weeks to set.

I gazed at the manuscripts for a while and let my imagination slowly transport me to another era. I looked at a 17th-century manuscript which turned out to be *Ari The Learned's Book Of Icelanders*. Originally written in the 12th century, the book describes in great detail the Settlement of Iceland, the nation's conversion to Christianity and the development of the old parliament. It even lists all the Law Speakers until that time. One of the biggest manuscripts in the room was *Flateyjarbok* ('Book Of The Island Of Flatey'), which was written in the late 1300s by clerics and contained stories about Nordic kings, Eirik the Red and the Settlement of Greenland. (The Vikings had settled in Greenland and shared it with the native Inuits for a while, making their way from there across to America.)

After viewing the manuscripts, I took a walk up to Hallgrímskirkja, the ambitious concrete church built in memory of the 17th-century national poet Hallgrím Petursson. The structure took 40 years to complete and its space-age, rocket-ship shape suggests it might be able to carry a congregation up to the heavens rather than simply provide a place of worship. Along with Perlan, the revolving restaurant set atop four huge water containers on the outskirts of town, it is the most adventurous – and the most contentious – building in Reykjavík. Its 73m (80 yard) steeple stands way above any other building in the city, and the bell tower at the top naturally affords some inspiring views. The interior of the church, designed by the state architect Gudjon Samuelson, is impressively spacious and full of light, emphasising the Lutheran principles of sparseness and simplicity. The most dramatic feature is the huge organ, which dominates the front of the interior, an immaculate contraption with over 5,000 pipes and 72 stops. It was built from proceeds donated by the local community and has ensured that the church is now something of a cultural hotspot and the envy of church organists the world over.

Outside the church is a large concrete effigy of a Viking man looking proudly out towards the city and sporting all the accoutrements of the day: axe, sword, chain mail, helmet, cloak, virile demeanour. He looked impressive. I read the inscription on the back of the statue and learned that it was a gift from the USA on the 1,000th anniversary of Iceland's parliament in 1930. The statue was of Leifur Eiríksson, the first European to have discovered America, some 500 years before Columbus. Leifur's discovery of America was news to me.

I walked back along Laugavegur to Reykjavík's Phallological Museum, the only institution of its kind in the world. When I walked in, I discovered the owner, Siggi, sitting alone behind a small reception desk near the door. A slightly rotund fellow with a grey beard, a friendly, square face and braces stretching across his portly stomach, he was surrounded by phalluses. The room was literally chockablock with schlongs. They sat in jars, protruded from walls, dangled from the ceiling. They had been removed from whales, elephants, bulls and a range of other animals.

The collection, Siggi told me as I absorbed the bizarre décor, contains over 150 penises and penile parts belonging to almost all the land and sea mammals that can be found in Iceland. 'We have 38 specimens belonging to 15 different kinds of whale, one specimen taken from a rogue polar bear, 19 specimens belonging to seven different kinds of seal and walrus, and 93 specimens originating from 19 different kinds of land mammal.'

Aside from real-life flesh phalluses, there also were imaginative penis-shaped furnishings and gadgets made from all kinds of materials, which Siggi had crafted himself. I asked him how he got started in such an idiosyncratic business. 'It all started with this,' he said, leading me across to what looked like a thin leather strap on the wall. 'I used to be a headmaster in a school in Akranes for almost a decade and taught history. One day I threw a party with some of my teachers and we were talking about the utilisation of the animals in the old days. Icelanders used everything on an animal, you know, often out of necessity. What they couldn't eat they used for toys. One of the teachers who came from the countryside remembered that he used to have a bull's penis as a whip when he was younger. Someone else said he was going to slaughter some of his bulls soon and the following week he bought me four penises to show me. They tan them in the factory like leather. I kept them and a little while later some of the teachers working at a whaling station brought me some whale penises, and the idea to go on collecting came to me from there.'

The whole museum smacked of dedication. I learned a lot. I discovered that some mammals have bones in their penises while others don't. Apparently all carnivorous animals have them apart from hyenas, and all primates have them except the species *Homo* (humans, chimps and so forth) and a couple of types of ape. Siggi showed me how humpback whales have special muscles for retraction. 'Free Willy?' I suggested.

'No, no, it was very expensive,' he chuckled.

I found myself gazing at a human foreskin. It was a forlorn-looking thing in a jar. It was the closest the museum had to a human penis so far, explained Siggi, although there were a few signed pledges on the wall from individuals offering to donate their 'goods' just as soon as they didn't need them any more. One German gentleman had enthusiastically supplied two photostats of his intended gift, which were also pinned to the wall. He had named each image: one was called 'High Emotions', the other 'Low Emotions'. The difference between them was marked.

'The German gentleman has been visiting the museum every year for the last 20 years,' enthused Siggi. 'All these letters of donation are from people who have been here before. We put a rule in place a while ago that all pledges have to come with some kind of sample, a mould or a picture or something, which proves their donation will be bigger than our legal length of five inches [13cm]. Anyone under size could potentially go into the dwarf section.'

He wasn't joking, either – there really was a section for dwarves. And elves. And trolls. The elf and dwarf jars seemed to have nothing in them, although Siggi explained that they were invisible creatures, so naturally their penises were also invisible. 'Some girls claim to see them, though,' he said. 'They all seem to agree on the shape and length of it, so I believe them.' In the troll jar was a stone. 'Trolls turn to stone if they get exposed to light,' Siggi explained. 'This one was obviously caught whilst hurrying on his way home or something. Any humans from outside Iceland, like the German guy, would go into our Foreign Penis section, as they do not qualify as Icelandic mammals.'

Siggi led me to the Foreign section, which included an undeniably impressive phallus from an African elephant amongst other assorted international appendages.

'But we do have one prospective donor from Iceland.' He showed me a page of writing, which turned out to be written evidence from a local lady who not only attested to the appropriate size of the donor's tackle but also its capabilities. 'He's a famous womaniser from Akureyri in the north,' explained Siggi. 'He's 87 now but still going strong. He was actually one of the pioneers of Icelandic tourism and was the first to organise large tours to the Icelandic Highlands and Italy back in the '50s. He always was far from being a modest man and he still likes to be in the limelight.'

I had gone to the museum because it was recommended by the folklore professor Terry Gunnell that I meet Siggi. He had told me that he was one of the last true Vikings, whatever that meant, and that he also knew his onions about history, having taught for a while and written specialist essays on Latin-American history. I reckoned he might be a good person to ask about Leifur Eiríksson.

I waited patiently for him to enthusiastically demonstrate to me a 2mm (½in)-long hamster penis and then asked, 'Siggi, what do you know about Leifur Eiríksson?' Siggi raised his eyebrows. Not his penis, I explained, his discovery of America.

'Ah yes,' he said, looking slightly relieved and taking a seat behind his desk. 'The name of Columbus is taboo here because we have proof in the sagas that Leifur discovered America, or what he called Vinland, which is today known as Canada, before Columbus did. He discovered it 500 years before Columbus, who robbed us of the honour of discovery. Some say that Columbus actually got his ideas to sail there when he came to Iceland but I'm not so sure. The so called "proof" is just ten lines in a letter he wrote to someone to say that he had sailed beyond a place called Thule, which was the size of England. Thule was one of the old names for Iceland, and from these ten lines Icelandic historians say that not only was Columbus here but that he learned about America from us. I don't think you can draw all these conclusions from such small evidence, personally.

'We had some problems with the Norwegians trying to claim that Leifur was from there and that it was they who discovered the place, but that's rubbish. Leifur was born here. The Settlement Era goes like this...' Siggi wrapped a large paw around the thick shaft of a penis pen made from wood and began to write on a scrap of paper. 'The Vikings came from Norway and settled here between 870 and 930, which is what we call the Age of Settlement,' he said. 'We then founded a commonwealth at the Althing in 930, which was the first parliament in Europe. After that point we could not be called Norwegian immigrants any more. If passports existed then we would have had Icelandic passports in 930 and anyone born after that would be Icelandic, even if they had Norwegian descendants. Leifur's father was Eirik the Red, who discovered Greenland in around 980 and was born around the 930 mark. His son was born around 970 or something, which makes him definitely Icelandic.'

Siggi told me that, while most of this was based on the sagas, it had been backed up by archaeological evidence. In the 1960s, he said, a Norwegian couple discovered a Viking site at Epaves Bay in Newfoundland. This site was called L'Anse aux Meadows and offered incontrovertible proof of an early-11th-century Norse settlement. The sagas don't mention any particular area except Vinland, and the exact location of it was always tricky to determine, especially since the details in different sagas seemed to conflict.

The discovery of the Norse habitation at L'Anse aux Meadows obviously lends credence to the theory that Vinland was in Newfoundland, but the remains of the 'settlement' appear to have been small and may have been just a base camp used for further explorations along the coast. The general consensus among scholars is that Vinland was not a specific site but a whole region, which incorporates Newfoundland and extends into the Gulf of St Lawrence.

However, everyone agrees that, although the Vikings are the first recorded Europeans to land there, they never settled permanently. They were certainly in places like L'Anse aux Meadows and maybe other areas, but they seem to have left again quite soon. This could have been due to many reasons, including the fact that Vinland was far away and involved a risky journey and that there may have been some native inhabitants who put up a fight for their land. Both of these could be true.

But because they never settled, the Vikings never had any impact on the development of North American culture, and this has lead many historians to dispute the term 'discovery'. What seems certain, though, is that an Icelander was the first European to set foot on the 'new continent' and makes Oscar Wilde's famous quote just as poignant. 'The Icelanders are the most intelligent race on Earth,' he quipped, 'because they discovered America and never told anyone.'

5 Rimur

Iceland is not just a nation of saga literature; it is also a nation of poetry. Although the sagas came into vogue in the 12th century, the Vikings had long before mastered the art of poetry. As far back as the first century AD, the Roman historian Tacitus noted that the only form of history the Germans had were poems. This extended to the Norsemen, too, as the two cultures overlapped and shared many similar characteristics.

Poems were composed constantly and handed down through generations in Iceland right from the time of Settlement. The oldest surviving poems were composed in Norway but, as with the sagas, the style became more popular in Iceland during the ninth and tenth centuries. The original poets were called *skalds*, and Icelanders wrote skaldic poetry to please the Norwegian King, not being put off by the fact that the poetry was known for its mind-boggling complexity and possibly went straight over the King's head.

When the sagas came into fashion, the poetry went into decline, but some of the verses and the technical structures were remembered. In the 13th century, Snorri Sturluson, reckoned to be the greatest writer of the Saga Era, lamented the fact that this once-noble tradition was fading, so he wrote a textbook that explained the complex structures and metres of the poetry to the younger generation. He hoped that the readers of his book would help revive it by bringing it back into practice. This work became known as *Snorri's Edda*, or the *Prose Edda*.

Snorri lived in Iceland between 1179 and 1241 and belonged to a notoriously powerful family. This family were involved in a period of violence and turmoil which led directly to the loss of Icelandic independence in 1262–4. The era ended up bearing his family's name: the Age of the Sturlungars.

Snorri himself was a wealthy and powerful man and not much liked. He was once a Law Speaker at the Althing, and became embroiled in the politics of the Norwegian monarch King Hakonarson, until he managed to upset him and was assassinated in his own cellar in Reykholt.

Ironically, it was Snorri's work on the sagas (he was the acknowledged author of the lauded *Heimskringla*, as well as the suspected brains behind *Egill's Saga* and other works) that had helped diminish the influence of the skaldic poetry. His resuscitation attempts didn't quite work at the time, but in the 14th century the form of the old poetry was brought back to versify the sagas of the day, which were then chanted for entertainment purposes alongside readings of hymns and normal renditions of the sagas. These were known as *rimur*.

This tradition flourished in the 18th and 19th centuries and is still alive today. Because it is chanted, and because it has lasted an incredible six centuries, the *rimur* represent the most consistent musical form Iceland has ever had. In the rush for modernisation, *rimur*, like the old folk songs, were all but forgotten about, but 20 years ago they got an unlikely public airing when some of the members of the punk movement in Iceland – Purrkur Pillnikk, Theyr, Kukl and The Sugarcubes – asked Sveinbjörn Beinteinsson, then leader of the pagan Asatru society and an active performer of the old rhymes, to join them on stage.

The strange half-sung, half-chanted way in which he performed them entranced audiences all over. The atonal mode of chanting is known in Icelandic as *kveda* – a different word from the Icelandic word for sing, which is *syngja*. One of the principal protagonists of *rimur* in Iceland today is Steindór Andersen. Tall and broad-shouldered with a thick black beard and a deep, booming voice, Steindór seemed even more of a modern Icelandic Viking than Siggi.

I first heard of Steindór via Sigur Ros, whom he toured with in 2001. Their live collaborations were essentially updates of the old-school/new-school fusion that the 'Cubes and Beinteinsson first proposed two decades earlier but in new settings and perhaps with more fittingly melodramatic music. I never got to see Sigur Ros on that tour, but I heard stories of the mysterious man who appeared with them on stage, clad in a black suit and chanting eerie, hymn-like songs. No one knew what he was singing about, but his performances were by all accounts captivating.

One morning I caught the bus to Steindór's hometown of Hafnarfjördur, 20 minutes outside Reykjavík. Hafnarfjördur is built on a lava field at the confluence of several ley lines and is allegedly brimming with mystic energy, although there wasn't anything particularly mystical about the group of floppy-haired teenagers spitting and kicking each other at the bus station as I arrived. However, there was a pretty harbour, which I spent a few minutes admiring until Steindór arrived in his car to drive me to his house.

On the way, I was slightly taken aback at the scenery. I had seen lava fields before – Iceland is covered in them – but never with lots of houses built on top. Instead of green suburban lawns or nice concrete driveways separating each dwelling, Hafnarfjördur had craggy rock formations. Some of them looked seriously steep. Borrowing a cup of sugar from a neighbour here could be a life-threatening exercise involving sturdy climbing boots, crampons and grappling hooks.

As we drove, Steindór told me how he came to discover *rimur*: 'I first discovered the old rhymes when I worked as a child in the country. Later, when I was 40, my mother told me that my grandfather chanted for me sitting on his knee when I was two or three years old – something completely lost in my memory. It was not until many years later, after 20 years as a fisherman, that I recovered the *rimur* tradition and began to study the manuscripts. By then I was a fisherman on a stern-trawler. Three years later I bought a small fishing boat and gave her the name *Idunn*. Since then I have been captain on my boat, alone. Now I only operate on sea over the summertime and catch the fish with nylon line and rubber bait hooks. The radio on board has always been out of order, which doesn't matter because I chant all the time for myself and the seagulls. It's a fantastic way of living, especially in still and foggy weather.'

Steindór told me how, as he discovered more and more about *rimur*, strange things began to happen. He kept running into people connected with the tradition – especially Sveinbjörn Beinteinsson. 'Wherever I went, Sveinbjörn would suddenly appear,' smiled Steindór. 'In the National Library, walking down Laugavegur, in the pub – he was always there. I discovered a cassette tape with recordings from Sveinbjörn and he followed me through the first steps into this amazing world of *rimur* songs. At the same time, I met other people, also by coincidence, connected to the *rimur* tradition or related to old chanters. I have never been fatalistic, but now I'm confused as what I have been doing in the last few years is obviously not in accordance with what I had decided to do.'

Steindór's house was pleasant and roomy. Originally built in 1926, Steindór bought it in 1976 and reconstructed and enlarged it himself, keeping its original style. Most impressive was the elegant, sweeping staircase that led up to the bedrooms and his office. We went into the kitchen where Hilmar Örn Hilmarsson was waiting for us, a thin cigarillo dancing between his lips and adding curlicues of smoke to the fumes of sweet coffee. Hilmar is a distinguished character within the Icelandic music scene. He was heavily involved in Iceland's punk explosion in the '80s with an act called Theyr, and since then he has become best known as a soundtrack composer. He has more than 20 film scores under his belt, many of them for his friend Friðrik Thor Friðriksson, Iceland's best-known moviemaker. Hilmar, a creatively restless soul like so many in Iceland, has also produced albums for a dizzying range of artists from '70s counter-culture hero Megas to hip-hop crews and death-metal bands.

One musician once described Hilmar to me as a 'romanticist'. This presumably alludes to his being a motivating factor for a host of projects that aim to bring Iceland's ancient culture to the fore via music. A while ago he orchestrated a collaboration between Asa Ketilsdóttir and an avant-garde electronic producer called Kippi Kaninus, and he arranged and took part in an esteemed concert between Sigur Ros and

Steindór called Odin's Raven Magic, an emotive piece that set ancient poetry performed by Steindór to a bewitching musical and visual set produced by Hilmar and Sigur Ros. The show received positive criticism at both places at which it was performed: the Reykjavík Arts Festival and London's Barbican Arts Centre.

More impressively, the performance served to get the poem Steindór was reading reinstated into the new translations of the *Older Edda*, an ancient book of poetry that contains some of the main descriptions of the Norse mythology and which Snorri borrowed and built from in his own *Prose Edda*. 'A Norwegian scholar had decided it was too apocryphal,' Hilmar told me. 'For some reason, people listened to him, so we tried to bring attention to its majesty and relevance and got it put back in. It was a significant cultural victory, a bit like getting a book back in the Bible. I decided a long time ago that our ancient culture should be treated with the same reverence and respect as the Greek and Roman worlds.'

Steindór and Sigur Ros were initially brought together by a TV presenter in Iceland who contacted both parties and suggested Steindór teach Jonsi, Sigur Ros's lead singer, to chant some *rimur*. Steindór showed him some *rimur* melodies and a week later received a call from the singer asking if Steindór would meet the band at the recording studio during their rehearsal and try to record a song. Steindór agreed, chanting something that Sveinbjörn had taught him. It worked so well that they asked him to perform with them and recorded a limited-edition CD to sell at the concerts.

As we sat at the kitchen table, the light hum of the refrigerator providing an ambient backdrop, Steindór and Hilmar explained to me some of *rimur*'s complex structures. The rhymes, they said, adhere to a vast array of rules and regulations that are more or less strictly observed. One of the main rules is that the syllables of each line must be arranged in trochaic form – ie a long syllable is followed immediately by a short one, or a stressed syllable is followed by an unstressed one.

There are also laws that relate to the lines in the individual stanzas, or verses. The amount of lines can vary from two to four. In a four-line stanza, the first and third lines almost always contain seven syllables each, although eight syllables are sometimes used. In the second and fourth lines the number of syllables may vary from four to eight, although the most frequent number is six or seven. In a three-line stanza, the first line is always the longest, possessing anything from 10 to 12 syllables. The second line has seven or eight syllables and the third line has from six to eight syllables. In a two-line stanza, the first line must consist of 11 or 12 syllables while the second line varies from 7 to 12 syllables.

My head was reeling slightly as I absorbed all of this and tried to imagine how it might sound in English. I was no Shakespeare, but I could tell things were already getting tricky. The principal metres of the verses, they continued, then differ from one another in the number of lines, the number of syllables in each line and/or in the final rhyme combinations. Each *rima* (the singular of *rimur*) is the equivalent to a chapter in a book, using the same principal verse form consistently but containing individual stanzas within it so that the individual *rimur* are clearly separated.

Another of the principal characteristics of *rimur* is that they are highly alliterative. Alliteration must always occur in the accented syllable of the trochee. It must also appear for the third and last time in the first trochee in the second half of the couplet.

By now, any hope I had of keeping up was long gone. When Steindór added that it was possible to have either consonant or vowel alliteration, that the *rimur* also contained several other forms of internal rhyme and that sometimes entire stanzas can be palindromes – that is, they are intelligible when read both forwards and backwards – I exhaled the long, awe-inspired gasp that been building up inside me for the last few minutes: 'So the Vikings really had enjoyed playing with words...'

Steindór and Hilmar nodded gravely. They had the slightly haunted look that accompanies men who have spent a great deal of time battling with complex rhyme structures. I had to ask what had made them so drawn to such an incredibly complex art form.

'The different patterns and ornamentation in so many forms of the metrics fascinated me,' said Steindór, clasping his large hands together in front of his face. 'Through Sveinbjörn I discovered the Rimur

Society, which had been formed in 1929 by people from the countryside who moved to Reykjavík but wanted to preserve something that had once been their way of life. The idea of the Society initially was to collect as many of the *rimur* melodies and styles as possible and to keep them living. We now have around 500 *rimur* preserved in the collection, which is a lot more than we had before. We use many of the same rhymes that were used in the 14th century, even though we perform from many different sources.

'The Society has become a sort of living museum, with people from different parts of the country coming forward with different strands of the tradition. The Society meets once or twice a month in the winter, as they used to in the old days, and we chant and listen to the recordings we have to try and keep the old traditions alive. We also collect and preserve manuscripts like these here...'

He gestured towards some antiquated books that were lying on the kitchen table. I picked one up and browsed through its yellowing pages. Considering it was printed in the 17th century, it wasn't in bad condition. On the raggedy paper were lines and lines of ancient Icelandic poetry. I paused on a page and tried to see if I could glean anything. There was more chance of being bitten gently by a snowman. 'The poem you're looking at was probably written in about 1820 or something and is called "Andrarimur",' explained Hilmar, '"The Rimur Of Andri". Andri is the central figure in the story, but it's about a large fight between families and has a lot of heroes, magic and murder in it. Lots of the *rimur* derive from the sagas. "Gunnarsrimur", for example, is about Gunnar, one of the main characters in *Njal's Saga*.'

Olafur Davidsson put the first printed versions of *rimur* melodies together at the end of the 19th century. Bjarni Thorsteinsson then published 250 of them in his book. Some of the melodies were fixed, but many others were updated and changed with each performer. The earliest extant text goes back to the 14th century; the most modern was written this century. The texts vary in length, from single *rimur* of less than 100 stanzas to sets of 20 or more *rimur* which add up to thousands of stanzas.

The *rimur* poets versified the literature of the day (the sagas) and had to handle the passages skilfully and master all of the different meters that were involved. Hence the rhymes contain many of the same themes as the sagas: dramatic accounts of battles and heroes, supernatural stories, tales of chivalry and romance.

Due to the widespread appeal of the *rimur* style throughout the community, contemporary 'gossip' stories were also common. Much of the *rimur* poetry carries with it heavy metaphors which allude back to the Viking mythology. These are known as *kennings*. A typical *kenning* might be 'beer of wounds', which, for example, means 'blood'. 'Swords maple' means 'soldier'. 'Wave steed' is 'ship'. Some of these metaphors are relatively easy to deduce but others are, as Hilmar pointed out, 'about as penetrable as a cryptic-crossword puzzle'.

'During the period at which the *rimur* were at their peak of popularity, our nation was in a bad way economically,' explained Steindór. 'We suffered from plagues, volcanic eruptions and poverty. The old turf-houses that people lived in were cold and dark and the people hungry and helpless. Their relief was in the romances of chivalry as well as the sagas from the glorious Viking age in Iceland. National pride and also some comfort were derived from the *rimur* and from the sagas that told of the ancient Republic of Iceland – the good old days. These were stories of battles, love and defection, rewards of victory and so on, and they brought the illusion of brightness and warmth into the cold and dirty living rooms. The living rooms were called the *badstofa* and were where the family worked hard and listened to *rimur* during what was called the *kvöldvaka* in long winter evenings, where clothes were made from wool and carving and splicing ropes.'

This *kvöldvaka* tradition survived as a general custom right up until the early 1900s. The family would gather in the *badstofa* after working outside. The adults would sleep through the twilight and then wake up again and work indoors, making ropes, mending nets, carving tools and so on. The performer of *rimur* usually sat by the only lamp in the room with a copy of a text. Good *rimur* singers (*kvaedamenn*) were usually available for the performances and could even gain employment in households as nightly entertainers.

Before the *rimur* were performed, there would traditionally be something called *mansöngur*, a short lyrical introduction to each *rima* in the same metre as the *rima* itself. The subject matter of these introductions depended on the *rimur* chanter, since they composed them themselves, but usually they were respectful odes to the ladies in the room and lamentations of the poet's lack of skills and success in the affairs of the heart. Often, the audience would request their omission so they could get on with the main story.

Rimur were performed and appreciated by all levels of society up until the end of 19th century. At the beginning of the 18th century, an administrator of the Danish Crown, Magnús Stephensen, attacked the *rimur* and called for it to be replaced with other forms of poetry and happier tunes. Eventually the style gave way to the influx of new, foreign tunes and melodic music. The more Iceland modernised, the more *rimur*, and the old folk tunes that Asa and others sang, became an embarrassing relic from old times. The founding of the state radio in 1930 brought with it a wealth of new music, although it did retain some of its programme for *rimur*.

'Poetry has been a mainstay in Iceland,' commented Hilmar. 'We missed out on at least 200 years of European evolution, going straight from farmhouses to modern buildings, etc, and so a lot of our older culture is still very much intact. We had influences from the Enlightenment, but that was mainly amongst the intelligentsia. No one really rammed Christianity down our throats, which is how these pagan traditions have survived. Sometimes the Christian and pagan worlds have produced offspring like the mythical Christmas children we have, which are unique to Iceland. They are dirty, scruffy little people who steal and cheat and lie and they turn up every year at Christmastime. They often disturb visitors. In fact, Yuletide itself was a pagan festival originally but was adopted by the Christians. People used to say we didn't have any music here in Iceland, but thanks to the revival of the *rimur* and our folk songs the tide has turned now and people are starting to realise that we have a vibrant musical heritage.'

6 Poetry In Motion

Since old Icelandic music has more to do with words than musical instruments, one of the most obvious links between Iceland's modern and ancient musical cultures is to be found in the Icelandic language. The most creative usage of the country's linguistic heritage in a modern musical context can be found in the rap scene.

For many years, Icelandic hip-hop has been heavily influenced by the international market, particularly the USA, which instigated and developed the style. Emulation of American rap is not rare in countries outside the US. In the same way that a young guitarist learning his art begins by playing the tunes of his heroes, so rappers study the styles and approaches of the originators as part of the process of discovering their own individuality and uniqueness. In this way, rap music has continued to maintain its impact across the world and remain one of the most potent forms of urban musical expression.

Iceland was relatively late to develop its own native-tongue rap scene. Prior to 1998 most local rap groups wrote their lyrics in English, but since then there has been a vogue for working with the Icelandic language, a process which culminated in the recent explosion of XXX Rottweiler. XXX Rottweiler were formed in spring 2000 at Iceland's annual 'Battle of the Bands' (aka 'Músiktilraunir'), a competition that pits local artists against each other and rewards the winner with studio time to make a demo. In recent years the bands that have won it have been rock-based, but XXX Rottweiler proved that you can dish out just as much attitude with a sampler as a guitar. The group describe themselves as 'the white-trash massive of the North' and offer the slogan, 'Buy our record or we will kill you!' Controversial, yes, but to their credit, it has worked. Their last LP went platinum, selling 10,000 copies in a market where most artists sell one-tenth of that figure.

The lyrical links between rap and *rimur* have not been lost on Hilmar, who has been working hard behind the scenes to bring the two styles together. 'A lot of the things that are coming out of the rap scene at the moment are just brilliant poetry,' he enthused to me at Steindór's house. 'Many of them have been introduced to the old poetry tradition by their parents or grandparents.' Hilmar told me about a project called 'Rap and *Rimur*', where he has invited *rimur* and other folk singers to perform over a rhythmic backdrop, and some of the city's rappers to perform *a cappella*. In this way he is crossing over the musical traditions of his country.

'It all boils down to poetry,' he maintained. 'Rap music is good poetry and breaks up a lot of the rules that are applied to *rimur* so it has modernised the poetic use of the language in a way. In many ways the rappers are re-inventing it. They're taking over from one of our finest national poets, the singer Megas, who also raised the standards of poetry within our music by using specifically Icelandic slang instead of imported words. A lot of the rap here pokes fun at American attitudes and is very Icelandic in that sense. The links between *rimur* and rap are also to be found in the content despite the fact they are separated by centuries.'

But what kind of links? I couldn't see on the surface what could possibly connect old Viking poetry with modern-day rap apart from the language. 'Many *rimur* contain more blasphemy, pornography and violence than your average Ice T record,' explained Hilmar. 'It was our nightly entertainment, performed every night before people went to sleep and while they were working, so people were especially encouraged to tell juicy tales of sex and violence. It was the sex and drugs and rock 'n' roll of a former era – party music. The whole sense of poetry has been codified in our language, so whether we want it or not, Icelanders have an innate sense of metric structure, even in their every day speech and conversation.'

Hilmar invited me to come to see the concept transformed into reality at a special showcase he had put together for the prestigious Carnegie Arts Awards. The award ceremony is the biggest annual event for visual artists across Scandinavia. Tonight's show was to be attended by the upper echelons of Icelandic society. The president and prime minister were amongst those in attendance and the event was broadcast live on national TV. Halfway through the ceremony, Steindór; XXX Rottweiler's main man, Blazroca (Erpur Eyvindarson); and a guitarist with giant curly hair took the stage.

Steindór, impeccably composed and with the requisite amount of *gravitas*, chanted some sections of *rimur* in his inimitable style over a rolling hip-hop beat. Giant Hair, meanwhile, let loose some seriously psychedelic guitar. Erpur, decked out in striking red and white B-boy regalia, had been standing as still as a statue next to Steindór, but when his verse arrived he came alive in a tumultuous blaze of rapid-fire motion and words. Up until this point the ceremony had been a fairly polite affair, but Erpur took proceedings into a more raucous dimension with a performance that was truly galvanising. The audience was visibly taken aback. It was a powerful way of illustrating these two connected yet distinctly different uses of the Icelandic language via music, and once the initial shock had abated the applause came loud and long.

A couple of days later, I met Erpur in Café Solon. He was almost as animated off stage as he was on. His energy is in-yer-face urgent and is a big factor in why XXX Rottweiler are such a big success, although the combined weight of the band on record is irresistible. They are aggressive, uncompromising and decidedly irreverent. 'Since we started doing this, we have rap groups all over Iceland doing it,' said Erpur, referring to his band's use of the Icelandic language. 'The action now is not just in Reykjavík but all around in small villages like Selfoss and up in the north. We have even been playing Sveitaballs, the traditional Icelandic pop circuit around the country, where people just want to get drunk, girls get their tits out on stage and sailors get their cocks out. One of the band got punched in the face by a 15-year-old girl the other day because he crowd surfed and must have landed on her. We have a whole range of bands here too. Some are really dark, like Vivid Brain, who talk about monsters rising from the dark and eating your children, and others have more emotional lyrics that you really can't listen to if you're distressed. There are a lot of songs with wordplay, of course, because Icelandic is one of the best languages in the world to rap in.'

'Why is it so good, Erpur?' I pressed. 'To my ears, Icelandic rap sounds very much like German, but harsher.'

'We do have a lot of harsh words,' he agreed, 'but they have a lot of natural rhythm. Maybe it's not a good language for R&B singing, but who cares? We make hardcore rap so it really fits what we are doing. I have a feeling that Icelandic rap may work well in other Scandinavian countries. They're making fantastic hip-hop in Finland and Denmark, and even though those countries can't understand our language, they like the flow. I feel that we're unifying. We didn't think we would sell any albums in Iceland but we were proved wrong. We sold 10,000 records and I don't think it's the case that 10,000 people in Iceland enjoy hip-hop. That can't be true. But Icelanders like poetry, they like lyrics, and they like the attitude we bring. Like, we say in one of our songs, "Fuck hip-hop, we're punk rock."'

I wondered how Erpur originally got involved in an event like 'Rap and *Rimur*': 'I met Hilmar Örn through my father. They were together in the Asatruarfelagið (a pagan society), and when Hilmar asked me to take part in this I agreed on checking it out at least. Afterwards I felt it was just another perspective of the same thing, the old Icelandic rhymes are very similar to rhymes I make when I'm MC'ing. Some of the *rimur* come from a saga called *Sturlungsaga*, which is the most violent part of Icelandic history. They are some serious gangster shit. Back in those days, the 1200s, families in Iceland were killing each other all the time. There's a show on our national radio station called *Hagyrðingar*: it's for older people who are good at making the old rhymes. One person starts and then another answers back and it's all broadcast live like a freestyle show but with these old guys who are brilliant. They often get more than naughty, too. Sometimes it's totally pornographic.'

I asked Erpur what he got out of the collaboration himself. Why would a modern rapper want to be bothered about 600-year-old traditions? Surely that would be boring? 'I like the power the combination has,' he said. 'It's mysterious and it seems to be much more than just words of the moment. I feel now like part of a heritage where Steindór is the old school and I'm the new. That's the main difference and also justifies the differences of methods of "rhyming". Rap is kind of an update of *rimur*, but only coincidentally. I mean, all old cultures have a way of getting stories and feelings out in a similar way as *rimur*, from Greenland to Africa. All inhabited continents have this. My lyrics can be technical but there are no unbreakable rules and no system like in the old *rimur*, so most of the time the old *rimur* are more technical. *Rimur* are old of course, but everything becomes old and that doesn't mean a thing. They remain a keeper of a world hidden to most.'

Erpur's brother, Eyjolfur, is a rapper, too. His pseudonym is Sesar A and he is commonly regarded as the grandfather of Icelandic rap, even though he is only 27 years old. Sesar lives in the flat below that of his brother, up past the harbour. There was hardly a soul around as I followed the gentle uphill curve of Vesturgata, breathing in the clean, fresh air and admiring the prettiness and neatness of the houses along the way. I pondered how it must be to live permanently in such a slow-paced, pretty little town. Did it feel like a Utopia? Was it as dull as dishwater? Though I hadn't been in Iceland long, it didn't seem the kind of place where much crime occurred, at least none that generated shocking news headlines. It didn't even seem to be a particularly political place. What, then, did Icelandic rappers rap about?

Sesar A is a curious contrast to his effervescent brother. He has a deep, baritone voice and a saturnine disposition. When he greeted me at his home he wore quite straightforward clothing, nothing that suggested he was the grandfather of rap. He looked more baker than B-boy, yet his recordings and live shows testify to his versatility and talent as a solid, all-round rap artist. Like many musicians working in Iceland, Sesar has broken new ground on his projects, working with everyone from veteran crooners to celebrated opera singers. He creates his own videos, does his own distribution, produces, mixes and engineers on his own. The only things he doesn't do are his cuts and scratches, which he drafts in professionals to take care of.

Sesar directed me into his living room, which had been all but converted into a studio. The only lounge furniture that remained was a two-seater sofa and a chubby cat that regarded me coolly from the windowsill. The rest of the space was taken up with records, turntables, a mixer, a mixing desk, a bookcase, CD racks, a computer, posters of concerts and an impressive portrait of him in sedate pastel colours. 'That's the artwork for my album, the first hip-hop album to be released in Icelandic,' he said proudly, taking a seat in his producer's swivel chair. 'It's called *The Storm In The Wake Of The Calm*. I put it out on my own label, Boris. Actually, it was released just the day before XXX Rottweiler's. We both managed the feat together, but the newspapers keep calling mine the first one, so it has stuck. My brother, Erpur, is in the band so we aren't in competition in that sense.'

Since the first time I heard it, I had been curious about the Sesar A name. 'It's the name I got before I was baptised,' he revealed. 'A friend of my mother called me Sesar when she was babysitting for me because I had been delivered by a caesarean operation. And the A stands for Afrikanus, which my dad added because I was conceived in Tunisia, in North Africa. I used the full name for a while but then cut it down to Sesar A.' I digested this piece of idiosyncratic information silently and asked Sesar when he had decided to become a rapper.

'I started to write rhymes in 1989 to 1990, initially in English because it was the language of the rap I had been listening to and buying since 1988. My father lived in Denmark for a while and I used to go and visit him there. They had a big rap scene early on and I found this record shop and started buying hip-hop tunes there and began collecting them. By 1991 I was a regular subscriber of *The Source* magazine and had all these records here. One day I got home from school and put on an Ice T record I had bought. It had an instrumental side on it so I started putting my own lyrics to it. Erpur and myself actually recorded our first song in 1993 in English. Then, in around

1995, I started writing in Icelandic along with English. Since then my own language has prevailed, maybe because I feel that I can express myself better in it.

'I wasn't very popular at first,' continued Sesar. 'When I went to secondary school I started wearing hip-hop clothes and got picked on for it. I was asking for it really when I started wearing gold chains, but I had been inspired by a picture of Big Daddy Kane. I then wore an African medallion, which one guy tried to smash on a door handle. I stopped after that. When I first started rapping in Icelandic I thought it was about time we did it as other scenes in Europe had been rapping in their own languages for a while. People didn't take it too well, though, and at various times I thought I would quit. Thanks to my brother, who also began to write in Icelandic, I decided to carry on, which is a hard thing to do when the world seems against you. Another inspiration was our father, who is an author and a poet. Both my parents are teachers, but my father has been more active. Ten or fifteen years ago he decided to fulfil his dream to write a novel, which ended up winning the Halldór Laxness book prize in 1997, when the prize was only in its second year. To win that award here in Iceland is a real honour.'

Sesar crossed the room to the bookshelf to get me a copy of his father's novel. The cat blinked back at me sagaciously. How is it that cats just seem to *know* sometimes? The book was called *Landid Handan Fjarksans*, by Eyvindur P Eiríksson. 'He also published this,' said Sesar, handing me another, smaller book. The title of this was *Oreidum Augum* and it had a CD with it. On the back of the CD I noticed Hilmar Örn's name on the credits. 'It's a book of pagan poetry,' explained Sesar. 'My father wrote the poems and then had Hilmar compose the music to it.' Hilmar certainly liked to keep busy with interesting projects. 'My father was an influence on both myself and my brother,' continued Sesar, lowering himself back into his studio chair. 'We would have conversations where he would explain the heritage of a word, tell us where it came from, etc. He's a natural-born researcher and has done a lot in the field of linguistics. I realised that I don't have the vocabulary to be able to express myself properly in English. I'd have to be reading dictionaries constantly to do this, so why not just do it in Icelandic?'

Icelandic seemed like such a difficult language to me. Erpur had pointed out that it sounded good for hardcore rap, but were there any other advantages? 'Lots,' he confirmed. 'In English, the origins of words aren't as transparent as Icelandic words. What I mean is, English words have lots of different sources, but in Iceland the language is the least developed out of all the languages in northern Europe. We can read the sagas and understand them, but there's a lot of scope to make new words in Icelandic, too. We have something in our blood which makes us want to cherish our language and modernise it to an extent, in our own way. If someone makes a grammatical error on TV, people will always pick up on it. They like to hear perfection in the language here.

'Words like *diss* and *chill* have come from hip-hop and are now in common use, but we have our own words for things, like *síminn*, which initially meant "long thread" and which went out of use until we brought it back in for the telephone. I try to make up my own slang where I can. Some people might say "step up" in an American way, but I try and make my own version by using another word in Icelandic, maybe the word that means "confront". This kind of purism comes from the influence of my parents, I think. The notion of protecting our language somehow was brought up with us because of them. I always keep this in my head and now love making my own words. I think that reinventing old words and using them instead of Anglicising slang is cooler than the other way around.

'This tradition is not new, even in Iceland. My father told me about our ancestors, who come from the Westfjords. They would throw rhymes at each other in the old style. In Greenland, too, they have rhyme battles where they have a drum each and sing nasty songs about each other, saying how the other guy's penis is small and how bad a hunter he is. This form of communication over a beat has been present in different cultures and societies, but through technology and through the misery in the Bronx it became the most modern form of it.'

I asked Sesar about the subject matter of his songs. Did he rhyme about universal subjects, or were they more Icelandic? Was he political at all? 'I want my lyrics to be political,' he said. 'I think it's important to realise that this music is a powerful way of communicating information to the people. If I use the music to talk about my ego or how many cars I have, I will be misusing it.'

So what does he talk about? 'Well, there's not much point in talking about crime because there isn't much crime here. There is some, of course, but the police don't carry guns or anything like that. We don't even have an army. I could make a whole record that talks about my fans, my money, my Bentley, but I might as well shoot myself in the head because I would be missing an opportunity to get a point across. I ask things like why we have a NATO base here still which may have atomic weapons. And why do people keep saying Jesus is white when others say he isn't? I also take influence from Asatru in Iceland, which is the pagan society here in Iceland. My father and Hilmar are members of it and I joined when I was 25, though I'm not a strong believer. In one of my songs I say thank you to the gods who gave us poetry, like Odin, who is one of the best poets. This is the god my ancestors prayed to and so it's much closer to my culture than talking about Jesus or whatever. I like it because it doesn't raise humans to this superior level; it has a lot more proximity to nature. I sing about fishermen and Asatru and nature rather than the ghetto and guns.

'Iceland is a rich country and the youth have a lot of conveniences now.' Sesar was on a roll. 'We have mobile phones, we can go to movies, order pizzas and all this stuff. But a couple of generations ago it wasn't like that at all. I want to remind people about that. I want to show people the roots of where they came from. People now go and buy a pint of milk in a shop without having any idea about how it got in the bottle. I want to restore some of those links and put people back in touch with their past. I write songs also about what the media and politicians get away with here. We have government and media corruption like everywhere else, sometimes worse, as we are so small and everyone knows each other. There are more backs being scratched.'

'Sesar,' I asked, 'what would you like to achieve with your work? Won't rapping in Icelandic limit you to your country and alienate you from audiences abroad?'

'Well, Sigur Ros have lyrics which are very much their own and they do okay,' Sesar pointed out. 'I think the best way for me to promote myself outside of Iceland is to stay Icelandic. If you sound English you can do okay, but good luck if you want to try and take on America. The queue for the music industry starts at JFK Airport. I like the spirit of people like the Orishas from Cuba and Saian Supa Crew from France, who manage to translate a universal energy while still rhyming in their own languages. It's not as hard as it sounds to rhyme in Icelandic. In fact, it's very easy. People might not understand shit, but they'll be curious.'

In terms of keeping it real, Sesar A was doing a good job. He was determined to avoid direct emulation of other rappers to create his own brand of Icelandic rap music. During our illuminating conversation, I was surprised to learn that Iceland had a gangster rapper. His name was Móri, and he was to be playing a gig with Sesar at Grand Rokk in a few days. I made sure I was there. The idea of 'gangster' appearing in the same sentence as 'Iceland' seemed absurd. After Sesar's funky set, Móri stepped on stage with a distinct lack of fanfare or glamour. He was tall and skinny and dressed in a casual jumper and denim jeans. He had no gangster accoutrements – no big gold necklaces, flashy bottles of champagne, large-breasted women dancing beside him. He didn't sound or look aggressive at all. But when he dived off stage after his set and sprinted angrily towards the sound man, I saw that there might be something in the epithet. I was a little worried that he would suddenly pull an Uzi, or perhaps a knife. As it happened, he pulled the sound man's hair. Then he shouted at him and walked moodily back towards the stage.

I had never heard of a gangster pulling anyone's hair before. I told Móri so when I met him in a bar the next day. 'That sound guy just shouldn't have been there,' he said, rotating his pint of beer slowly with his hands. His eyes flashed for a second. Móri didn't look like a tough man, but he obviously had a short fuse and looked like he could handle himself if he had to. 'I was supposed to have my own sound man in there, but this other guy just turned up and put himself in the mixing desk. He made my set sound awful. I kept telling him to move out of the way, but he didn't.'

So Móri had pulled his hair. I wondered how he had come by his gangster tag. Was it one he himself had conjured up, or had other people given him the title? Did he really regard himself as a gangster? 'If you count selling weed as being a gangster, then yes, I am,' he smirked.

'Do you have a gun?'

'No, but I have a knife, which I carry everywhere.'

'Do you come from a ghetto?'

'I've been around,' he said, 'and I've seen the darker side of life. I lived in Breiðholt for a while. There is a drug dealer in every house there. There was also a gunfight there last year. But now I live in a nice area with my girlfriend and pet turtle. I used to have two pet turtles but one of them died after the police raided my house and forgot to feed it. They didn't even have a warrant.'

Móri has been arrested twice for possession of cannabis. On one of those occasions he was sentenced to eight months in prison. The experience, he said, was dismal. He is an avid campaigner for the legalisation of cannabis in Iceland and has used his role as MC as a platform from which to air his views. On his solo album, which grew out of the ashes of a band called Delphi, there are a number of songs that talk about the rough side of life in Reykjavík, about drug dealing, working in shitty jobs, burglaries. One song, called MC Panic, is about a rapper who owed Móri money and fled to Sweden. Another is a love song about his girlfriend. Most of them have references to cannabis in some shape or form. Given its debut status, the beats and flow on the LP are all extremely self-assured.

Next to us in the bar, a man who bore a remarkable resemblance to Popeye was playing chess with a younger man. Móri didn't seem to notice them, but they looked frighteningly surreal to me. 'Móri, tell me about the life you've had – you know, the one that you draw on for your songs...'

'I was a bit fucked up when I was younger,' said the rapper. 'I didn't meet my father until I was eight years old, though now he's coming through; he's helped me finance my album. I lived with my grandparents, who were born at the turn of the century. I was raised old-school. I remember one day I was walking to the hairdressers with my grandfather. He always went to the same place to get his hair cut and I still go there now. The wind was blowing in our faces and it was hard to walk. Then he stopped dead in his tracks, turned to me and says, "You know what? You should never let the wind overcome you. You should always just face it straight on and just scream at it."

'He was telling me, no matter how much adversity there is, you should always fight. I've spent a lot of time growing up and working in crappy jobs. There's a lot of manual labour here and you can never earn enough money from it because the government want to make sure no one can leave this rock. People don't work nine to five here; they do eight until six and then do some overtime to get decent money. I have worked in plastic factories and done construction work, but I hate it. I've never gone as low as working in the fish factory. I do jobs for three months at a time and then have to leave. It damages your soul. They should get robots for those jobs and pay people just to exist. Iceland is like a small place in the States – everyone is looking for a way out.'

Móri told me how he started listening to hip-hop and dance music back in the '80s, 'when everyone else here was wearing leather jackets and listening to punk'. As we were talking, he suddenly announced that he has a picture of himself naked in bed with Björk. I almost choked on my drink. 'I'm only two years old, though,' he grinned. 'She used to babysit for me. In fact, she is the reason I smoke. When I was about five years old, our families were staying in a summer cottage, and when the parents were drunk Björk and her friends were outside smoking cigars. She gave me this cigar and I turned green and puked. She never babysat me again after that.'

Móri tells me that things have picked up since he put the LP out. It has acted as a business card for both his music and his extra-curricular activities. He also told me I would be surprised at how many people in

Iceland smoked weed, including national celebrities. He glanced around the café. 'At least four people around here are smokers,' he said. There were only about ten people in the whole place. 'The thing is, alcohol is much worse than cannabis and it's legal. Doctors use speed, dentists inject cocaine. I want to bring attention to cannabis. No one ever committed a violent act when they were stoned. We're going to raise money for the campaign through some live shows. The money will basically go into growing a load of weed and then we can bring the market price down.'

Drugs, paganism, religion, unemployment, modernisation, crime, politics – it seemed there were a lot of topics to rap about in Iceland after all. Although Móri was perhaps mild compared to hardened gangsters in other countries and maybe even in Iceland, he was nonetheless reflecting his life as he has lived it – and it really had been a life of drugs, crime and dysfunctional families. In that sense he was more of a gangster than many of the supposedly ghetto MCs from the US, whose constant *braggadocio* about guns and crime was often based more in their imaginations than any kind of reality.

Móri had really been to prison, and he had found religion there. 'My grandfather wrote a book about his life, which I had never read,' he said. 'He was a sailor and a hero who saved lots of people from drowning once. One day in prison I was reading and I just stopped for some unknown reason. I was in the middle of a really good chapter, but I walked over to the bookshelf and went straight to a copy of the book my grandfather had written. It had never been opened. It was placed right there, just for me. It made me realise that God works in mysterious ways. I felt like there was someone over me watching. I felt that someone understood.'

7 Asatru

The first time that I set eyes on the Sacred Ash was while I was standing outside Reykjavík's falafel shop at 6am on a Saturday morning. Purely out of professional duty, I had undertaken an investigative trawl through the town's bars and found myself in a queue, behind a man who had been served but who was now fighting with his jacket. He was trying to put it on but was failing heroically. The jacket simply kept getting the better of him, slipping under, over and away from the strange, contortionist shapes he kept moving his arms into. After a two-minute struggle, he gave up, placing the coat on top of his head like an African bundle and staggering off along the road.

The man at the serving hatch answered my request for a falafel sandwich in a broad cockney accent. This was something I really wasn't expecting. He informed me that he had moved to Iceland from Surrey, England, importing his hole-in-the-wall takeaway business with him. Judging by the line of people that snaked along the wall behind me, he was evidently doing okay.

As I looked around, I came face to face with a man in his mid 20s whose face was framed with a mane of blonde hair and a beard. He was dressed in jeans, shoes and a tweed blazer, and was puffing on a Sherlock Holmes-style pipe. He seemed to be smiling at me as if I knew him. 'Hello,' he said, his pipe bobbing up and down in the corner of his mouth. He must have heard me speaking in English to the shop owner.

'Hello,' I responded.

'Have you seen a heavy lizard?' he asked. I turned around to pick up my falafel sandwich, wondering when I would ever learn that conversing with eccentrics at six in the morning invariably ended in insanity.

Just as I was making off to leave, he tapped me politely on the shoulder and repeated his 'Hello' again. I didn't want to be rude but the man was obviously raving. He removed the pipe from his mouth. 'Have you ever seen Eddie Izzard?' he repeated. 'The comedian.' Guilt washed over me. The poor man wasn't a lunatic at all, just difficult to understand with a mouth full of pipe.

'Yes, yes, yes,' I said enthusiastically. 'Very funny man. One of my favourites.' I could feel the warmth of the falafel sandwich seeping through its wrapping onto my hand. I wanted to go home.

'He's great, isn't he?' said the man contentedly, placing the pipe back in his mouth and leaning back.

I now understood where his accent was coming from; he was imitating Izzard's vague English drawl. I was about to say goodbye when I spotted a badge pinned to his blazer with a strange symbol on it. I asked him what it was. He looked down at his appendage proudly: 'It's the Sacred Ash.' Sacred Ash? 'It's the symbol of the old Norse mythology. I'm an Asatruer, a member of Asatru. It's a pagan religion here in Iceland that goes back many years. But I'm not religious, though; I'm an atheist.' My head began to hurt. I made my excuses and left.

I started to research Asatru. I learned that, when the Vikings came to Iceland, they brought with them not only their poetry and farming methods but also their customs and beliefs. Although some of the original settlers were Christian, the dominant religion in Iceland until the year 1000 was paganism. Asatru is an 18th-century Danish term which means 'faith in the Aesir', the Aesir being the Norse deities who were worshipped by pre-Christian Scandinavia. The Christian cosmology says that God invented the Earth. In Asatru, the gods were invented by nature.

It all started, as these things so often do, with a void. The void was called Ginnungagap, icy cold on one side and burning hot on the other.

When the two sides met, two beings were born. One was a giant called Ymir and the other a cow called Audhumla, who nourished the giant. While Ymir slept, a male and female frost-giant grew from his armpits, and a six-headed troll was born from his leg. Audhumla survived by licking ice-blocks, and by the evening of the first day there appeared a man's hair where she licked.

By the second day, a man's head appeared. By the third day, from the ice emerged a whole man, who was called Buri. Buri had a son named Bor, who married Bestla, the daughter of the giant Bolthurn. Bor and Bestla had three sons: Odin, Vili and Ve. There was a lot of tension between the offspring of Ymir and the children of Bor and Bestla. Odin led his brothers against Ymir and they killed him. Ever since that time, the gods and the giants have been bitter rivals.

From Ymir's body, the world was built: mountains from his bones, seas from his blood, trees from his hair and clouds from his brain. Odin and his brothers also discovered maggots living in what had been Ymir's flesh. They turned these into dwarves and dark elves, who reside in the depths of the earth, mining ore and minerals beneath the mountains and hills.

There were also some creatures living in the soil formed from Ymir's flesh. These were named light elves and placed in the world known as Alfheim. As Ymir's blood flowed, it created a flood that killed all the giants, save one, Bergelmir, who made an escape in a hollowed-out tree trunk. The sons of Bor then took Ymir's skull and fashioned from it the sky and set it over the Earth.

The sons of Bor then took some sparks and burning embers and cast them into the midst of Ginnungagap to light the heavens and the Earth. They gave stations to all the stars and planets and fashioned a world for the families of giants called Jotunheim. Away from this land, they made a stronghold to surround the world and defend it from the giants. This land was fashioned from Ymir's eyebrows and is called Midgard, or 'Middle Earth'.

Now that the Earth was made, all that was needed were some human beings to populate it. They were formed when Odin and his brothers were walking one day and came upon two tree trunks.

The gods saw great beauty in the trunks and so decided to bring them to life. Odin gave them soul, Vili gave them motion and sense, and Ve gave them life. These proto-humans were named Ask and Embla, and Midgard was given to them to inhabit.

With the creation of Earth and humans out of the way, the gods then focused on a home for themselves. They built a stronghold for themselves in the middle of the world, which was known as Asgard, and forged a bridge (Bifrost) to connect Asgard and Midgard. Asgard is sheltered by the great Sacred Ash, Yggdrasil, which touches upon all of the worlds. The roots of Yggdrasil extend to incalculable lengths. One section goes up to the gods, another one up to the giants, and a third down to the world of men. Beneath the Ash sit the three Faiths, or Norns, called Urd, Verdandi and Skuld – the past, the present and the future. The Norns are responsible for man's fate.

The creation story ends with Ragnarök, a great and final battle between the Aesir and the giants during which both groups are annihilated. The giant Surtur (who gave his name to the newly formed island of Surtsey in the Westman Islands) sets fire to Earth and all life except for two humans that take refuge in the Sacred Ash. These two humans repopulate the new Earth, which rises from the sea, and so the story begins again.

I found the story of the creation pretty intense and deeply imaginative. It is described in vivid flashes of poetic inspiration in the *Older Edda*, from which Snorri Sturluson borrowed for his own *Edda*. As the Viking poetry was closely bound up with the old Germanic poetry, the *Older Edda* has a German counterpart called the *Nibelungenlied*. Aside from the creation story, known as the *Völuspá*, the *Older Edda* also contains a poem known as 'Havamal', a more ethical poem that preaches moderation in all things.

Snorri's Edda, in fact, provides the main source of knowledge for Asatruars about the old ways and mythology. Snorri took the poems of the *Older Edda* and built them into a living, breathing cosmology in his own textbook of poetry. He was more or less forced to give this comprehensive account as the kennings in the skaldic poetry were so tied up with it. It is ironic that the poetry he tried to save continued to go into decline while the world of the Viking gods that he described so thoroughly, yet cared for so little, is now the primary source for the Norse mythology in the world.

Central to Asatru is the idea of regeneration and nature. This is presumably what allowed the Norse gods to stand down in favour of the new Christian god when the Norwegian kings arrived and demanded that the country sign up for the new religion. Iceland was one of the last countries in Europe to be converted to Christianity and hence one of the last vanguards of Norse culture. According to Ari The Learned's *Book Of The Icelanders*, when the Norwegian converts arrived, the Law Speaker at the Althing simply asked the gods what they wanted to do. They agreed to step down, making the event the most bloodless religious conversion in history.

Historians have endlessly argued about the motives behind such an easy acquiescence. Some say the Law Speaker was bribed. Others say that, since most of the countries that Iceland was trading with were Christian and increasingly traded only with other Christian countries, it simply made economic sense to be Christian too. Whatever the motive, the Christians did not fully wipe out the pagan belief system in Iceland as they did elsewhere. The Catholic Church was notoriously lax, possibly because they realised what a difficult job it would be to police a population as remote and isolated as Iceland's. People were allowed to worship their old gods as long as they did it in private. Many subsequently simply threw away their statues but kept their beliefs.

In 1972 Asatru was officially reinstated in Iceland thanks largely to Sveinbjörn Beinteinsson. Sveinbjörn, who passed away a few years ago, fought hard to bring back Iceland's ancient beliefs. He was by all accounts an ascetic character who chose to live on a farm in the countryside with no hot water or electricity, happy to be at one with nature and the gods. Sveinbjörn Beinteinsson's successor is Jormundur Ingi.

I spoke to Jormundur on the telephone to arrange a meeting. He had an impressively deep and hoarse voice which at times descended almost to a growl, and I imagined an immense, bearded Viking of a man attired in tunic and battle helmet. When I met him in the National Library, he was indeed tall with a full white beard and a more than generous moustache, but was dressed smartly in a black suit and carrying a leather briefcase instead of a blood-stained axe.

He possessed a disarming scholarly charm. As we shook hands, I noticed that on his blazer was pinned the same badge as the pipe-smoking gentleman at the falafel shop. I also noticed that he was wearing a ring with a runic symbol on it. I wondered if it was magic. Jormundur led me into the library café, where a few students and some older gentlemen that looked like professors were drinking coffee and talking in muted tones. Jormundur's booming voice soon cut through the quiet atmosphere, causing a Mexican wave of curious glances.

'I'm currently transcribing a book by an author called Finnur Magnússon,' he told me as we queued for some coffee. 'It's a similar thing to *The Golden Bough* by Frazer, but Magnússon wrote his 60 years earlier. He went through the mythologies of Iceland, Europe, Africa, India and indeed the whole Indo-European world, making comparative observations about all the religions he found in those places. People didn't have that much information on these things back then, but he managed to get more information than anyone has ever found since. It's a very important book.'

Jormundur was looking directly at me as he was speaking, but his fingers fiddled distractedly with a bar of chocolate on a shelf next to him. It looked like they had a life completely of their own. 'Although it's a comparative work on religion, it's really all about Nordic paganism. Magnússon started that particular science, so to speak. People had been documenting it, of course, and working with the old texts and publishing books and so on, but it was virtually forbidden to use Nordic mythology as a basis for art at that time. The authorities said you had to use Greek and Roman refined myths for art, as they were more civilised.

'When Magnússon started his research, it was mainly out of a passion to see Scandinavian myths used to make art, and he got his way after he helped thwart a revolution in Iceland in 1809. This gained him some popularity with the King of Denmark, who commissioned him to give lectures at the Royal Academy of Fine Arts in Copenhagen. The book on the Eddic Lore was, however, a commission, or rather a gold-medal-winning thesis on the connection between the cultures and mythologies of Persia, India and Scandinavia. It was directly because of him that Wagner wrote his great Ring opera. All the pagan art that's been created in Britain, Germany and Scandinavia over the last couple of centuries is all because he had this crazy idea that it's okay to use the Norse myths as inspirational material. It was written in Danish and parts of it were translated into Russian. My job is to translate it into Icelandic.'

The modern manifestations of the Norse myths on modern art and thought are numerous. Interest in the old myths started in the 17th century and continued discreetly for a while before exploding in the 19th century under the banner of Romanticism. The Romantic movement began in Germany and England in the 1770s, but by the 1820s it had swept all through Europe. The Romantics rejected order and rationality, sought a deeper appreciation of nature and celebrated emotion over reason.

The Romantics also idealised the past, holding up the folk tales and myths created by the 'uncultivated' common man as high art. The Germanic and Viking myths were routinely plundered by various Scandinavian nations suddenly desperate to show off their illustrious cultural heritage. The most famous collectors of folk myths and tales were the Grimm brothers from Germany. In 1835, Jacob Grimm's *Deutsche Mythologie* (*German Mythology*) used peasant poetry, fairy tales and mythology to reconstruct the pre-Christian religion of the Germanic people, which was essentially the same as Norse mythology, apart from a few name-changes – Odin became Woden, or Wotan in the Germanic versions, and characters such as Sigurd and Brynhild become Siegfried and Brünnhilde in German.

One of the greatest of the Romantics was Richard Wagner, whose immense four-opera cycle *Der Ring Des Nibelungen* drew heavily on the Norse mythology. About 80 per cent of the material he used was from the Icelandic *Older Edda* and other Icelandic works, and the remainder from the Teutonic epic *Nibelungenlied*, which had its Icelandic counterpart in the *Völsunga Saga*. The opera is divided into three acts, with a dramatic dénouement known as *Götterdammerung*, 'The Twilight Of The Gods'. The whole opera is a rollercoaster of betrayal, love, violence and heroism and has a cast that includes Odin, Freyja, Thor and Loki, as well as the occasional dwarf.

Generally speaking, the Teutonic versions of the tales weren't as violent as their Viking equivalents, and Wagner certainly tempered them more to fit in with his own ideas and views. Despite his tweaking it, there were still enough tales of heroes performing brave deeds in the face of certain death to make the opera appeal to one Adolf Hitler.

When Hitler quit school and was kicking it around Linz, he visited the opera every night and became hooked on Wagner's work, which was played a lot there. Hitler once boasted that he had seen *Tristan Und Isolde* and *Die Meistersinger* over 100 times each. He was inspired enough by the dramatic tales of the Ring to buy books on German history and mythology, which he would read for hours at a time. He also tried to compose an opera based on an old theme that Wagner had toyed with, although it didn't amount to anything.

When Hitler gained power in Germany, both he and his henchman Heinrich Himmler remained deeply affected by the old sagas. Himmler worked closely with a man named Karl Maria Wiligut, who had spent time in a Viennese mental institute and claimed he was an oracle-clairvoyant descended from an ancient German family. He said he could 'see' as far back as 280,000 BC, to a time when the world had three suns. It says everything about Hitler and his cohorts that this man became an SS employee and an active advisor on their policies.

Many of the codes and practices of the Nazi party and the SS referenced the old mythology. The symbol of the SS itself – two lightning bolts twisted together – is a runic symbol which has unfortunately been linked forever with the Nazi regime. Hitler also organised secret initiation ceremonies which utilised the old myths, held at midnight on 20 April, to coincide with his birthday. Also, when the Nazi party decided to promote childbirth out of wedlock, Himmler instituted a 'secular christening' which involved wrapping the child in a blanket embroidered with swastikas and runes and set before an altar. These children were given candles on their birthdays each year as gifts – manufactured free of charge by prisoners.

Asatruars are obviously not best pleased about the Nazi Party's appropriation of their mythology's symbols and rituals to assist his evil deeds, and neither should they be. The central messages of the mythology couldn't be further away from the fascism, racism and genocide that Hitler's iniquitous regime represented. Asatru is an eminently peaceful religion that respects all nature and all life and follows a loose moral code (loose because Asatruars are wary of dogmatic teachings) based around 'Nine Noble Virtues': Courage, Truth, Honour, Fidelity, Discipline, Hospitality, Industriousness, Self-reliance and Perseverance.

A more positive plundering of the myths was carried out by JRR Tolkien, who used the Eddic poems to build the fantasy worlds of his *Lord Of The Rings* trilogy. Gandalf, the book's main wizard, takes his name straight out of the *Elder Edda*, as do Bilbo's 13 dwarf companions in the series precursor, *The Hobbit*. The name of Tolkien's Middle Earth derives directly from Midgard. Although he happily used the old Scandinavian myths, Tolkien also had a range of other influences: the Finnish Kalevala, Anglo-Saxon poetry and writers such as George MacDonald and GK Chesterton.

Jormundur and I paid for our coffees and chocolate and carried them across to a table. 'Jormundur, how trustworthy is *Snorri's Edda* as a source for Asatru if Snorri was a Christian?'

'A lot of people think that Snorri was actually a pagan,' he countered, 'but I think that the fact he was a Christian makes the mythology all the more accurate, since he would have known exactly what was Christian and what was not in the mythology. In a way he would have filtered all of the Christian elements out of it, as it would have been easier for him to keep them separate and thus write a more accurate portrayal.

'Much of the mythology is kept alive through other poetry, too, as well as the *Edda*. You simply couldn't make a poem in Iceland up until the 15th or 16th century without knowing the myths because all the word usage came from them. When it comes to physical evidence of the Viking religion, we don't really have a lot. There are some Thor's hammers, less than ten small statues of what could be the gods. If we didn't have the *Edda* and the other poems we wouldn't have the faintest idea of what the Scandinavians had believed.'

'Where does Asatru come from originally?' I asked. 'And what applications does it have on a modern level? What are the advantages for followers today?'

'Well, like Hinduism, Asatru is a classical pagan religion and a classical ethnic religion,' answered Jormundur, licking the tips of his long fingers and dabbing at the last scintillas of chocolate that lay in the wrapper. 'All ethnic pagan religions are individualistic, which means they are not dogmatic. There are no teachings in paganism that you have to adhere to in order to become a member of the religion. If you want to join, you do so entirely as you are. Whatever you want to believe is okay by us as there is no authority in Asatru to tell you to believe anything else.'

'Unlike Christianity, which is very precious about its rituals and beliefs?' I asked.

'Asatru doesn't work in a straight line like Christianity,' agreed Jormundur. 'The Church decided early on that straight-line thinking was the only right thing and declaimed what we pagans call circular thought as heretic. Christians say that God created the world, God then gave it to humans, God has the power to end life and to send their souls to paradise and that's that. The end. Pagans believe that the gods and the world were already here. We believe that the sun comes up every morning, and that the seasons come back every year. We also believe that the world will end, but that it too will come back. All of our thought processes are circular. The gods to us are all part of the world. The Christian idea that God is outside of the world is very wrong to paganism.'

I told Jormundur about the man at the falafel shop who had said he was an atheist and a pagan. He chortled heartily. 'The whole idea of atheism is absolutely unknown within a pagan society. You can decide that you don't want to worship the gods and want to rely on yourself, that's no problem. But to say the gods don't exist...well, people would just laugh at you because the next thing you'll be saying is that you don't believe in the wind or rain. Our gods are so much a part of nature that you can't simply separate them. The whole pagan idea is that there is no difference between religious thought and secular thought – it all follows the same logic and is intertwined along the same lines. The idea of having two systems in a state – a religious one and a secular one – is a Christian idea.

'In a pagan society, the differences between the humans and the gods are very thin. The gods definitely live longer, but they're not eternal. They're definitely stronger than human beings, but they're not omnipotent. They know more than humans, but they don't know everything. In Christianity, there is such a difference between man and God that you cannot even compare them. Our gods are more human, and also more humane. They can also be crueller, sometimes. One of the eternal questions for Christians is, "If God is so good, why does he do things that make us so miserable?" Paganists have the answer. We know that the gods do bad things because, whoops, they got drunk. They were very sorry afterwards, of course, and tried to patch things up, but hey, they screwed up. We can accept this because we know that our gods have a very human way of looking at things. The world is not perfect because the gods were not perfect in the beginning. The gods have to go back on their word sometimes.'

Jormundur told me that many of the attitudes of the gods can be illustrated through modern examples. He offered the analogy that both the gods and businessmen like to try to cut corners on the contracts they are given, that they are sometimes swindlers and like to get away with things. He also compared the ending of the world, *Ragnarök*, in which the gods fight to the death even though are going to lose, to a modern business dilemma: 'If an executive sees that the company he runs is wobbling and is going to fall, he runs and tries to get out as fast as he can. Then he watches it crash around him and get everything ruined. Everyone around him loses money. The gods use their wisdom when the world is wobbling and starting to collapse. Instead of running away, they acknowledge the problem and try and make the best out of it. They want to try and build a new company on top of the ruins of the old one, but in order to do that you have to stick with the company that's falling. You can't just run out and sell your stock, and this example works on all levels of existence. You must not run away from your responsibilities, even if you know you're going to lose. You can approach it in a way where other people can build on what you've lost.

'It's long-term thinking. The gods are not perfect, like humans. They make the same mistakes over and over again, but they always hope that it will be a little bit better next time. The worst crime is stagnation. Things must be built and then be destroyed in order for evolution to occur. Perfection is no good because it causes stagnation. Look at the postal service. It's a perfect system and it has now stagnated because the Internet and the electronic revolution have made it ridiculous to send letters. No matter how perfect things are, they can still go the way of the dinosaur.'

When I enquired as to whether there was any kind of ritual connected to Asatru, Jormundur told me of something called a *blot*, pronounced 'bloat'. There was one coming up in a couple of weeks. Jormundur wouldn't be there, but since Asatru is open to anyone I was welcome to go. A *blot* can be performed alone, Jormundur explained, though mostly it's a communal affair. The ceremony, he said, was a way of saying thank you to the gods and a way of offering the gods gifts in the shape of food and drink in order to strengthen the bonds between gods and humankind. After discovering this new world, I felt I was ready for a drink with the gods.

On the designated evening, at the appointed hour, I pulled up in a taxi at the official Asatru building in Reykjavík. The car stopped at the address Jormundur had given me, but there were no signs of life anywhere on the street. Everything was pitched into blackness. Had I got the wrong address, perhaps? The wrong night? Then my eye caught the flickering light of a candle placed on the floor outside a glass door. The Sacred Ash symbol was stamped on the window. The door gave way when I pushed at it, and I stepped into a foyer area with a large staircase that spiralled upwards.

At the top of the staircase was a small, brightly lit room inside which a dozen or so men and women sat around on small tables, drinking, smoking and chatting amiably. The place had all the mysteriousness and spiritual atmosphere of a roadside café. I don't know what I had been expecting, but I felt a little disappointed. A voice to my right made me jump. A girl smiled at me from behind a small table upon which sat a plastic tub full of money. Alarm bells began to ring in my head. 'There's a charge?' I asked.

'Yes, it's a contribution for the meal and the drinks,' said the girl. I explained that I hadn't brought any money. I had paid for the taxi by credit card – did they take plastic? 'No, but it's no problem,' she said cheerfully. 'You can be our guest for the night as it's your first time.'

I wasn't quite sure what to do next. At the back of the room, near a tiny kitchenette, I spied a corridor. I wandered over and saw that it led through into a much larger room. I walked down towards the room and came across a huge tent and totem pole placed just off to one side of the main doors. On top of the pole sat a stuffed raven. It contemplated me with beady black eyes. My imagination began to give way to thoughts of witchcraft and human sacrifice. Would I make it out of here alive? Had I been let in free because I was the main course for the evening? My body rippled with an involuntary shudder.

In the spacious main room were ten large tables, arranged in a slightly disorderly fashion. Each table had at least two or three people sitting at it. The walls of the room were adorned with tapestries that depicted scenes from the mythology. My eye followed the never-ending branches of the Sacred Ash, coming to rest at the front of the room, where there seemed to be some kind of ceremonial table. A man and a woman wore Medieval-style tunics and looked like they were going to host the *blot*. At the back was a row of tables on which, I was relieved to see, stood trays of food.

A rotund girl wearing an apron came over and greeted me with a grin. 'I'm a bit pissed,' she announced.

'You're wearing an apron,' I observed.

'I'm the chef. My mother and grandmother were cooks too. I can skin a sheep but I'm not very good with horses. Too much blood. I can't cook without drinking, though, which is why I'm a bit drunk. Is this your first time? Have you had any of the food yet?'

Icelandic food is an acquired taste at the best of times. One of the nation's favourite snacks is *hakarl*, putrefied shark meat that has been buried underground for several months to ensure sufficient decomposition. It smells of ammonia and tastes like shit. Apparently you can leave it anywhere outside since no self-respecting animal scavenger would touch it with a very long barge-pole. My newly acquired host led me across to the trays at the back of the room and showed me some more of her country's culinary delights.

'This is raw horse meat here,' she said. 'And this is *sursadir hrutspungar*, which are rams' testicles pickled in whey and pressed into a cake.' We came to a tray full of sheep heads. They were boiled to the bone and looked utterly macabre. I knew what I would be dreaming about later that night. 'We eat everything from the head,' chirped the cook. 'We usually leave the eyes in but take out the brain. From the meat that we get from around the head we make *svidasulta* – head cheese. And these are *slatur*, which are sheep leftovers tied up in a sheep stomach and cooked.'

I never thought that food could physically scare me, but I found myself trembling by the time I reached the last tray. I thanked the lady for her guided tour and took a seat as far away from the 'banquet' as I could. I looked around and saw that the room was filling up. There was a good spread of people: men and women, young and old, all mingled together. It could have almost been a normal family get-together if it wasn't for the large drinking horn, the tunics and a trio of Hell's Angels. I had never seen such harmless-looking bikers. They looked almost shy, as if they had been ticked off and told to sit in the corner. Perhaps it was their first time, like mine.

A young blonde man, wearing the kind of woollen patterned jumper one normally receives for Christmas, sat down next to me. 'Welcome!' His grin grew a mile wide. His aura was intense and I felt a little uncomfortable, although I could see he was obviously trying to be friendly. I smiled back and said, 'Thank you.' He stayed beside me for a few seconds, saying nothing, just grinning and staring at me. Then his features turned a little more serious and he said, 'This is our home here. This is where we come to enjoy ourselves, to enjoy each other's company.' He threw his arms open and gestured around the room. The grin grew again. 'This is not a religion,' he said. 'This is fun. This is life. Religion is for the others – for the people with crosses. Welcome to the feast.' With that, he gave me a friendly whack on the back and walked over to the back of the room for some dinner.

The *blot* got under way. There is a ritual at the blot known as *sumbel*, a kind of toast where a drinking horn full of mead or ale is passed around the group and people give speeches to the gods, as well as to their fellow humans. The general idea is to hail the god or goddess being honoured and then begin your own hail. The *sumbel*'s other aspects are oath-taking, poetry and song. Any words given at a *sumbel* are imbued by the nature of the holy rite and therefore carry some serious weight. This rite, Jormundur had explained, connects us not only with the gods and goddesses, but also with our ancestors, our community and, to a degree, with ourselves.

Eventually, everyone was hushed and seated. The lady in the tunic offered what looked like praises to the gods and poured some ale into a large drinking horn. She passed the horn to the people on the table nearest to her. A man stood up and shouted, 'Hail, Odin!' before taking a sip from the horn. The man passed it to the next person who did the same. This was repeated until the horn was passed to the chef, who decided to give stand up and sing a little song. She had a pretty good voice and managed to slur only once or twice.

Asatru is a pantheistic religion in which Odin, the ruler of runes, the occult and poetry, is the boss. Odin, who is hardly ever to be seen without a glass of wine in his hand, dwells in Valhalla, the place where all warriors who die in battle are invited to go. He has only one eye, having given up the other in exchange for wisdom, and rides an eight-legged horse named Sleipnir, who never gets tired. Odin owns two ravens, which give him information about all the worlds. One is called Huginn ('Mind') and one called Muninn ('Memory').

Odin's family is large, with each member being responsible for different aspects of life on Earth. Odin's wife, Frigg, protects the home and marriage. Their son, Thor, is the god of lightning and thunder, the protector of mankind and of planet Earth. He is a strong, heroic character armed with a hammer named Mjolnir and spends his time travelling across the sky in a chariot drawn by goats. The hammer (the name translates as 'The Crusher') is an important symbol in Asatru.

There are other gods. Tyr is the god of valour, bravery and war; Freyr is the goddess of fertility, corn and all plants that grow upon the Earth; Freyja, Freyr's sister, is the goddess of love and war; Njordur is the father of Freyr and Freyja and is the protector of fishermen and merchants; Baldur is the master of all things handsome and fair. And of course no pantheon would be complete without a bad guy. The Aesir have to put up with the evil Loki, a malicious and troublesome character who constantly undermines the activities of the gods.

The chef finished her song and passed me the horn, motioning urgently for me to stand. 'Hail someone,' she said. There were so many choices! I hailed Freyr. 'Now drink,' she urged. I took a sip. It was lager. I wondered if it was Viking. The ceremony continued like this for a while, with more and more people joining up into small groups, talking, singing and drinking. I ended up sitting with the Hell's Angels and another couple, none of whom said much at first. After a couple of drinks, they became more verbose and I found myself being congratulated on my new pagan status. I asked if anyone had a badge. No one seemed to have one.

This was the closest I had been to anything religious for at least 20 years and I was thoroughly enjoying myself. It was far removed from the stifling confines of the churches I remembered as a child. Asatruars seemed to hang out a lot more and were free to make up their own minds about a lot of things. The gods didn't seem to ask much of you and it was comforting to know that they weren't perfect and all-powerful. I was also very drawn to the fact they respected nature. I went home feeling quite tipsy and surprisingly liberated.

8 Hidden People

'I see elves and hidden people all the time,' claimed Erla Stefansdóttir. I was sitting in her front room. Bright sunlight poured in through large bay windows, illuminating a piano in the corner and reflecting off the wooden coffee table that occupied the space between us. Bookcases around the walls groaned with the weight of thick tomes. Next to me was Hilmar Örn Hilmarsson. He had brought me here and introduced me to Erla because I had wanted to know more about the mysterious hidden world of elves, dwarves, trolls and land spirits that I had often heard talked about in Iceland. Erla is Iceland's most renowned psychic and seer of these people.

'I was born with the ability to see them,' continued Erla. Her energy was relaxed. There were no dark lights in her eyes and no sense of sorcery or witchcraft about her. She looked at me through eyes that were ever so slightly closed, which made it look as though she was squinting. 'For me they have always been there. Most children can perceive them but your surroundings dictate the form they take, and in societies where people say there is no such thing people become stripped of the ability to see. It is possible to unlearn what you once knew. I don't make a point of communicating with them when I see them, but if they ask me, then I do it. I don't stop and chat to every character I meet on the street, but I often talk to them when there are problems between them and human beings. If someone is building a house or something, for example, and there is an inhabited spot of ground or rock, I will act as an intermediary and negotiate with them to help them and the humans co-exist in harmony.'

I had never interviewed a psychic before. Hilmar had given me a lift to her house, and on the way I caught myself wondering if she would already know what questions I was going to ask. As it turned out, Erla is not the mind-reading type. She simply sees things invisible to most. Stories abound in Iceland of hidden worlds and hidden people. It all felt like a bit of a cliché, but after hearing several sensible people refer to them, I realised there must be at least a kernel of truth in the claim that Icelanders are heavy believers in these and other supernatural occurrences.

The newspapers in Iceland have often reported stories about humans attempting to construct houses or roads on rocks and stones in which hidden people are alleged to live. Many inexplicable occurrences had prevented these projects from continuing: machinery had broken down; workmen had suffered mysterious injuries; builders had been visited in their sleep by elves and hidden people telling them not to continue. There are roads in Iceland that go *around* rocks because workmen are too frightened – or respectful – to move them out of the way.

As we drove, Hilmar, a perfectly rational and highly intelligent man, told me a story. 'A friend of mine was trying to build a hot pool,' he said, 'but everything broke down when they tried to move a certain rock. It didn't break down in any kind of ordinary way, either – some of the metal drills and bits of equipment seemed to literally melt away when they tried to use them against the rock. The workmen got scared and wouldn't work on it any more. Then we got Erla to come in and negotiate and everything was okay.'

On the coffee table were two maps, which Erla passed to me wordlessly. They were 'elf maps'. One was for Hafnarfjördur, the area where Steindór lives, just outside of Reykjavík. The other was for Ísafjörður in the Westfjords. I unfolded the Hafnarfjördur map onto the table. It was a hand-drawn map of the region that featured roads, mountains, hills, forests and other landmarks. The map was marked with the areas where hidden people are purported to live.

Running along the perimeter of the map were boxes with drawings of the elves, dwarves, gnomes and light fairies that Erla had seen there, and the homes, churches and communities in which they lived. The maps are sold at the tourist office in Reykjavík and Hafnarfjördur so that ordinary people who lack psychic skills can get a glimpse of where they are and what they look like.

Elves, according to the map, range greatly in size and type. One drawing showed a tall, skinny fellow with legs up to his neck and a shock of bright red hair. Another looked more feminine with wild blonde curly hair and a colourful patchwork dress. The hidden people resemble humans and are often colourfully dressed. They are allegedly very social creatures that live closely together and can often be seen in large groups.

Gnomes looked tiny – apparently they are 10–12cm (4–5in) tall – and extremely jolly. The drawing of a light fairy looked very much like Tinkerbell from *Peter Pan*. The dwarves looked like a weird and unpredictable bunch, some ugly and frowning, others with pointy hats and big smiles. Dwarves, I presumed, could be very temperamental.

Erla told me how she sees these beings everywhere: in the countryside, on the streets of Reykjavík and in her home. Some of the creatures, she said, are just 1mm tall, others 100m (110 yards). Some have the shapes that are on the maps, others – mountain spirits, for example – are just auras. 'Most of them are in the countryside, though,' she said. 'Iceland's farmhouses are built on top of hills which contain these communities, so it always looks very busy to me, even though these beings cannot see each other. They just walk through each other without realising anyone else is around; they have no perception of anything but themselves. As far as most humans are concerned, too, there is nothing going on, but believe me it can get incredibly busy.'

I asked Erla how long these beings have existed. 'They have always existed,' she replied. 'In our Icelandic fairy tales, it says that the hidden people are the unclean children of Eve, and that when God saw them he said, "They are too dirty to lay eyes upon," and so he hid them away. Then, in the old Norse mythology, there are also different races, like elves and giants. Some of the elves aren't really that different from men in appearance but they have special skills. They are great smiths for example, good at manufacturing things. Dwarves can be as tall as men, but they live in burrows in the ground and in stones. Sometimes you go downtown and there are people who you can't be sure are hidden people or not. The elves and the hidden people are related but the main difference is that the hidden people, whom we call *huldufólk*, resemble the race of men more closely. Then we have *landwights* which are more like *devas* – huge thought forms which are more of an elemental power than individual consciousness.'

Jormundur had told me about landwights. Asatru has at its core a profound respect for nature and its forces. Landwights are a key part of the Viking cosmology. They were, and still are, invisible beings that protect the land. 'My theory is that the landwights are a development which came with agriculture and evolved through Shamanism,' Jormundur had explained. 'Asatru came from the Indo-European religions on the one hand, and Shamanism on the other. The landwights originally came into the Viking religion as the mother of the game that hunters were hunting. You had the mother of the bison, the mother of the stag, the mother of all living things. But in Iceland there was no hunting to be done because we had no animals to speak of. Instead, we had the mother of the fish – of the salmon and the flounder and so on. These mother ideas are described in very much the same way all around the pole, from Siberia to Greenland. Back then you had to hunt, kill and process the animals in a very special way, otherwise this mother spirit will get very pissed off. When she becomes angry and irritated, she will keep the animals away from you because you've been doing things in the wrong way. This is probably the same goddess that was worshipped by the people who painted the great cave paintings during the Ice Age. When people settled, they were not depending on animals for hunting, so the mother of animals became the mother of the Earth, and it is she who is the main protector and the principal landwight in Iceland. She is always female and always represents the fertility of the Earth.'

I had talked to Jormundur about the beliefs of Icelanders. I wasn't sure whether a lot of people really did believe in these spirits and beings or whether it was just people *saying* that everyone believed. Was it a media cliché, or was it true that people in the country had these beliefs? 'A friend of mine, a retired professor of ethnology, did some studies on the beliefs in hidden people,' he replied. 'He came to the conclusion that Icelanders didn't believe in them. He was a very pragmatic man and, as scientists do, he was trying to prove something that he thought he already knew. He sent out some general questionnaires to people and sneaked in the question "Do you believe in hidden people?" 90 per cent of people said no. Then he drew his conclusions. But then, just to double-check, he changed the question to "Do you know of anyone else who believes in hidden people?" This time 90 per cent of people said yes. He then asked if they believed the stories that the other people told them and again they said yes.

'My view is that people don't believe in hidden people; they accept them. Nobody *believes* in the wind and the rain, do they? That's a ridiculous question to ask someone. It's just there. Pagans don't believe in the gods in the same way that the Christians are supposed to believe in their god; we just accept the fact that He is there, just as we accept the sun and gravity and so on. Even if Icelanders don't worship the pagan gods or Christian God, Icelanders will still accept the fact of the land spirits. When I hold pagan ceremonies and ordained priests are there, how do I make them take part? I tell them about the landwights and they pray to them rather than the gods.'

The folklore professor Terry Gunnell, who has lived in Iceland for 20 years, gave a slightly different spin: 'If I asked a class of my students how many of them believe in elves, only two would put their hands up. Then, if I asked how many of them don't believe in elves, there would also only be two that put their hands up. That immediately leaves you with the middle area, and that's the area that's interesting. It's not that Icelanders believe or don't believe, but that they are *ready* to believe. It's been shown that Icelanders also have strong beliefs in ghosts, or rather spirits, and strong figures to suggest that they believe in God. I think they believe in a power, that something out there controls their fate. There is a big market for clairvoyants and fortune-tellers here. Many of them believe that dreams tell you something about your future, and they do certainly dream differently to other people, I think. A lot of Icelanders, like my wife, will have abstract dreams, which they discuss with their friends. The theory is that when you dream you are in contact with something somewhere.'

I had asked Jormundur how he expected someone like me, who had never seen an elf, a ghost or even had a supernatural experience, to believe that they were really there. 'Around 30 years ago there was a five-year-old boy who had a Marxist mother,' he said. 'She was an absolutely convinced communist. One day the boy went to school and they started teaching him about Christianity. He came home and asked his mother about God. His mother said, "Well, you study what they tell you to study and you can make up your own mind, but I don't believe in him."

'"Why not?" asked the boy.

'"I only believe in things I can touch," responded the mother.

'About two hours passed and the little boy came into the kitchen, where his mother was washing the dishes. He pulled on her skirt and said, "Mummy, are you a communist?"

'She said, "Yes, son, I am."

'"So you believe in Karl Marx?"

'"Yes, I do," she said.

'The boy asked, "Have you touched him?"'

Jormundur chuckled fondly at his anecdote. 'The thing is,' he said, 'you simply cannot believe everything your eyes and ears tell you.'

Before I was even ready to begin to believe that elves and hidden people existed, and that they could interact with selected humans, I needed some questions answered. I asked Erla what their relationship with humans was like. She shrugged: 'Sometimes it's okay; other times they don't like each other much. It's different in the countryside, where people are living more with the land. The interaction there is much more fluid than with city-dwellers. Maybe it's us humans that are closing down the means of communication. If a hidden person wants a human to see them, they can do that. I have been giving workshops that teach people how to get in touch with different areas of their lives and with the hidden people, and sometimes they show up. I've had as many as 10 or 20 people seeing them at one time. Sometimes just going along with people and describing what I see enables people to see themselves. As humans, we exist on different planes. We have the physical body and the spiritual layer. Parts of us are flesh and parts are hues and colours. We have different perceptions in different dimensions.'

So were elves on a similar level to, say, ghosts? I had the same feelings about ghosts as hidden people, namely that I have never seen one or felt one, and therefore could not readily believe that they existed. At the mention of the word 'ghost', Erla let out a cynical laugh. 'To me, the concept of a ghost is very negative,' she explained. 'I can communicate with people who have passed on, but I don't call them ghosts because it has such negative connotations. A ghost is something that comes out on Hallowe'en. They're like pictures from the past that don't have the inner light of the person you are seeing. I was attending a funeral this morning of a good friend of mine, and there was a light over a choir in the church. I could feel her presence wash over the place. There was nothing spooky or negative about that; she was just saying that she was happy and letting everyone know she was on her way somewhere else.'

I asked Erla if elves and hidden people could be found only in Iceland. Erla shook her head. 'I have travelled all over the world,' she said, 'and seen them in Greenland, Germany, France, all over. There is a species in the north of Spain that are similar to the ones I've seen in Ireland and Wales, so there could even be emigrations of different species. Many races of dwarves and elves breed and they live together with generations, especially dwarves, as they live longer, and so you get great-great-great-great-grandparents living together. There are the same amount of elves everywhere else as there are in Iceland. Each area has a distinctive race of beings or type of beings. Wherever you find nature, you can also find them – they are proof that nature is a living entity.

'We keep on poisoning the planet, chopping down trees and spoiling the oceans, and we kill a lot of these beings when we do this. Nature finds ways of fighting back, though, which is why we have earthquakes and floods. Some people say that we are the guests in the world of the hidden people, but we aren't very good at behaving like guests sometimes. The lesson we can learn from the hidden people is to open our senses and to try and get in touch with them and with nature. It's a question of being aware and respectful towards nature and she will be respectful back. The fishermen, before they went to sea, would offer up prayers or talk to the sea mother. If we can learn similar ways of interacting with nature, it will help us.' And if someone – me, for example – found it difficult to believe that I co-existed continuously with invisible communities of tiny people? Erla chuckled as if she had been expecting the question. 'That's okay,' she said. 'If people believe, it's good, and if they don't, that's okay too. This thing just is, regardless of me or anyone else. The reality will always find a way of reminding people of it, and people will encounter it one way or another at some stage. Whether it's through my perceptions of it or not is really not so important.'

I still wanted to find out more about how deeply these beliefs were rooted in the consciousness of Icelanders. One day, as I strolled along Hverfisgata, I saw a door with moon and star symbols pasted all over it. It was on a corner and seemed to be some kind of shop, although there was no sign or anything. It had something vaguely mystical about it, so I walked in and found myself in a claustrophobic little space divided along the centre by a long counter. Behind the counter were shelves full of occultist paraphernalia. At the far end of the room was a tiny table which looked set up for fortune-telling or some such ritual. There were hordes of books on all manner of subjects from the *I Ching* to numerology, as well as tarot cards, crystals, incense, divination tools, lucky charms, crystal balls and myriad other things to enhance communication and interaction with the spiritual world.

Also behind the counter were two ladies. One was adding stock to the shelves, the other looked at me attentively. 'Can I help?' she asked. I told her I was looking for proof about psychic phenomena and the supernatural in Iceland. Did she have any? Both ladies offered me slightly bemused expressions. A young girl came in and asked for a palm-reading kit. The whole set-up was very commercial, but the ladies seemed to know of somewhere that psychics could meet. 'There is a place,' said one, 'called the Spiritual Society. They have a lot of meetings and also séances. Here is the telephone number.' She wrote it down next to a name: Magnús Skarphedinsson.

That same afternoon, I called Magnús, who is the founder and leader of the Spiritual Society. He explained that it is the largest organisation for supernatural occurrences in Iceland and had a remarkable 10,000 members. He said he could meet me, and a few hours later I was sitting next to him in a café. He was dressed in an off-beat mix of jogging bottoms, running shoes, shirt and blazer. He told me how he started the society in 1990 after he becoming interested in 'scientific signs of life after death'. At the society, Magnús holds weekly séances and collects people's experiences with the supernatural – ghosts, aliens, hidden people, elves, dreams and so on. Since 1995 he has also been running an Elf School, the purpose of which is to demonstrate to tourists what elves are, where they come from and what they look like.

'Judging from our very intensive research,' said Magnús gravely. 'I'd say that there is a 98–99 per cent chance of there being life after death. We have also learned that the worlds that the dead inhabit are far away, though it's easy to go there in mind. An overwhelming percentage also shows that elves and hidden people exist here, and there is also some evidence for aliens coming to the planet regularly, either through physical energy or mental energy. These are just some of the conclusions we've reached.'

Aliens? This was an interesting angle. I had heard from a few Icelanders about UFOs. When I interviewed the filmmaker Friðrik Thor Friðriksson, whose films often include ghosts and mysterious occurrences, he told me a story of how a flying saucer came towards him one day and frightened the life out of him. He had run away and never saw one again. 'But just a few days ago I got an SMS from my son,' he said. 'He told me he had just seen two of them in one night.'

'Magnús, how did you reach these conclusions?' I enquired.

'We have on file over 400 positive reports of people's experiences in Iceland. They're based on conversations. They're based on people calling us, or on things we have found out or heard about. We interview people, go through everything they say in fine detail, ask about their personal feelings, about what they saw, about other witnesses and so on. We go back and forth, forth and back, until we are satisfied with their stories. When we question the witnesses, we go really deep to divide the idea they have about a given experience from what they *actually* saw or experienced. We conduct our research in a very critical and scientific way. It's very open, not like in the new-age way. Those people don't look at figures and facts, that's their handicap – they're not very balanced. We have hundreds and thousands of people claiming things every month, but we have to weed out the convincing ones.'

'And what would a typical, everyday case for the society be like?'

'A majority of the material we get is regarding dead relatives and friends,' said Magnús. 'Lots of people have dreams where friends and relatives come and visit them and say things like, "You will have two children in two years," etc. Some of those predictions don't come true, but many do. Another typical dream is where a relative has died far away in another country or something and they appear in a dream and give a message about leaving, often saying, "I'm fine, don't worry, see you later." That's one of the most common experiences. Many of the dreams have to be interpreted, of course. The stories about elves and hidden people are also hard to research, but one thing that's interesting is that, when you find the witnesses and ask them about the details such as clothing, furniture, words, types of communication, many things start to match up and form a coherent picture. It would be out of the question to say that all of these things are coincidence. Our research shows that there must be a comprehensive truth behind all of this.'

But what about people reading other people's descriptions and adopting them? 'We've published less than one per cent of our findings so far, so it cannot be said that people are reading it and forming their stories around that. We've never showed our main results to anyone, and we're not going to until we've found nearly all of it.'

Why did Magnús think these beliefs are so widespread in Iceland? 'Many of them come from the country,' he replied. 'People in the country are less educated, less polluted by the educational system. The more education people have, the more prejudice they have about these things. I've met doctors and dentists and politicians that have told me in deep secrecy about all the experiences they've had, but they refuse to talk about it publicly. They say it's just insane people that have these experiences. Iceland and Icelanders, for the last 11 centuries, have been much more in touch with nature than other countries. The Enlightenment came here in the 19th century, two or three centuries later than other countries, and in the meantime Icelanders had to rely on their senses and on nature. Icelanders really respect nature a lot more than other countries because they've had to rely on it. They open their senses wide for nature and don't try and block it out like in other places in Europe. They had to sense the weather and things like that, and I think the fittest survived, and those are the ones with psychic abilities.'

Magnús told me that an opinion poll by Iceland's local newspaper *DV* discovered recently that 81 per cent of Icelanders believe in life after death. This, he said, compared to 28 per cent in Germany, 22 per cent in Denmark, 10 per cent in Sweden and 60 per cent in Ireland and the UK. Magnús pointed out that, back in 1978, the figure in Iceland was 77 per cent, which meant that 4 per cent more people believed now than they had 22 years ago. I asked if Magnús had ever experienced anything supernatural: 'I've had no physical experiences myself, but I have been told that dead people and elves, etc, are in front of me by numerous people. It's my feeling, based on other people's experiences, that the elves and the landwights existed a lot more in the past for people than they do now. I get the impression that, in older times, more people had physical experiences of them. Now it is more like some kind of myth or legend, unless you're psychic, but back then they were visible to many more people.'

I had been told by Erla and Magnús that humans and hidden people had communicated, but I was curious as to whether they had they ever managed to physically touch each other at all. 'People have not only touched them, they've screwed them,' said Magnús, looking at me with utter seriousness. 'You can fall in love with them just as with other people. It seems that hidden people can decide to be physical for a few seconds or some minutes or a few hours. They choose. They can pop between worlds whenever they want. Unfortunately, most of the people who have had these kinds of experiences are kept in mental hospitals.'

9 Landmannalaugur

All this talk about land spirits, elves and nature made me want to throw myself into Iceland's mysterious and alluring landscape. Icelanders have developed a strong relationship with nature ever since their Viking ancestors arrived in the country. Most other countries have developed at least one urban centre where people have all but forgotten about the natural world.

These people live in synthetic environments made of concrete and glass which produce so much pollution that they can't breathe clean air and which have so many artificial lights that they can't see the stars at night. In Iceland, nature and isolation have worked together to ensure no such urbanisation has occurred. Even in Reykjavík, Iceland's most built-up area, the sea and the mountains are constantly in view.

The forces of nature have manifested themselves throughout history to remind Icelanders of where they are and also who is in charge. The earth has routinely vibrated with the force of earthquakes or volcanic explosions; hot water comes gushing up from the bowels of the earth; strong gusts knock people off their feet; snow swirls make shapes in the wind; northern lights dance across the sky in winter. You simply cannot forget about nature in Iceland.

Hence Icelanders have learned, out of sheer pragmatism, to respect it a great deal. They are ardent environmentalists. There is pollution, of course, from the country's several factories and also from the large amount of cars that the population own (they are one of the highest car-owning communities in the world), but Iceland still shines a torch in terms of many ecological issues. Energy is generated naturally, either geothermally or hydro-electrically; there are no oil refineries; the waters are some of the cleanest in Europe; and there are constant discussions about the environment and how to keep it clean and safe.

Björk realised how natural her home environment was when she first travelled outside, to London. 'I kept washing, like, three times a day because I could feel the dirt on my skin,' she told *Sky* magazine. 'I was touching bricks and it felt like it was all grease. I got so claustrophobic and got obsessed with oxygen. I couldn't breathe.' In *Arena* magazine, she commented, 'People who are brought up in big cities come to Iceland and get dizzy. They are OD'ing on oxygen.' She also talked about how she liked to walk and camp through her native countryside. 'It was fantastic, waking up and coming out of the tent into an unspoilt landscape, singing and shouting and whatever you want. Freedom, total freedom.'

Björk is a confessed lover of nature and of paganism. Songs like 'Pagan Poetry' and 'Nature Is Ancient' give the game away, as does the fact that her son's name, Sindri, is taken from a Norse blacksmith in mythology who made weapons for the gods, including Thor's Hammer. Björk also has a 1,000-year-old Runic compass tattooed on her arm, and admitted on a recent TV documentary that she once thought she was '100 per cent atheist until I realised I had a religion…it was nature'.

On her third LP, *Homegenic*, she went as far as to attempt a direct fusion of her creative vision with the forces of Icelandic nature by sampling volcanic activity and transforming it into deep, rumbling, hard-edged beats, tempered by harmonious strings and sumptuous vocals to conjure up the majesty and the terror inherent in her native terrain.

I always found it difficult to bring up the subject of nature and art with Icelandic musicians. Most found it a difficult thing to talk about, commenting that nature is simply there and its effects cannot be measured nor described. The question almost always produced a nonchalant shrug or frustrated sigh. This may also be because they get asked about it constantly.

It has become a cliché to describe Icelandic music in terms of its environment, although it is tempting at times, no matter how hard you try and resist. The slowly unfurling sounds of Sigur Ros seem the perfect description of Iceland's vast, open landscapes, for example, as do Hilmar Örn Hilmarsson's emotive soundtracks, Múm's pockmarked fantasy worlds, Ilo's gorgeous electronic washes, Minus's violent thrash-outs and, of course, Björk's own dramatic compositions.

The best place to get to grips with glorious nature, I reasoned, was right in the heart of Iceland's forebodingly titled Interior. Much of Iceland's landscape is rugged and uncompromising, a fact that reveals itself as soon as you land in the country. Most visitors driving from the airport at Keflavík to Reykjavík for the first time are astounded at the barren, almost desolate vistas *en route*. These give a good indication of the rest of the country's topography: lava, rocks, mountains and a disturbing lack of natural vegetation. It's no coincidence that NASA chose Iceland as a place to practise their moon landings.

The Interior has all these features but on a more magnificent and awe-inspiring scale. Volcanoes, mountains, lakes, ice caps, glacial rivers and steaming hotpots are the norm in this place that is closed off from the public in winter for being too dangerous. Even so, it has still managed to claim many a reckless wanderer's life.

I signed up for a trek that travelled through the middle of the Interior, from Landmannalaugur to Thorsmork on a trail with the same name as Reykjavík's main shopping street – Laugavegur. The trail is reckoned to be one of the finest in the world, with enthusiasts bandying around comparisons with the Inca Trail in Peru and mountain walks in New Zealand and Nepal.

The full distance was 54km (33½ miles) and would take between two to four days, depending on levels of fitness and expertise. The most I had walked before was about 15km (9 miles), and that was across the gently rolling hills and easy-going fields of the English countryside. This was another league. The terrain was to be almost continuously mountainous and there were no facilities, apart from basic huts located at 10–15km (6–9 mile) intervals, which had cooking and sleeping amenities. All food and equipment had to be carried. There was nowhere to stop off for emergency supplies like toilet roll, coffee and chocolate.

To be on the safe side and better to enjoy the experience, I opted to tackle the range in four days. I booked up three huts, figuring I would start walking as soon as the bus dropped me at Landmannalaugur in the afternoon. It only cost the equivalent of £15 (US $24; €22.5) a night for the huts, and the bus fare was around £40 (US $65; €60) each way. It seemed such a minimal sum for what promised to be a maximal experience. I spent a couple of days buying things: new walking boots; waterproof clothes; nutritious but light-to-carry food; spare clothing; emergency medical kit; spare limbs.

I felt like a professional hiker as I made my way down to the bus terminal loaded up with equipment. Then I saw the group of *really* professional hikers with whom I would be travelling and felt a little deflated. There were three groups, and all of them looked a lot more convincing than myself. A trio of ultra-fit Germans looked like they might trek for a living. To my relief, soon afterwards an English couple arrived who also seemed to have the same hesitant, self-conscious air as I felt I had. Their presence made me feel better. I decided I would befriend them.

The bus drove us all east of Reykjavík and into the Interior. The weather was gloomy and the mountains and moss-strewn lava fields that we passed through looked harsh and unwelcoming. A swirling mist smothered the peaks of the mountains and silver streams snaked across their heavy bulks. The occasional lazy spiral of geothermal steam could be seen hanging in the air.

It started to rain. After an hour or so, our van pulled over. We were in the middle of nowhere. Everyone on the bus looked at each other with the same thought in their eyes: was this our starting point? All heads turned to the driver for answers, but he wasn't there. I spotted him out of the window, moribund cigarette tucked into the webbing of two gnarly fingers, a foot kicking despondently at something under the van. We had blown a tyre. A few of us stepped outside and helped the driver jack up the van. Fortunately there were two wheels on each side of the back axle. We pulled one off and replaced the blown one. The wind was fierce outside and was blowing dust into our faces. I looked up and down the road and watched it stretch on interminably in both directions. It didn't look like the type of place a mechanic would choose to start a business. We had been lucky to have an extra tyre.

We carried on winding our way up into the mountains, watching the weather deteriorate. By the time we arrived at Landmannalaugur it was truly atrocious. We disembarked from the bus and sprinted as fast as we could across to the hut. It was only 100m (110 yards) away, but by the time we got there we were soaked. These obviously weren't the kinds of conditions in which to be walking 12km (7½ miles) across exposed mountains. We would have to spend the night here.

I made friends with the English couple, Rob and Louise, in the kitchen, while the 50-strong group of adolescents who were already in the hut when we arrived caused havoc around us. I had never known a group of schoolchildren to behave so obnoxiously. They were loud and arrogant and kept stealing other people's food. I caught myself wondering how many of them I would be able to strangle with my shoelaces without their tutors noticing.

Rain lashed violently against the doors and windows. The door suddenly opened with a bang and a girl stepped into the kitchen wrapped in a protective silver foil gown. She was soaking wet and looked like she was in shock. She lit a cigarette with shaking hands. 'I got caught out there halfway to the next hut,' she explained, looking around at our curious faces. She had a French accent. 'We had to turn back because it was so bad.' I traded fearful glances with my new-found colleagues.

It was gravely disappointing to find out that the toilets were outside. I hauled on my coat again and prepared myself for the onslaught. As I stepped out the door, I was quite surprised to find two young men sprinting towards me along a wooden pathway in just their swimming trunks. My eyes must surely have been deceiving me. I was shocked enough to take a step back inside the door and wait for them to arrive – this looked like it might be interesting.

They barrelled through the door and pogo'd up and down on the spot to shake off the cold. 'Where have you been?' I quizzed. One of them pointed a shivering, wet arm towards the door. 'There's a-a hot pool just over there,' he said. 'It's v-v-very nice. You should t-try it.' No thanks. Not in these conditions. In truth, I had not thought about packing any swimmers or shorts. No one had told me that there might be hot pools.

Out of morbid curiosity I walked over to take a look and found a collective of young people relaxing in the naturally heated water. They seemed fairly oblivious to the storm that was giving me a pretty good soaking. In fact they looked positively cheerful. I had experienced similar things in the Blue Lagoon, Iceland's largest thermal pool and the country's premier tourist attraction. I knew what it felt like to be in warm temperatures while the wind slowly freezes your face over – kind of pleasant and sort of comfortable too. I had felt like my head might snap off if I stayed too long. I left them to it and fought my way against the winds to the toilets.

By the time I got back to the hut, I was relieved to find that most of the kids had dispersed. The warden, a young man who enjoyed spending time in the mountains because 'Reykjavík is too hectic', told us that we might have to sleep in the kitchen as the hut was full and we hadn't booked. It was all he could offer. But by evening there had been some cancellations, which thankfully meant we could have a bed. The dorms were basic, just long mattresses that stretched along the walls of an attic shaped room. We were sharing a room with a group of Americans who had travelled to Landmannalaugur just for the night for an outdoor barbecue. We all went to bed slightly disappointed.

The next morning brought renewed optimism. The weather was clear and, although none of us had slept too well, a few seconds of being outside made the thrill of the challenge come back to us. The three of us felt fit and adventurous again. We had spent quite a lot of time deviously trying to ascertain the route of the school children so we wouldn't have to encounter them again. When we climbed the first peak, we saw them springing across the terrain in front us. It was an uplifting sight – almost as good as the views themselves.

I had decided to pool my resources with Rob and Louise. They, like me, had planned to start walking immediately on arrival. The poor conditions meant that we had all lost a valuable day's rations and now had to cover two legs of the trip to make up for lost time. 24km (15 miles) in one day. Just the sound of it made my feet swell. The views, though, made us immediately forget about any mundane reservations we might have had about levels of fitness, supplies of food and so forth.

The mountains came in a variety of pastel shades: greens, browns, pinks and oranges. I didn't know mountains could look so gentle yet so splendorous all at once. They were composed of rhyolite, a normally rare mineral that's rife along the Laugavegur trek. The shape of the mountains were unique too – all delicate folds and mellow contours that merged mellifluously with the bright blue sky and the white, sparkling glaciers. From the top of a burnt-orange peak, we looked out across the range and saw majestic wilderness stretching out before us for miles and miles. It felt somehow like we shouldn't have been there, that we had no place amongst this incredible vastness and were really walking through some beautiful and abstract dream.

We trekked carefully across slippery ice caps and through mini-deserts made of black volcanic sand. The scenery changed every hour or so and, with it, the terrain. It was incredible that so much variety could exist in a place as remote and barren as this. We marvelled at huge, natural steam-pools and an hour later were admiring the scattered lumps of shiny black obsidian that coruscated like black jewellery in the hot sun. The climbs were steep right from the start, and the ups and downs of the trek felt merciless in places. We soon started to feel pain wrack our bodies.

The three of us fell into our own natural paces, becoming separated for a while, then waiting for each other and exchanging comments and observations. At one point, when I was alone and Rob and Louise were far behind me, I put my rucksack down and looked all around me. I was so overcome by the scenes that I let out a loud, involuntary laugh. It felt good. I kept going, laughing louder and louder, like a madman, but feeling instinctively that it was the right thing to do.

I listened to my voice falling into the deep canyons all around me and wondered if Rob and Louise would be able to hear it from where they were. If so, it would probably have scared the hell out of them.

Perhaps I needed to fill the landscape with some sound. The irony wasn't lost on me that these mountains, which provided constant inspiration for so many musicians, were completely silent. No birds, no sheep, no horses, no traffic, no factories, no other people. Just man and mountain. Pure and magical.

By the time we reached the second hut, a few hours later, I had blisters. One on each heel. They were big, bad and bloody – the size of 7in record centres. This was not the place to be breaking in new boots. The weather had gotten worse as the evening had worn on and had made the last part of our walk quite miserable. The three of us had stuck together for the last couple of hours for moral support, walking with our heads down against the relentless drizzle that rained on us.

Once again I knew how it felt to be at the mercy of the elements. We struggled through it more or less wordlessly. To our dismay, the hut warden had left for the night, leaving the sleeping quarters open but the showers locked. We couldn't work out quite why someone would lock the showers in a place as remote as this, especially when they knew how badly people would need them. What were we going to do? Steal the showerhead? We had to settle for a strip-wash in the toilet before more or less collapsing into bed. We were the only people in the hut.

The next morning, I discovered that someone had come in during the night and replaced my flesh with wood. Rob and Louise were equally stiff. Just the thought of putting our boots back onto our sore feet, let alone walking on them for another 12km (7½ miles), made us speculate about the cost of a heli-taxi back to Reykjavík. Our shoulders and backs were aching severely from our heavy rucksacks. And the threateningly overcast weather outside wasn't helping.

We had no choice. Turning back involved walking just as far as moving forwards. We were halfway through; we had to continue. Summoning up some extra energy from somewhere, we started off once again. We started to get comfortable with our pains and blisters again after an hour or so. They became a part of us. The weather got a little brighter and the grandiose views once again reminded us of what we were doing here. We walked more slowly this time, stopping at the odd spot to enjoy a snack and watch the clouds race across the sky like thoughts.

Five hours in, we came to a river that measured a few metres across. We looked up and down, but as far as we could see there was no bridge – and the water was travelling quite fast. We tested the depth with our hiking sticks – they sank a good metre or so, but it was impossible to tell how deep the water might be in the centre. The few boulders that poked through the water were too far apart to form decent stepping-stones. The only option seemed to be to wade. If we waded with our boots on, we would have to walk the rest of trek in wet boots – obviously not a good idea. Before I had time to think too much about it, Rob and Louise were already untying their shoelaces.

Fifteen minutes later, the three of us were knee-deep in glacial water, boots tied around our necks and trousers rolled up as far as they would go. We held hands to make sure no one fell in, since the current was strong enough to tug someone downstream. The water was the coldest I had ever experienced. It numbed my feet and legs completely, which was halfway to a blessing since my blisters were so raw. Our natural inclination was to run through as fast as we could, but since we didn't know what we were stepping on in our bare feet, we had to traverse slowly. It was a mini-ordeal, but a couple of minutes later we were on the other side, dabbing at our tortured feet with towels.

Two hours later, we met another river, twice as big. We sat on some rocks in protest. There were no modern conveniences to get us out of this. No shops selling long ladders, pole vaults or rafts. We just had to do it all over again. Wearily, we once again removed our footwear and socks and linked hands. The previous crossing had been intense – this one was unbearable. The water came up almost to our waists and the current felt dangerously strong against our legs. Halfway through, some kind of kooky defence mechanism bade me to howl like a wolf until I reached the other side. This was the first time in my life I have ever experienced any such lupine tendencies. I never want to again.

For a couple of hours we walked across a desolate landscape of black dust. The afternoon stayed gloomy and there wasn't much to look at, but at least it was fairly flat. Our bodies enjoyed the respite, but not long afterwards they were being pushed again by a series of volcanic canyons which dipped down into narrow streams and ice packs. The steep and rugged downhill passes were harder on the legs, in some cases, than the uphill slogs. We came across a glacier that had melted underneath and formed ice caves and took a break to investigate. They didn't extend too far in, but the formations of the tunnels and caves were full of unexpected curves and shapes. They looked unreal, as if they had been carved by visitors from another planet.

When we arrived at our final night's hut, the warden was there and the showers were thankfully open. They even had hot water available for a small charge. We haggled with the warden to give us a constant supply for a little extra money so we could take our time. The shower was in a tiny wooden hut behind the accommodation quarters. It was incredible to feel hot water gushing over my body after walking for 40km (25 miles). I didn't emerge for a very long time, and when I did I hit the sack immediately and slept right through until the next morning.

The last part of our trek was the least dramatic in terms of views, but was still tough going. Our amateurish physiques were still hurting from the previous two days, but our rucksacks were lighter and the thought of finishing the trail was an added motivating factor. I had bonded with my friends a great deal over the previous two days. We already knew it was an experience we would never forget.

We came out at Thorsmork and revelled in the woods and trees and vegetation that marked the area. The sun started shining on us as we pressed on to get our 3:30pm bus, the last one of the day. There was another river to wade through, but by now we were veterans and the solar heat on our faces and exposed legs made a considerable difference to the experience. We crossed with impressive speed and a lack of howling, and then proceeded through the woods up to the final section.

I pressed on ahead to make sure one of us was in time for the bus. It was 2pm and we still had a couple of kilometres to go. The smell of the trees and plants assaulted my senses. I was already thinking about how many massages I would need when I got back home to remove the knots from my back. Even my blisters had blisters, but by now my body was used to the pain. I saw our destination in the distance and pushed on almost at a gallop towards the end. I could almost taste the culinary delights I was going to reward myself with when I got back home.

I could see some huts that seemed to be the finishing point, but they looked strangely deserted. As I got closer, I saw a girl was sitting outside in the sunshine, her fingers typing away at a laptop. It was a strange sight after three days in the wilderness. I checked the time. It was 3pm. I slid my rucksack off my back and walked across with the self-assured swagger of a man who has just performed a heroic task. I asked her if we were still in time for the bus.

'The bus to Reykjavík?'

Yes, that'll be the one.

'That goes from the other huts. They're about half an hour that way,' she said, pointing back the way we had just come from. 'Didn't you see the signs?' I felt as if someone had just removed my spine. I almost crumpled onto the floor in front of her. I could see Rob and Louise bounding happily towards me. I motioned frantically but they couldn't understand. I met them halfway and broke the bad news to them. There was only one thing for it.

The final half an hour of our challenge was thus spent transporting our tired and broken bodies as fast as we could towards the real finishing point. It was a painful experience. Twenty minutes later, more huts came into view and we could see the bus shimmering behind them. We could also hear its engine running. We were all sweating profusely by now and ready to collapse. The bus was literally pulling out as we arrived but the driver saw us running after him. He was grinning as we clambered on board. We must have looked quite a sight.

We sat on the bus, smelling of sweat and mountains and blisters. We looked at each other and laughed. It had been harder than we expected, but the rewards already felt exquisite. We experienced the self-satisfaction of a lifetime's challenge met. We had marched through the Interior of Iceland. We had seen things that not many people get to see. Not one of us had seen an elf.

10 Rock 'n' Roll Revolution

I took a stroll down to Austurvöllur so I could sit on a bench and think about the Icelandic revolution. There had never been a political revolution in Iceland, but there had been a musical one. It took place around 50 years ago and was part of a bigger, worldwide uprising. There was no fighting involved; the only thing being thrust towards the establishment were hips; the only weapons in sight were electric guitars; the only thing being overthrown were attitudes. The revolution was rock 'n' roll, the sexiest musical rebellion ever.

Austurvöllur is the closest Reykjavík has to a bustling square. Set just off from Austurstræti, this pretty, well-tended area is the perfect place – weather permitting – to indulge in a spot of sedate reflection, newspaper-reading or people-watching. I sat on a bench and took a look around. Dominating the square was a slightly rusted statue of Jon Sigurdsson, one of Iceland's most revered national heroes. Sigurdsson was an ardent campaigner for Iceland's quest to break free finally from 700 years of foreign rule – 'the Lost Years', as they are oft referred to.

The movement for independence began slightly before Sigurdsson stepped onto the scene. In Copenhagen in the 1850s, a ragtag group of Icelandic artists and intellectuals – linguists, academics, politicians and poets – got together to form a cohesive group. Inspired by the nationalist fervour set in motion by the Romantics, they campaigned via letters, magazines and manifestos for home rule in Iceland.

Sigurdsson stepped in a little later, starting his own magazine and pleading for independence at a higher political level. He had also been studying in Copenhagen and had spent a lot of time studying the old manuscripts that had been collected by Árni Magnússon and were held at an Institute there. His main argument to the Danes was that in 1262 the Icelanders had made a treaty with the King of Norway, consenting as a free people to have him as their ruler. Control by the Danes, however, had been enforced by the latter rather than arising from the voluntary will of the Icelandic people. The Icelanders, he said, had recognised the Danish King out of respect but had never belonged to Denmark in legal terms.

The logical conclusion of his argument was that Iceland should therefore rule itself. Through his outspoken leadership, he managed to end the trade monopoly in 1854 and get domestic autonomy established in 1874. This was followed by home rule in 1904 and sovereignty in 1918. The Romantics posited that the country should re-establish their parliament at the original site of Thingvellir. The more level-headed Sigurdsson pointed out the impracticality of the location and argued instead for its reinstatement in Reykjavík. He got his way. His statue now gazes solemnly over the grey basalt building in Austurvöllur, which has housed the parliament (Althing) since its re-establishment in 1843.

The building looks more like a town hall than a national parliament, but its symbolic value is huge as it represents one of the first victories in the long struggle to shake off colonial power. In 1918, the Act of Union between Denmark and Iceland was signed in this building, although the final stage of independence occurred during World War II. When the Nazis occupied Denmark, Iceland declared itself a free republic. The auspicious date was 17 June 1944 – the date of Sigurdsson's birthday.

As the war rolled on in Europe, Iceland found itself increasingly popular. After centuries of being ignored by all and sundry, this little north Atlantic country was suddenly deemed to have an advantageous location. It was observed that whoever controlled Iceland could have a gun pointed at Canada, Europe and America. The Nazi occupation of Denmark had proved handy for independence, but the flipside was that Iceland might now be on the German hit list. (Indeed, it was later discovered that there were plans by Germany to include Iceland in the Third Reich.)

The British, concerned that the Germans might take over Iceland before they did, offered military support to the island. The Icelanders categorically refused, preferring neutrality, so the British invaded the defenceless country anyway, on 10 May 1940. Without an army to fight with, there wasn't a lot Iceland could do; when the British deigned to make contact with the government, they came to an agreement that they could maintain a minimum force there.

The Germans began to attack Britain, though, and the troops based in Iceland had to leave in order to defend their own shores. Unwilling to risk having the country occupied by the Germans in their absence, the British negotiated a deal between Iceland and America for the latter to position troops there. The Americans duly arrived and built an air base at the town of Keflavík. The original deal with the US troops was that they would stay until there was no longer any threat to the country. But when the Germans capitulated, the Americans decided that they didn't want to leave.

A year or so later, the government agreed to join NATO, a decision that motivated the normally placid Icelanders into a mini-revolution – they threw eggs and stones at the Althing. It was one of the only times Icelanders have rioted. The Americans were forced to leave for a while, but then they came back. In May 1951, 5,000 soldiers returned to the base. The US had persuaded the Icelandic government that they needed to be there as the world order was under threat again: there was a war in Korea.

The Keflavík military base has been a source of controversy since it was built. Outbursts against it are frequent, although they have calmed over the years. For the first few decades, the target was a permanent source of public anger, mainly because the army's airport was also the civil one. Anyone wishing to leave or enter the country, including Icelanders, had to pass through barracks and endure military checkpoints. This was too much for many to take, especially so soon after achieving independence. In 1987, protests were significantly lessened when the Americans agreed to build a new civil airport away from their military base. This is the one that most visitors to Iceland arrive at today.

The subject of the base has continued to remain a favourite topic for political musicians such as Sesar A, Megas and Bubbi Morthens. But although its presence has been resented and rejected by the majority, it was here that Iceland's musical revolution began. During the '50s and '60s, the air base's radio station introduced rock 'n' roll to Iceland. Icelandic radio had started in 1930 but was run by a bunch of greying classical-music enthusiasts who allocated just one hour a week to 'popular music' and hogged the rest for 'civilised' music and educational programs. The youth wanted something more exciting and, thanks to the air base, they could now listen to Elvis, Chuck Berry, The Kinks, The Beatles and The Rolling Stones. It wouldn't be going too far to suggest that the base played a major role in spawning Iceland's first-ever youth-culture movement.

It had been impossible not to notice at Airwaves how many of Iceland's hottest bands had a lot of traditional rock influences. A multitude of acts during the festival offered varying takes on the blueprints of the swinging '60s, from the energetic punk funk of Maus, the fierce hardcore fusion of Minus and the raw country blues of The Funerals. One night I found myself at the custom-built nightclub NASA, also in Austurvöllur, watching Singapore Sling, Vinyl and The Leaves. All these bands had been hyped as Next Big Things, with The Leaves having already procured a good deal of international success following tours in the UK and Europe.

Vinyl let rip with a thrilling alacrity that echoed early Rolling Stones or Stooges gigs, the lead singer strutting around confidently in a sharp black suit and the drummer kicking over his kit. Singapore Sling had more than a little bit of The Velvet Underground about them, and the lank-haired bass player had a cigarette hanging loosely from his bottom lip, *à la* Keith Richards. The Leaves, meanwhile, were slightly calmer, issuing forth a slowly building set of introspective indie rock that wasn't a million miles away from the sounds of bands like Coldplay or Radiohead. All of these bands were modern manifestations of the rock 'n' roll revolution which had taken the world by storm and which gave Icelanders their first taste of a pop-music scene.

World War II did not affect Iceland in the same way that it ravaged other European nations. In fact, it brought a lot of prosperity. Suddenly, the island's domestic products were in demand from the other war-torn countries, particularly England, which it kept supplied with large shipments of fish. So lucrative were these years, especially compared to the harshness of previous decades and centuries, that the war is still sometimes referred to as the Blessed War. Teenagers in the '40s and '50s found themselves with extra cash to spend, as unemployment all but disappeared and a consumer-based society began to form. This was embellished by the US Marshall Plan, which gave post-war European countries loans to revive themselves and cash 'gifts' to spend on American goods. Although Iceland had suffered relatively little hardship, compared with other European and even Scandinavian countries, it ended up with a great deal of free cash. No one was heard to complain.

Overshadowing the Althing in Austurvöllur is the Lutheran church Domkirkja, which stands out due to its size and its distinctive, pale-green corrugated exterior. Even more imposing is Hótel Borg, the very first hotel to be built in Reykjavík. Borg is an institution in Reykjavík and still possesses some art-deco charm as well as excelling at serving up overpriced breakfasts to tourists and wealthy Icelanders. In the first part of the 20th century, the building provided a convenient venue for the country's first popular musicians.

People of all stripes came to Borg to hear the latest styles of music imported directly from Europe and America. There were no schools dedicated to music in Iceland at the turn of the century, so most of the country's musicians were learning their trade abroad and bringing their education back with them. Crowds got to listen to the latest Broadway musicals, Tin Pan Alley sounds, swinging jazz, Scandinavian Vaudeville and German dance music. This trend for importing foreign music had begun back in the latter part of the 19th century, when Iceland's voice-based folk songs took a back seat to the new melodies coming from Europe.

The heady combination of money, consumerism, urbanisation, independence and modernisation and the sudden influx of pop music literally electrified Icelandic youth in the '50s. The older musicians ignored the new music: their acoustic repertoires were too far removed from the raucous rhythms in form and attitude to enable them to absorb it easily. Some Icelandic bands had found gainful employment at the base, though, and the soldiers there began to demand rock 'n' roll. The bands that obliged them then carried the sounds out onto the streets of Reykjavík and the revolution began. It wasn't long before Icelandic kids were listening to US music on jukeboxes while sucking on milkshakes and wearing denim.

'There were a few rockers in Iceland as early as in 1957,' recalled Thorsteinn ('call me Stenni') Egertsson one day. Stenni was born in Keflavík, and was at one point a hip-swivelling Elvis impersonator. His main role in the emerging music scene, though, was as a prominent lyricist. 'One of the first ones was Barrelhouse Blackie, an Icelander who had travelled the world over as a shipmate on an ocean liner,' he continued. 'He'd play the piano standing up. He was a bit of a Little Richard. Well, he was just copying him, really. Then there were other rockers like Siggi Johnnie, Haddi G Haralds and myself. The closest we ever came to singing ballads was Siggi Johnnie's version of The Platters' song "Only You". We were considerably wild, I think, jumping all over the stage and even from the platform into the audience.'

Thorsteinn had his own band, The Beatniks, but was employed as a lyric writer by the band Hljómar, who formed in the early '60s and who went on to become one of the first Icelandic pop superstars. By 1964 the geographical emphasis of the rock scene had shifted away from America as The Beatles stormed the States and put the spotlight on England. The screening of The Beatles' movie *A Hard Day's Night* was a big event in Reykjavík and introduced 'the beat' into the country. Hljómar were dubbed 'the Icelandic Beatles'. Their first releases sounded like The Beatles but were mixed with other, more disparate influences. In 1967 and 1968, they made two LPs which combined cover versions with original material and made them one of the most exciting and beloved Icelandic groups of the '60s.

While Stenni wrote the lyrics, guitarist Gunnar Thordarson wrote the songs. Gunnar, who went on to form the hippy band Trubrot after

Hljómar and is today a part of jazzy-folk trio Guitar Islancio, is regarded as one of the most distinguished songwriters in Iceland. He has written music in most genres, from mainstream pop and rock to theatre and soundtrack, jazz and disco, and even classical music. He has written some 400 tunes, many of which have seeped deeply into the nation's consciousness. As a musician once noted to me, 'Gunnar Thordarson makes the most hummable tunes in Iceland.'

Gunnar lives in a spacious two-floor apartment near the harbour. The top floor of the flat is reserved for a fairly elaborate home studio. I had seen photos of a young Gunnar sporting flowing locks on his '60s albums and, although he was a little more gaunt, I recognised immediately his long, sophisticated features. The centre of his studio was taken up with a large mixing desk, speakers and two computers. On the walls were various platinum- and gold-plated discs which his various bands had racked up. In January, Gunnar had been awarded the esteemed Order of the Falcon for his contribution to Icelandic music.

'The Americans had a TV station before we had our own too,' Gunnar recalled. 'It was broadcast all over, and through that we watched shows like *Shindig*, which was a kind of American *Top Of The Pops*. I remember watching James Brown on there in his heyday. Whether through the radio or the TV, it all came from the States, initially. First off there was Elvis, but the musicians here were mainly into jazz and they hated him. It was us younger generation who really liked him. I had a job on the base, which is how I got to hear it. I was driving officers around in a pick-up truck that the army gave me. I didn't like the job, really. There was a lot of anti-American sentiment at the time. We had the feeling that the soldiers looked down on us. We didn't like the base – but we liked their music.'

Hljómar were the first band to be popular right across Iceland. Although there were some acts in the '50s – Haukur Morthens, for example, the uncle of contemporary troubadour Bubbi Morthens – who were mobbed by girls and revered by boys the island over, Hljómar took things to another level. They played to sell-out audiences everywhere they went, playing remote villages midweek and large halls at weekends. Thorsteinn had recalled to me the reactions to the band:

'Hljómar had perhaps the wildest groupies of them all. If their most enthusiastic girl-fans couldn't get in, they would climb up on the roof of the venues where they were playing.'

The novelty of this new pop scene generated a lot of positive feeling in Iceland. Before the rock 'n' roll boom and independence, the country was remote and isolated and had no youth culture to speak of. Now it had found a way of connecting with the world through music. A lot of importance had been placed on music education during the first half of the century, with music schools being built all over the country from the '30s onwards, but now it was simply a case of grabbing instruments and going for it. Hljómar's bassist, Runar, couldn't play the guitar when he joined the band – he was Gunnar's classmate and football buddy. Gunnar told him to get himself an electric bass, taught him how to play it and Runar went on to become one of the best bass players of the mid '60s.

At Gunnar's place, I asked him how Iceland was in the '60s. Did it feel that a whole new youth culture was emerging? Was it rebellious?

'It was in a way,' said Gunnar. 'The main draw for the music for us, though, was that it was simply a fun atmosphere. We weren't really saying "fuck the government" or anything like that. The long hair, the clothes...it was all just a good laugh. It was the only real entertainment we had, anyway, as we didn't have TV, as I said. It was really easy living, a carefree lifestyle back then which involved football, music and school. It was the first time we had a real youth-culture movement, people were richer than before and we just had a good time walking the main street and playing football and handball. There was a feeling that anything could really happen. Being a young republic, there was a real feeling of optimism. Our parents and grandparents didn't know what hit them, but it was all good-natured, I think.'

Since recording facilities in the country were limited and often under par, Hljómar recorded their songs in London, and one of their two LPs was made in the studio next door to a then-unknown band called Led Zeppelin. Hljómar ruled the scene for a few years until some heavy competition showed up in the shape of a hippy band called

Flowers. The two bands both provoked a fierce loyalty from their audiences and became intense rivals. This was the '60s Icelandic version of the famous Oasis–Blur divide in '90s England, but the Icelanders got around it in typically democratic fashion: they dissolved both groups and formed a supergroup called Trubrot, who went on to become one of the hottest bands of the '70s.

The first step for the Icelandic rock 'n' rollers was to emulate, but the time soon came when they wanted to write original songs and produce music that could be called Icelandic rock. To do this, Icelandic lyrics were needed. Enter Stenni, who has written the lyrics for around 420 songs to date. 'My reason for writing words to music was that all the older Icelandic songs sounded so outdated and used such queer Icelandic words,' he said. 'I wrote mine in an ordinary street language, using words that people would use in their speech. I also wanted the words to suit the music and be a part of it, rather than just putting them there separately, if you know what I mean. Eventually I made songs that would make no sense but would exist just for themselves, something like the 'Jabberwocky' of *Alice In Wonderland*.

'Gunnar and I made about 40 or 50 songs together. One of them, called "Heim I Budardal" ("Home To Budardal"), was our greatest hit, a country-and-western tune about a remote place up west in Iceland. The place became known overnight to the whole nation after the song was released, in 1975, and the population of Budardal doubled instantly. I find it interesting that Paul McCartney had a similar idea about three years later when he came up with the song "Mull Of Kintyre". Once, in 1968, I had to put Icelandic words to the Aretha Franklin song "Think". I had to do it before nightfall. I told the man that this was a difficult song, so needed a bottle of whisky to do it. I was driven to a fine discothèque that was closed during the day, someone was asked to be at hand to play the record as often as I needed to listen to it – and I started writing. By the time I had finished the words, the bottle was empty.'

I had heard about another legendary Icelandic songwriter who went by the name of Magnús Eiríksson. Magnús writes his own lyrics and has excelled in adapting the national language to the blues, the music that preceded and influenced rock 'n' roll. Magnús, alongside Gunnar, is also regarded as also being one of the nation's top songwriters. He got into music when he was 15 years old, playing Elvis Presley songs and rockabilly music, and by the age of 20 he had started songwriting. He began to play with a popular dance band called Ponik, who played mostly cover songs, and then began to write original compositions for his new band, Mannakorn. Magnús also went to London to record; he used the same studios that The Kinks had used back in the '50s. His first EPs, which were influenced by The Beatles and The Kinks, became popular in Iceland and kickstarted Magnús's career. In 1968 he formed his own blues band, which was influenced by players like Jon Mayall And The Blues Breakers. Afterwards, he picked up on the likes of BB King and Albert King. After eight LPs, Mannakorn are still going strong.

Magnús works in Rin, a music store in downtown Reykjavík. One sunny morning I decided to drop into the store. Marked out on a residential street by a large neon sign, it wasn't hard to find. On the way, I passed Jappis, a large record shop on Laugavegur. There was a sizeable crowd standing outside. As I walked over to investigate a heavy tumble of rock music came rolling out of the shop doors. I managed to squeeze my way in and found myself in front of a local stoner band called Brain Police who had decided to throw a Saturday-afternoon impromptu mini-concert.

This kind of thing isn't rare in Iceland, by any means. Bands are often seen playing in record shops, art galleries, shoe shops, cafés – anywhere they can persuade to let them make some noise. The town's main record shops – Thunder, Hljómalind, 12 Tonar and Japis – are part of the independent word-of-mouth network that keeps the scene thriving and writhing, acting not just as sales points but also places to hang out, exchange tips, instruments and demos, and play shows. On more than one occasion I had received a phone call to tell me this or that band would be playing here or there in a few hours. In a small community like Reykjavík's, who needs costly advertising campaigns when a quick jaunt along the high street and some phone calls will suffice?

Brain Police's show was good. It was certainly loud. I was deafened when I left the store and walked up the road towards Rin, but I also had a jauntier swing in my stride from the basslines that were rolling around in my head. Rin was deserted apart from a customer in the front of the shop gently strumming an acoustic guitar. He didn't look at me. I saw the counter, but there was no one behind it. I waited to see if anyone emerged, scanning the rows of synths, electric and acoustic guitars, accordions and other musical paraphernalia while I waited. Five minutes later I was still standing there, alone.

Behind me was an office. I walked in and found two men deeply absorbed in paperwork. The loudness of my presence disturbed them. 'Hi!' I said. They both looked up at me. There was an awkward silence during which I smiled weakly. Normally I would have found this rude but I was used to these Icelandic practices by now. Icelanders don't come rushing towards you with open arms, but if you hang in there for a minute or two they will usually respond.

My best Being-Studiously-Ignored-By-An-Indifferent-Icelander experience happened in the antiquated bookstore on Vesturgata. I had dropped in there a few times and found it like entering a time machine which transported me back a few decades. The higgledy-piggledy spread of books, paintings, posters and random *objéts d'art* scattered around the shop give it a wonderfully eccentric feel, and the soft, soothing sounds of the radio that played constantly at a low volume helped make the atmosphere a little magical. I wanted to meet the owner, but every time I went in there I encountered only his attentive son. 'My father is usually here from 11am until lunchtime,' he told me when I finally asked. Then he called him to make sure he would be around. 'He'll be here,' he confirmed.

I returned the next morning and was delighted to find the shop deserted apart from an elderly man with a shock of white hair, typing something on an old '50s typewriter and wearing a pair of slippers. I introduced myself and asked him how long he had been running the shop. 'A long, long time,' he smiled. The door opened and a young man in a leather jacket walked in. 'Ah!' cried the old man. 'Now here is a writer you may want to talk to.' The man had the demeanour of an intellectual or a poet. 'He is an intellectual and poet,' cried the owner of the shop. The guy smiled good-naturedly, walked over and silently shook my hand. Then his phone rang. And so did the shop-owner's. They both chatted, leaving me to take a seat next to the shop-owner's desk and browse through a magazine. I found an interesting article and became absorbed. A few minutes later I became aware that neither of them was talking any more. The young man had left and the owner was typing again.

I decided to sit there and see what happened. Five minutes passed. Ten. Fifteen. The old man got up, humming a tune to himself, passed right by me without any sign that he could see me and started putting some books in the window display. I felt like a ghost. I almost had to pinch myself to make sure I was real. I coughed. His humming got louder. 'Are you busy now, then?' I asked.

'Yow, yow, yow, very busy now,' he said. He didn't seem too bothered about re-arranging another time to talk, so I decided I should leave the inner workings of the magical antiquated bookstore a mystery. I could still hear him humming to himself as I closed the door quietly.

At Rin I stood obstinately at the door. I wasn't going to give up so easily this time. I had worked out to an extent why Icelanders seem so famously taciturn. The things is, particularly in 101, people are so used to seeing each other around that it simply wouldn't make sense to greet everyone they meet on the street like long-lost brothers. If anything they keep their heads down to avoid spending their whole day saying hello to people they know. This slight emotional coolness also extends to foreigners, most of whom they know they probably won't be seeing again. But the warm and hospitable characters that lie underneath this veneer comes out very soon if you make a genuine effort. Icelanders might be a people of words rather than music, but they are also a people of actions rather than words. They are incredibly independent, and if they feel that anyone is trying to make them do something they don't want to do, they automatically put up a barrier of glacial stubbornness.

'Is Magnús here?' I asked in a slightly cracked voice. The older of the two men looked up again and nodded. I introduced myself and asked if he had some time to spare. More silence – and a sigh. I feared I'd overstepped my mark by coming into his office and demanding his time like this. But then he spoke. 'I have to post some letters in a minute,' he said, 'perhaps you'd like to take a ride with me?'

A couple of minutes later, he was driving me to the outskirts of 101. I asked him how long he had been running Rin. 'About 60 years,' he said. 'I have owned it for 20. It was originally an accordion shop started by my wife's father. The other guy in the office was my son, Stefan. He is also a musician and next in line to take over the shop.' The rock 'n' roll boom over the last 50 years had helped the shop survive, Magnús said. 'Especially recently. It's unbelievable how many bands there are. We handle all the Marshall Amplification line from Britain and sell guitars like Gibson and Epiphone. The sales of these have been going through the roof of late.' The revolution was evidently still under way.

Despite his good sales, Magnús was having some business problems since there wasn't a great deal of parking on his residential street. 'Everyone drives here in Iceland,' he explained. 'This may seem strange on a sunny day like this, but when you come here in the middle of a snowstorm, you'll see why.' Magnús dropped his letters off and drove us to an inlet where we could look out over the harbour. We pulled over and Magnús lit up a cigarette and opened the door to admit a fresh breeze. For a few moments we both admired the sedate views across the water, looking at the tiny island of Videy and its picturesque farmhouse, which used to be part of a working farm but is now a tourist attraction. In the distance, the town of Akranes glistened prettily in the sun. The visibility was so good we could even see the great glacier Snaefellesness, which had inspired Jules Verne to write his *Journey To The Centre Of The Earth*. 'You should try out the motorised sleds,' suggested Magnús. 'I tried them a few weeks ago with my family and had a surprisingly good time.'

'Magnús, how much business was your shop doing in the '60s, when the rock boom erupted?' I asked. 'Was everyone buying instruments?'

'The electric guitar had an enormous influence on music here in the '60s,' he confirmed. 'The shop's sales went through the roof in around

1968. We were selling 20 times more than Denmark, which was 20 times bigger. People were just grabbing guitars and playing. Most of the bands were copying the stuff from abroad until Hljómar came along. They had a big influence on a lot of bands, including me. I had no ambition to be a songwriter but it kind of happened. I started writing my own lyrics as I wasn't satisfied with the work of the poets. They were good but they weren't speaking the language of the day, so to speak; they were more classically orientated and using advanced words not spoken in daily language. I wanted stuff which was more casual, the way that people talked.'

I asked Magnús why he thought music was such a popular pastime in Iceland these days. 'Music is maybe a language which can bring people together,' he said. 'We tend to be quite isolated here. Even though we are a small community, the different generations don't often mingle unless it's for music. When I play, I am always surprised to see 20-year-olds in the audience, some just to see what the old farts are doing these days, but others who enjoy our music. I don't encourage my children to do it, because there is not a lot of money to be earned in this profession and there never has been, but they all end up in bands anyway here. I accept they play as it's a nice and good pastime, but it's hard to do it professionally in a small market like Iceland. That's why I still have a day job. Even if you are a popular songwriter, like I am, and have a lot of rights coming in through being played on the radio, I don't earn so much as to be a professional songwriter and never have done. It's really impossible. But the kids are fucking up certain rules lately, which I think is a good thing. They don't give a shit about traditions, and you know what? They really shouldn't.'

But looking back at it, the traditions were starting to be broken before the modern alternative scene began. In the early '70s a band called Stuðmenn were formed. Their initial motivation for getting a band together was solely to take the piss. They wrote all their lyrics in Icelandic but made them as tacky as possible, satirising the hippy rock which had become popular in Iceland through bands like Nattura and Trubrot. They occasionally wore rubber animal masks on stage. They were an immediate and massive success and, 30 years later, are still going strong. During the celebrations of the new millennium, Stuðmenn were chosen as the 'Best Dance Band of the Decade', having in a previous poll been elected the millennium's 'Most Outstanding Group'.

Stuðmenn are often described as Iceland's most Icelandic band. I went to watch one of their concerts at Iceland's National Theatre. I couldn't understand a word, but they were certainly accomplished and energetic musicians covering a range of styles from rock and Latin to jazz and pop. They had a fun, light-hearted approach to performance, ensuring that the seated audience were clapping and stamping their feet throughout. I could see why people compared them with Finland's Leningrad Cowboys.

A few days after their concert, I called Egill Olafsson, one of the band's founding members, who invited me to his house to meet him and the band's co-founder, Jakob F Magnússon. At the concert, something had bugged me about Egill. I felt that I knew him from somewhere but couldn't work out where. When he opened the door to me, the feeling came back, but where could I possibly know this tall, bald, tanned block of a man from?

He led me through into his kitchen area where his equally hairless son was sporting a purple blazer and tapping away at a computer. Egill fixed me a coffee and I suddenly realised I'd seen him in the Icelandic movie *Angels Of The Universe*. He explained that acting is his other passion, aside from music. He has been in over 20 films to date. I was by now getting used to meeting Icelanders who had more than one string to their creative bows. In fact, Egill and Jakob exemplify to an extent the Icelandic effort of freeform creativity. Both are in their 40s but look ten years younger (Icelanders enjoy some of the longest life-spans in the world). Egill is an actor and a charismatic singer in Stuðmenn while Jakob is the band's keyboard player and has a range of solo musical projects, also having enjoyed a spell as cultural attaché for his country. The band's other singer, Ragnhildur Gísladóttir, has also appeared in feature films.

Jakob turned up a few minutes after me, dressed smartly in a blazer and slacks and sporting some slick shades. The three of us moved into

Egill's back garden to enjoy a rare burst of sunshine. Egill noticed me eyeing the large building along one side of the garden. 'That place was among the first recording studios in Iceland,' he said. 'My son now lives in there. We had a studio in there from 1980 which was used by many people to record their songs and albums. Björk did a lot of stuff in there and The Sugarcubes recorded their first material here, too. We also did the music there for the documentary called *Rokk I Reykjavík* that covered the punk scene here in Iceland.'

The mention of punk provoked an anecdote from Jakob. 'I remember going to London in 1976 and seeing The Sex Pistols' first concert,' he reminisced with a smile. 'It was a shock. We were playing totally different music at that time, but we were recording in England as there were no studios in Iceland until we sorted this one out. Our bass player, Tomas, ended up being managed by Malcolm MacLaren actually for a while, but it didn't really amount to anything. His visa ran out and he got deported. The scene over there was amazing back then, though. Everything was edgy and sexually charged – a little bit like Iceland is these days, actually.'

I asked the pair about Iceland's musical milieu when they formed. 'The '50s music here didn't exactly mirror what was hip in the popular-music scene either in Europe or in America at the time,' commented Egill. 'We had this strange mixture of patriotic and heroic songs about beautiful landscape and brave sailors. The music was a mixture of Schubert *Lieder* and vaudeville, very often in the lullaby style and sometimes with a military-march flavour. My theory is that this popular marching music had something to do with our young and newly independent nation. When we formed we took a lot from that kind of music. In the '50s, people weren't going abroad here very much as it was really expensive and hard for normal people to get foreign currency. You had to have a business reason to get foreign money from the Icelandic banks at that point. It wasn't until the late '60s that this changed and Icelanders all became sunshine holiday-makers.'

'We grew up here being a former colony of Denmark,' put in Jakob. 'We weren't really very wealthy until the '60s. Our parents started enjoying life then, allowing themselves the luxury of going on holiday to Spain and bringing back horrid pop songs, which were infiltrated into the radio here, along with the stuff from the American air base. When we started out, we were a real mixture of everything. We were influenced by everything from Monty Python to The Beatles and we were pretty much a tongue-in-cheek stab at the musical taste of our parents' generation, twisting it around with ironic and acidic lyrics. We dressed in black suits like The Shadows but 15 years too late. We then went even further and hired a costume lady with a wicked sense of humour and were rightfully and deservedly dubbed in America as "six Icelandic fruitcakes in ugly clothes".

Stuðmenn's debut album, *Sumar á Sýrlandi*, was an immediate success on the local market. After their second album, *Tivoli*, which set new records in sales in Iceland, the band went on to shoot the musical *Með allt á hreinu*, which is still the most successful film in the history of Icelandic cinema. Stuðmenn then released a book with their graphic work and lyrics before going on to do another film, *Kókóstré Og Hvítir Mávar (Cool Jazz And Coconuts)*. On their promotional tour for that movie, Ringo Starr joined the band at a festival and has allegedly been a fan ever since. In 1986, Stuðmenn accepted an invitation from the Chinese government to go on tour in China. They were the second Western band to visit the country after Wham!. They are one of the most popular bands in Iceland ever.

'Lots of people have tried to figure out the Stuðmenn formula, the magic key to such long-standing success,' said Jakob, obviously not one to shy away from a spot of self-promotion. 'Ultimately, I think it's been about always going against the mainstream, taking conscious giant steps towards being ultra-square when everyone around us was struggling to be cool. But in the end it boils down to the tunes, the anthems, the transparency of the lyrics and the melodic hooks.' The contemporary scene had plenty of those, though.

Finally, I asked Jakob and Egill about the effect they have had on younger generations of musicians. 'I think by taking chances and being bold we have managed to convince the younger musicians that great musical adventures can take place in Iceland, as long as you are willing to work hard, record low budget and put your imagination to work.'

11 Sveitaball

I wanted to get more of an insight into Iceland's pop-buying public. The best way was to attend an Icelandic Sveitaball. Sveitaballs are far removed from the philosophies and dynamics of the 'cool' Icelandic music scene. The bands, although often skilled musicians, are not attempting to create fabulous works of sonic art. They are simply making songs that people can get drunk and dance to. Some make their own music, but many play cover versions of popular rock and pop songs and tour remote villages around the country.

I had heard that Sveitaballs could be rough. Someone told me how the audiences sometimes tied bottles of alcohol around their necks so they wouldn't lose them when they fell down in a stupor. Gunnar Thordarson had reminisced about these curious events to me. According to him, they had started when politicians used to give speeches in villages around the countryside. Afterwards they would often have a band to play. The political rallies died off, but bands have continued to tour the same venues.

There may not be much money in the recording industry in Iceland, but bands that tour the countryside can supplement their incomes with the proceeds from live gigs. Sveitaball bands often start out touring then proceed onto recording their own LPs. Some of them end up recording original songs; others stick with the traditional favourites. Outside Reykjavík, the Sveitaball concerts are the musical mainstay of the villages. Many of the young people living in these isolated places are tuned into the local pop radio during the course of the week and then get their live fix over the weekend from the Sveitaball bands, some of whom have their songs played on the radio.

It is extremely rare for an overseas band visiting Iceland to play beyond Reykjavík, although some of the bigger local pop acts do. Bubbi Morthens, for example, has made a point of staying in contact with his core audience, but the most regular slots are filled up with bands like Írafár, Salin Hans Jons Mins, Papar and Men In Black. Men In Black are one of the younger, spunkier bands to have emerged on the scene of late. I contacted their manager, Einar, who is also the band's keyboard player. He sent me through a list of dates that they were set to play around the countryside and said I could come along whenever I liked.

A couple of weeks later I found myself heading for Reykjavík's domestic airport to board a flight with them to a remote village called Egilsstadir in the east of Iceland. When I arrived at the airport I realised I had forgotten to get any descriptions of the band. I thought I would test the band's mainstream notoriety by asking the woman at the airline reception if she had heard of them. Her eyes lit up in instant recognition of the name and she led me to a table where a group of young men were casually munching sandwiches and swigging on tins of beer.

Contrary to the picture of the band my imagination had set up for me, Men In Black were not middle-aged men playing soul numbers in Blues Brothers-style suits. In fact they used to be suit-wearing funkateers, which is how they came by their name initially, but they have since relaxed into a casual bunch of 20-somethings who play covers of Abba and Europe songs to masses of drunken teenagers. They invited me to take a seat and offered me a beer. Einar, a softly-spoken and mild-mannered guy, introduced me to the rest of the band: Jonsi, the lanky lead singer; Aki, the bespectacled bassist; Palli, the drummer; and Hrafnkell, the blonde-bombshell guitarist. He must have noticed the look of a perplexed foreigner on my face. 'You can call me Kelli,' he smiled. 'You'll never pronounce it properly. It means "raven", if that helps.' There were also two roadies, Dadi and Bjarki, a true mark of a successful band.

On the small passenger plane, I sat next to Einar. As we took off, a smiling stewardess asked us if we wanted something to drink. Einar pointed to his bandmates and asked if he could get a beer from them. I was expecting him to get a reproachful look but instead she walked across to Kelli, grabbed a can from his holdall, opened it, poured it in a glass and brought it back to Einar, all with a radiant smile. I was gobsmacked. If I had tried that on a British Airways flight I would have been ejected without a parachute. Iceland could be refreshingly accommodating sometimes.

As the plane got airborne, I asked Einar how he had gotten into doing the Sveitaball circuit. 'If you're bought up in the countryside and play music then you tend to naturally go into the Sveitaball,' he said, sipping his beer from its plastic container. 'If you come from Reykjavík then you get more influenced by the international trends. It's a unique culture, really, in that it has these two sides. I grew up in Blondous, on the west side of Iceland. We had just the one state radio station, but in Reykjavík they had a few more. We used to climb to the top of our roofs with the receivers and try to pick up the signals. When these other channels became nationwide, we could suddenly listen to pop music every day, even after midnight until 3am.'

I asked Einar what growing up in the countryside had been like. 'Blondous has a population of around 1,000 people, and kids there are either into sports or they're losers,' he smirked. 'I was into sports and also went to the music school and got a classical education in piano. When we were teenagers we formed a band and then I moved to Akureyri, which had 15,000 people. That was like moving to the big city for me. I met a lot of people there with common interests. We played football every day and competed with the other smaller towns around. It wasn't a bad childhood, but I wouldn't want my kids to grow up in a town so small, because in Iceland the distances are so long that it's much more isolated. Five thousand is the minimum amount of people I would go for. In England, if you live in a 1,000-person village, you can drive to a town in 15 minutes, but not here. In our village we had one supermarket, one grocery store, a hotel, a bar, a cinema and a sports hall. We had everything except a population. We were actually in a good position in the village, as my parents owned the grocery store, so I had as much candy as I wanted.'

I was reminded of my conversation with Asa in the Westfjords. The relationship between the countryside and the city has obviously been a big theme everywhere in Iceland over the last few years. Iceland's fast-track modernisation has forced a lot of changes, and a lot of people are still struggling to deal with them by the sounds of things. Traditional ways of life have been uprooted and replaced by new modes of living.

Einar told me that people have been leaving the countryside for decades and were still leaving now. 'No one wants to live there any more really, these days,' he said, picking vaguely at the seat in front of him. 'People are moving away because the farmers are not making any money. The structure of the fishing industry has changed and there are fewer jobs in the fish factories. Everything is now part of a co-operative so it's hard for individuals to make money. It seems to be coming to a halt. There is a lot of talk about the aluminium and the power business boosting employment again. There are hopes that international investors can build factories which are powered by hydroelectric power and which are environmentally friendly in local areas. Some people worry that waterfalls and rivers will disappear, but I think, as long as you don't let Gullfoss disappear, it's okay, as then it won't damage tourism. No one has been to the place where they are planning to build the next power plant and there have never been any tourists there.'

Not everyone felt this way about the building of a new aluminium plant in Iceland. It was a controversial issue and most of the people I had spoken to opposed it on the grounds that it would be damaging to the environment. While appreciating it would bring more money into Iceland and create much-needed employment in the countryside, most felt it would be a short-term solution to a long-term problem. Björk's mother, Hildur Hauksdóttir, felt so strongly about it that she went on hunger strike. 'I don't believe that Alcoa or the Icelandic government should underestimate the will of the Icelandic people,' she told the BBC. Comprising a clean and healthy countryside for money just doesn't seem worthwhile for many people. But then, the people I spoke to were living in Reykjavík and had jobs already. They weren't fighting for their homes.

'How do the older population in the countryside view Reykjavík?' I asked Einar.

'My grandfather has lived all his life in Blondous, and when he comes to Reykjavík, he is a little perplexed by things we take for granted, such as the traffic lights,' said Einar. 'He stops and he's not sure what to do. But he's in a minority. It's hard to find farmers that haven't been to Reykjavík now, but 10 or 15 years ago most of them hadn't been there. My parents, the next generation, are much more up on the city. I moved to Reykjavík when I was 20 and now I have a job managing the band and have two kids, so I don't think I'll be moving home anytime soon. Maybe we'll move to Akranes soon, as that's where my girlfriend is from.'

We landed at Egilsstadir with a series of small bumps. It felt like we had been airborne for only 20 minutes, but it had been over an hour. Night was falling so it was difficult to see anything aside from a few lights and the shadowy contours of mountains in the distance. Egilsstadir is a small place with a population of just a few hundred people. It is also dependent on fishing and is suffering the same problems as the rest of Iceland's countryside. It's a typically remote town that boasts few facilities, heaps of attractive natural habitat and a fairly isolated community. When I asked the band what usually happened here, they shrugged as if to say, 'Nothing much.'

After collecting our luggage, we all piled into a van outside the airport and headed to the venue for a soundcheck. The club resembled an English working men's club, complete with '60s-style décor and dartboard. A pervasive smell of ale and cleaning fluids set my olfactory nerves on edge. The band helped the roadies to unload their equipment and then got down to a few games of darts. A man armed with several pizzas arrived and the band took a dinner break.

Aki, the bass player, came across to me and drew up a chair. 'This is our work,' he said, gesturing around at his bandmates and through into the main hall. 'We make a living by playing this music, so it's like our job. Three or four of us are studying different things right now, and even though this isn't our favourite music, it keeps us going financially. I studied jazz, that's the music I love, but you can't make a living playing jazz here in Iceland, or many other places, for that matter. We don't listen to this stuff at home or anything but we still have the ambition to play it well. We are all trained in music. Kelli has been playing violin since he was five. Einar is classically trained. Our drummer has been playing in jazz bands for ten years and our drummer before him studied jazz in Miami. Jonsi sings and he also plays drums.'

Curiously, many of the alternative bands I had met didn't have this kind of skill level. But then, they were based in Reykjavík and had many more influences. The fact that Iceland had been big on building music schools around the country since the 1930s had evidently paid off. There wasn't a lot to do in remote places, but it was always an option to get classically trained in music.

Jonsi, at the mention of his name, came and sat down. From the start it was obvious that he was the natural leader of the band. He was the loudest out of the group and, as the night went on, became increasingly theatrical and hyperactive, to the point where he resembled a young, camp David Bowie. He was a star in the making. 'This is just a lot of fun,' he said in his eloquent Queen's English. 'Seeing and meeting new people, having a good time – that's the essence of what we do, really. We're entertainers. People here in the countryside just want to go to a big place, get drunk and have fun. They don't want to sit down and stroke their chins. We are making our own record now so we don't just do cover versions. We won't make any real money from it but it'll be a good business card. If you have a record out you can charge higher prices for admission so you get some cash that way.'

Was it true that the Sveitaballs could get a little aggressive?

Jonsi smiled. 'Yes, they can be. I've had ashtrays hit me in my arm, and so have the guitar players. It's just because people are drunk and it seems like a great idea at the time – like, "Oh look, there's an ashtray. What should we do it with it? I know, let's throw it at the people entertaining us." I've been punched, too. A guy came up and asked if I was a homosexual. I said, "No, I am engaged to be married to my wife." He said, "I'm going to beat you anyway," and punched me on the nose. I just got a tissue out and carried on.

'It's not just the countryside though that's rough. Last night I almost got into a fight in Reykjavík. A guy started shoving his finger into my eyes while I was singing, for no apparent reason. I made it very clear that he shouldn't be putting his fingers into my eyes as it was very dangerous. He didn't understand, so I kicked him in the stomach. He really had to be kicked, as he had to understand that what he was doing was dangerous to me. He then got really pissed and wanted to beat me up, but they threw him out. Two other guys were fighting behind the bass amplifier and they shoved the bass down from the pedestal and it dropped onto the floor, so we don't have a bass amp tonight. I kicked the guy in the shoulder and said, "Stop it! This stuff is expensive." Then they got thrown out and started fighting outside.'

I hadn't heard these kinds of stories from the other bands I had spoken to in Iceland. I felt I was getting to the real heart of Iceland here, to the nitty-gritty of day-to-day life, which was not about looking cool, being in a band and hanging out in bohemian cafés; it was about working hard through the week, getting some money, going out at weekends and getting drunk and maybe having a fight. There was, as in every country, ups and downs, times to have fun and times to have fights. Obviously, not everyone behaved like this at weekends, but from Jonsi's tales it seemed like a pretty regular occurrence.

'It's the Icelandic way,' he confirmed. 'They're like football hooligans – there's just a few people spoiling the fun for everyone else. Also, Icelanders really don't know how to drink. It's a very new thing for us. The crowds here don't touch it through the week and then at weekends they get out of their heads, dance, hit on girls and guys, have fun and throw the odd ashtray. There's often no respect for the bands. But as long as they've had a good night, we've done our job.'

'The Sveitaballs are actually in decline,' commented Aki as Jonsi wandered off in search of more pizza. 'There used to be really big groups like Stuðmenn and Hljómar doing this circuit. The scene was a lot bigger then, but these days there are a lot more ways to entertain yourself than there were 20 years ago. Now there are more TV stations and radio stations and the market is much more competitive. It's much more expensive to hire a band. When Stuðmenn or someone did a

Sveitaball, they would usually get all of the money and that would be it, but now we're a proper company and we pay tax and it's all legitimised now.

'We have to play a lot sometimes to make it work out. We played 28 gigs in March. Jonsi almost lost his voice three times. There are only five or six bands who can make a reasonable living out of this, and that's it. We're just happy to make an affordable living from this. It would cause a fuss and a lot of extra work to go abroad and play. We have families and we all study, so it's all full-time already. One day, when we quit, we'll be happy and satisfied with what we've done. We don't want to be The Rolling Stones or anything. Just being a cover band is enough work, as the performance has to be explosive and have some impact.'

The band got called into the main hall for a soundcheck, and then we went to the hotel for a quick nap. At midnight we were picked up in a large bus to return to the venue. The band scattered and jumped around in the seats like boisterous school children. The driver was a friend of theirs from the area, and they asked him to turn up the radio. It was a song they all knew and they all joined in and played air guitar. 'This is Bubbi Morthens,' pointed out Kelli. 'He is the Bruce Springsteen of Iceland.'

I had expected to see maybe a queue of people outside, but there was no one. The place was deserted inside, too. It was only open until 3am. Was anyone going to turn up? The young bouncer standing at the bar assured me it would be okay. 'No one wants to be the first one to turn up,' he explained. 'Sometimes the crowds meet somewhere else because they don't want to be the first ones to arrive and then they end up having a party wherever they are. That's happened before. But tonight should be fine.'

A man appeared behind the bar wearing a kilt. It was the night of a football match between Iceland and Scotland. Iceland had lost. His fellow workers burst out laughing at him, pointing at his bony legs and making him blush. I think it was the first time I had seen an Icelander blush. The kilt showed that Icelanders do recognise their Celtic roots, as well as their Viking ones. 'The thing is,' said the man in the kilt, 'we usually say we are Vikings, but when the Norwegians are pissing us off, we claim to be Irish or Scottish just to annoy them.'

Fifteen minutes later, the bouncer's promise came true. The place was suddenly teeming with young Icelanders, mostly aged between 16 and 25, with a few older people scattered around here and there. They didn't arrive in dribs and drabs; they came *en masse*, sweeping in from the cold night outside and hitting the floor already grooving. Legs and arms flew everywhere as they leapt and flailed around belligerently. By half past midnight, the place was completely full and rocking. The band, illuminated dramatically by the stage lighting, pulled power moves on their instruments and kicked up a storm with their version of Kenny Loggins' 'Footloose'.

The front of the stage was reserved for the girls, who started grabbing at Jonsi, Kelli and Aki, the members of the band nearest to them. Jonsi lapped up the attention, dropping down to kiss their hands and singing seductively into their ears. One girl climbed up onto the stage and groped in the air dangerously close to where Jonsi's hips were swinging and thrusting. The bouncer ran across and physically unstuck her from the singer's leg.

I was reminded of some comments that Thorsteinn Egertsson had made about the girls at concerts in the '60s. 'One girl practically tried to rape Runar Gunnarsson, of the group Datar, while he was on stage singing,' he chortled, 'but the bouncer got hold of her and took her away. There were lots of scenarios like that, but parties in houses with several rooms were much more civilised. A musician would seek out his groupie and they would use the normal sign language. She'd look lustily at him when no one else was looking and indicate with the movement of her eyes that she was going into a certain room, wanting him to be there a short while later. But I don't think that sort of a body language was only Icelandic,' he concluded. 'I've also seen it in Denmark.'

Men In Black had assured me that they were all very well behaved young men. I believed them when they told me that most of them were married with families and hardly ever drank at concerts, but the crowds didn't know that and pubescent pandemonium still broke out all over the place. Couples were snogging and running their hands all over each other in dark corners. 'If you ever saw a woman sitting on a man at a dance hall, you could guarantee they were having sex,' Thorsteinn had said. These couples weren't, but they were equally brazen in other ways. A young man mischievously reached around a door and pulled at the bra strap of a girl sitting nearby. *Thwack!* The girl screamed loudly and gave chase. Near the toilets, an extremely intoxicated young lady tried to dance sexily around a pillar. Her skirt rode up to her waist, revealing her underwear for a second, before she fell down on the floor with an ungraceful crash.

Sveitaballs, I realised, were enlarged school discos fuelled by the traditional teenage elements of alcohol and young lust. Men In Black played Abba's 'Does Your Mother Know' and the crowd became even wilder. This was obviously an Egilsstadir favourite. It was only a matter of time before I got dragged in the mêlée. A girl wearing bunny ears walked up to me and punched me hard on the arm – a traditional female Icelandic greeting, I soon learned.

'What's your name?' I asked her.

'You'll never be able to pronounce mine,' she said. 'It's the only name like it in Iceland. It's named after someone in the sagas and it goes back centuries. There are only five of us in the whole country.' She rattled off a name that sounded suspiciously like Kelli's. I repeated what I remembered of his name in the hope it might be close. She looked at me strangely. I asked if it meant 'raven'. She stepped back and looked at me like I'd just slapped her in the face. 'Waaaahahahaha,' she screamed, and ran back into the crowd. Clearly, my days of charming the ladies were not over yet.

This random mayhem ensued for a couple of hours. Although it was pretty rough and tumble, there was no sign of any outright aggression. The boys seemed far more concerned with chasing girls than flinging ashtrays. When the band played Europe's 'The Final Countdown', the whole place erupted.

A man close to me with arms the size of legs had been resting his head on the table. Now he came alive, stepping unsteadily on the dance floor and swaying like a troll to the power-rock rhythms. Nirvana's

'Smells Like Teen Spirit' got an even bigger reaction. I took the opportunity to get to the toilet while everyone was on the dancefloor. There was an overwhelming smell of vomit. I wrinkled my nose and let out a groan as I entered the gents'. 'It's the girls,' sympathised a young man who was more or less slumped over a washbasin. He jerked his thumb behind him to indicate the ladies' toilets. He was wearing a bright-yellow shirt and the focusing system in his eyes had completely shut down. The closest he could get to looking at me was staring vaguely at my chest area. 'The girls in Iceland just don't know how to drink,' he lamented.

12 Megas

Every country needs a counter-culture hero. Iceland has Megas. Troubadour and troublemaker, provocateur and poet, Megas is a musician who is both for the people and against the people. It's no coincidence that he is commonly referred to as the Icelandic Bob Dylan. The prolific Icelandic producer Vidar 'Viddi' Hakon Gislason was the first person to fill me in on Megas's status in Iceland. 'I can't really compare him to anybody to do him justice,' he said. 'Some say he invented punk in Iceland, but that's just the surface. He's a provocative poet first and foremost and an experimental musician second, with heavy roots in blues and folk music. His main contribution is to the Icelandic language and mentality. He broke the rules of what to say and what is taboo, and he always worked with great musicians, so the outcome was classic Icelandic rebel music.'

Classic Icelandic rebel music sounded pretty interesting to me. Viddi went on to mention that Megas was the 'original outsider, both socially and mentally', and that he manages to look at Icelandic society like a foreigner yet is still a master of the national language and at describing his country. 'He'll remain an outsider until after his death,' Viddi assured me, 'and then he'll be put on a pedestal next to Laxness, the sagas and all the other great cultural treasures of our fun little island.'

Viddi's comments may veer close to idolisation, but they echo many in Iceland. I don't recall getting a negative response from any musician when I dropped Megas's name. His reputation seems as forceful today as it was when he emerged unannounced on the scene and created havoc in the early '70s. His first, eponymous album, released in 1972, knocked the rock 'n' roll fraternity sideways. Until then, the trend had been to write good-time music to jump around and make love to. Icelanders were still discovering the joys of youth culture and an emerging Western-style hedonism.

Then Megas showed up with his softly plucked acoustic guitar and folkish melodies, on top of which he placed acerbic lyrics that criticised and mocked everything around him with an impish, irreverent glee. Or maybe 'intoxicated glee' may be a better phrase, since on his debut Megas sounds slurred, as if he's under the influence of either alcohol or narcotics. Some music critics have suggested that both wouldn't be out of the question.

Where Thorsteinn Egertsson and Magnús Eiríksson helped fit the Icelandic language into a popular music format by making it fun and palatable, Megas put it centre-stage, making full use of its diversity and flexibility to create new slang words and metaphors that were intellectually complex but wickedly entertaining. Through his linguistic orgy, he managed to get across his messages loud and clear: society was corrupt and its cultural values and riches were mostly just frail crutches for a lost and hypocritical civilisation. Dylan's famous quote might easily be applied to Megas: 'I might have been a protest singer,' he said, 'but I've never been into politics.'

Megas was the first musician in Iceland to rally against the Keflavík military base on record. He was fond of swear words and famously described the revered national poet Jónas Hallgrímsson as a syphilitic drunk. While many agree these days that he was, until Megas no one had dared to say it. Needless to say, the state radio did not dig the LP at all. In fact, they refused to play it.

On the cover of the album, Megas appeared smiling innocently in front of a crumbling concrete doorway – a metaphor, perhaps, for his own dystopian vision of society. He was 21 then and looking good in a casual black shirt and mop of hair combed neatly behind his prominent ears. When I met him, he was 30 years older and just about recognisable as the same man. His skinny, beaten frame was folded into a moth-eaten sofa in his Reykjavík apartment. He was sipping a

Biogen, aka the Icelandic Aphex Twin, one of the country's most esoteric and underground producers

Hallbjörn Hjartason, 'the cowboy of the North', stands proudly outside his country bar in Skagaströnd. Hallbjörn was the first musician in Iceland to champion country-and-western music. He owns a Texan-style eatery, a radio station and holds an annual country festival that pulls in up to 10,000 people each year

Gus Gus performing live at Airwaves. In typical Reykjavík style, Gus Gus grew out of a tangled web of filmmakers and musicians. They are now one of the best-known bands to have emerged from Iceland

Hilmar Örn Hilmarsson is one of Iceland's most prolific and diverse studio-based producers, and an all-round cultural hero. He has written scores for over 20 films, has enhanced a huge range of recordings with his magic studio touch and has dedicated himself to bringing Iceland's ancient traditions to the fore via music

Kitchen Motors – (l-r) Hilmar Jensson, Kristin Kristjansdóttir and Johann Johansson – are a thinktank organisation who arrange collaborations, put out records and busy themselves in ensuring that Reykjavík's music scene remains challenging and innovative

Jormundur Ingi, former leader of Asatru, the ancient Viking religion that Iceland's first settlers brought with them. Asatru has been preserved in Iceland for over 1,000 years

Magnús Eiríksson demonstrating his guitar skills in his music store, Rin. He is a dedicated bluesman and one of Iceland's best-known songwriters, having written over 200 songs

Men In Black, one of the younger, spunkier bands to have emerged on the Icelandic music scene and now well established on the Sveitaball circuit

Múm display their musical virtuosity at a concert in Reykjavík's National Theatre. The band are renowned for swapping instruments on stage and creating compelling fantasy worlds

The northern lights, seen here dancing in the sky above downtown Reykjavík, are visible during the winter in Iceland on particularly cold nights

A rare sign of human habitation in the rugged Westfjords, pictured by the author en route to meet Asa Ketilsdóttir, one of Iceland's last remaining folk singers

Sesar A, at work in his home studio. The grandfather of Icelandic hip-hop was officially the first MC to release a rap album in Icelandic

The President of Iceland's Rimur Society, Steindór Andersen, who brought Iceland's ancient poetry tradition alive for modern audiences when he toured with Sigur Ros in 2001

Stuðmenn performing at the Reykjavík National Theatre. The band is hailed as the most Icelandic in Iceland and is still going strong after 30 years of producing fun, provocative pop music

Tjorn, a lake in the centre of Reykjavík's 101 where locals come to stroll and feed the flocks of birds that hang out there

Trabant is one of the hottest new bands to have emerged from Iceland in recent years. Its members also play in other groups, underlining the incestuous nature of Iceland's contemporary alternative scene

Some of the slightly unreal scenery that is encountered on the awe-inspiring Laugavegur trail, which winds through the remote centre of Iceland. The mountains are composed of a rare mineral known as rhyolite, which gives them soft pastel shades

Bubbi Morthens, Iceland's original rock 'n' roll hero, is today one of the country's biggest pop stars and one of its most outspoken political musicians

can of beer at 3pm. It was a diabolical day outside. The streetlights were on even though it was only the middle of the afternoon. Rain beat ominously at the window. The scene was memorably gothic.

The front room appeared to be a cross between an artist's studio and a squat. It was full of what looked like a mix of junk, music equipment and memorabilia. Synths, guitars, a hi-fi and a computer took up the available floor space. Photographs of Bob Dylan, Marilyn Monroe and what could well have been members of Megas's family stared down from the walls, sandwiched between an assortment of paintings and posters. From the kitchen, the pitiful mewing of newborn kittens could be heard, and the smell pervaded the apartment. Megas offered me a beer with a slightly unsteady hand. I accepted.

Megas has recorded 11 albums so far during his long career. They are all about to be reissued by his label, Skífan, along with additional bonus tracks that Megas is digging out from his personal archive. The output is prodigious for an Icelandic artist, especially considering Megas went 'missing' for a few years. Rumours abounded around Iceland at one stage that he was dead because nobody saw him for a year or two, apart from the occasional, seemingly random emergence to play a live concert or appear as a guest on an LP. For a long time, he was battling against the stultifying effects of a flood of drugs and alcohol in his system. Sometimes he managed to get on top of it; other times he was dragged under helplessly.

The prolific and multi-talented Hilmar Örn Hilmarsson once told me that he considered his work with Megas 'among the most important things I have done, always challenging, edifying and, last but not least, incredible fun'. There was some music playing when I went into the apartment. Megas explained that it came from an album he had just finished recording with Hilmar called *Höfudlausnir* – '*Head Ransoms*'. It was actually released in 1988, but the 400 copies that were manufactured were shoddy and so, after waiting for 14 years, they had restored it to its pristine glory. The music sounded very different to the other Megas material I had heard. Hilmar had added a heavily effected brand of electronics and futuristic synths to the usual swinging rock beats and waspish vocals. Megas turned the stereo up so we could hear it better. There were some distinctive female vocals in the background. 'Is that Björk?' I asked. He nodded and smiled, revealing two deep – and deeply endearing – dimples.

Björk was, and allegedly still is, one of Megas's biggest fans. For a long time she and her sister performed as his backing singers, even when she became embroiled in the '80s punk scene. There was even a rumour, which was never confirmed, that she bought the apartment for him. Megas is often referred to as the grandfather of Icelandic punk, but aside from one or two precociously punkish tracks on his later albums he didn't engage with the style at all. Lyrically, however, he was more punk than anyone that preceded or succeeded him. He single-handedly created an alternative to the mainstream pop industry that had been born only a couple of decades earlier.

'These reissues are the first stuff I've worked on for a while,' he said, his alert eyes peering at me over his spectacles. 'Many of the tapes I've used for the bonus songs were in bad condition and had to be cleaned up. A lot of them were stacked against hot-water pipes and became unusable. Overall, though, the collection will contain almost everything I have left that's presentable. I used to write a lot of songs like demos, just kind of progress through the song, and then keep it if it ended up being okay. Some tracks are just strums, but the lyrics are the important thing. Going through these old tapes, I have gathered that I was a fine workman but also a very lazy one. Fifty songs a year is the minimum, even for a lazy artist. Anyway, I am glad I got this deal to put all the old stuff out. It happened because the man from Skífan was scared of dying and going to hell. He had treated me badly. He is getting old and I think the fear of dying and going to hell has a great impact on people. He told his successor to make a contract with me all on my own terms. He was afraid of the gods, you see. He knew he didn't have them on his side.'

I was struck by the fact that Megas looked so frail and so destitute, despite his iconic status and immense talent. While every other famous pop star in Iceland seemed to be at least living comfortably, Megas seemed to have fared less well. But then, he never made music to appeal to the masses. In 1977 he teamed up with Spilverk Thjodanna, a folk-rock quartet that had been formed with a couple of members of Stuðmenn, to produce the album *A Bleikum Nattkjolum* (*'Wearing A Pink Gown'*). Although he never actively sought popularity, this LP is often quoted by journalists as being the best Icelandic album of all time.

'The fans have come and gone,' Megas said with a nonchalant wave of his hand. 'They always have and they always will. There is always someone ready to be disappointed by new ideas. They have their own ideas of how I should progress, and when I don't meet those ideas, they go away. I've always been quite linear, in actual fact. Sometimes that means I am premature and other times I arrive long after everyone else. When you hit the NOW, people don't tend to understand, because it's too NOW. But the Icelandic music scene has never been remotely of interest to me because I've just done my own form of handicraft outside of the scene. My interest lies in making melodies and lyrics, and for that you have to know how to do things without any help or you make them awkward. It's a little like working with wood – you have to know the wood and you have to choose the right tools and know how you use them. People who practise music today don't think that way. They just think of the foreign trends and try and copy those. They're taking other people's woods and don't know anything about the tools they're using.'

Megas owed a lot to Bob Dylan's folk-rock style at the beginning of his career, but on subsequent albums he diversified into his own particular brand of rock 'n' roll and all the styles that informed it: blues, folk, country and western, R&B, jazz, boogie-woogie and rockabilly. He always kept his lyrical edge, though. Dylan once claimed that the beat writers Allen Ginsberg and Jack Kerouac influenced him initially. Similarly, Megas was influenced by Elvis Presley on the one hand ('He made me start and he made me keep on ticking') and the writer Halldór Laxness on the other.

'I found a world of verbal bacchanalia with Laxness which drew on the sagas and stories of the kings and our people,' he commented, clutching his can of beer to his stomach and looking more comfortable. 'I loved that. I loved how he made the language work by choosing just the right word and putting it in just the right place until he found something that worked, and something that was his. He knew all the traditions and used them, like any good craftsman who realises you have to know how your forefathers worked. You have to go through what's been done and work out how they create their own effects. You have to go through everything you can and make it your university, your school.

'Today that happens less and less, which is why so much stuff is similar. Laxness used tradition, but he broke with tradition, too. He was a true 20th-century man whose traditions went back to the 11th century and further, and if you have that spectrum, that timespan, everything is useable – especially in Iceland, as nothing has changed that much. We don't have so much of a pop culture to draw on so you need to construct from the core, from the original sources. We didn't and still don't have a central bank of pop clichés, so we need to make the clichés ourselves. If you write a song in English you don't even have to think about the next line; it's more or less self-evident, though in spite of that it can be very original if the concept is new. Otis Blackwell was asked to write a song about a coke bottle opening, and he came up with "All Shook Up". It was a challenge and he composed a hit song from it.'

Both Laxness and Megas are famed for stretching the Icelandic language to suit their own creative needs. Both are regarded as masters of wordplay; both are known for their immense vocabularies. Megas was ensuring that the rich literary tradition of his country was not only being kept alive, but that it was being continually modernised. 'At first I thought I wouldn't be able to write foreign lyrics,' he explained. 'Although I listened to them and took my inspiration from them, it was a challenge to make a rock 'n' roll language out of Icelandic. Everyone said you couldn't do it in Icelandic, that you had to translate English words. I started to show them you could make tough and cool lyrics in Icelandic, just like in old English. The toughest of them all is Shakespeare. If we have control of the highbrow and lowbrow cultures, then we have all the colours of our palette, and we can mix them all together. They mix very well in Icelandic, the highbrow and the lowbrow. The lyrical element of my music was always a mix. Everyone in my trade should be fascinated by words as well as music because this pop wave that started around 1960 is based upon words with music. Bob Dylan is a great musician and a great lyricist. He's not a good technician, but when he has good men doing that, it turns out all right.'

Placing a high emphasis on the lyrical structure and content of a song has been a habit of many musicians throughout history, and a laudable one at that, but when Megas was talking, it felt strangely poignant. This undoubtedly had to do with the fact that so many of my interviews and conversations had led in some way back to the written or spoken word. The Icelandic language is much more unique than, say, English or French, which are spoken across the planet. Icelandic is spoken amongst only one community in the world, and is hence more culturally defining. Megas was reacting against the fact that the rock and pop artists who preceded him did not treat their heritage with the proper respect.

'People translated English lyrics into Icelandic but not properly,' he explained. 'I remember one artist who just translated them in terms of how they sounded, not what was being said. Laxness took old Icelandic words and updated them, just like Jónas Hallgrímsson did before him. He took words that had dropped out of use and brought them back in parallel with their original meaning. We can make new words from the roots of the language. You can make many great poems from them too. And you need this for the progress of a language. If you are well enough connected to your language, you can make quite an impact with just a sound. You can also take a foreign word and make it an Icelandic word. But my theory is that a sentence that is completely right according to an encyclopedia is a thought borrowed from America or somewhere else and is thus not Icelandic, but a sentence based on Icelandic thought *is* Icelandic. It has to have an Icelandic thought-source to make the sentence special.'

One of the other prominent factors of Megas's work is his constant irreverence. He started out dissing society and has never really stopped.

His music has changed but his attitude seems to have remained the same. I wondered what the Icelandic government could have done to cause him to vent his spleen so much. 'There was nothing particularly wrong with the Icelandic establishment,' he said. 'It was just an establishment and it wasn't my favourite. It was just something that you had to spit on. I showed myself as a communist when I was young, though I was living an illusion because I couldn't stand anything Russian. All my culture was American; there were no pop songs in Russia. It was a controversy, this dilemma. Everyone hated Stalin at the time, and I found that someone had to guard his reputation, his good persona. He killed 100 million people, and Hitler just half of that – but then, Stalin had a longer time.

'No, I never tolerated the establishment; they are just like some kind of poison. I accept authority when it is real, but when it's just a title then count me out. I despise it when it is not real and [not] honest. I started badmouthing from the beginning and was set up like some kind of *enfant terrible*. A few people had a political approach before me, but they were pop idols that talked about peace and brotherhood without knowing what they meant. Bands like Nattura and Trubrot had love and peace on their cleft tongues. These bands didn't realise that lyrics were the most important elements in the new pop.'

The kittens chorused loudly from the kitchen as we listened to more music. Megas cracked open another tin. He offered me another but I declined. The wind and rain outside was still falling steadily outside and the music on the stereo, which had been turned down to a minimal volume long ago, had now ended. We fell into a comfortable silence for a few minutes.

I reflected on the difference between the public perception of Megas as a cult musical hero and his more destitute reality. I thought about the inner workings of the creative mind, how it can shine with brilliance one minute and lead you into darkness the next. And I thought about all the shiny happy pop stars with nothing to say in the world, who contribute nothing but more disposable rubbish to our lives yet who enjoy heavy financing by companies who care for profits but not so much for prophets. Here was a man who truly cared for his art, who made people dance, laugh *and* think, who could raise roofs as well as eyebrows. As I got up to leave, Megas stood up to see me to the door. We shook hands and he peered at me once more over his glasses, fixing me with his wise stare and dimpled grin. He looked youthful and vigorous. 'Remember,' he quietly. 'Falsehood is always ugly; truth is always beautiful.'

13 Rokk I Reykjavík

Without any warning, the striated image on the TV screen gave way to a picture of a man on a stage shrouded in smoke. He looked ancient and worldly with a big curly beard and wizened face. He was chanting something heavy and strange into a microphone. 'That's Sveinbjörn Beinteinsson,' said Friðrik Thor Friðriksson. 'He's chanting *rimur.*' The image changed, a heavy three-chord riff exploded through the speakers and a brief title sequence segued into a brightly lit stage on which a band were unleashing an urgent clatter of guitars and drums. The lead singer, shirt unbuttoned to reveal a skinny pink chest, twitched around frantically like a freshly severed electrical cable. He was screaming the words 'Reykjavík, Oh Reykjavík, Oh Reykjavík...'

The people in the front row of the seated audience were off their chairs and pogoing around excitedly. There were leather jackets, sneers, piercings. This was hardcore punk, Iceland style. 'This band is Vonbrigdi,' remarked Friðrik. 'In English, the name means "The Disappointments". I put them in the film first because they were a pretty powerful band. The song they are singing was well known and was written by Didda, a novelist and a good friend of Björk's.'

Friðrik Thor Friðriksson is the undisputed heavyweight champion of Icelandic cinema. The director of seven full-length feature films and several documentaries, no one has had a bigger impact on the movie scene in his country. His movies are visual reflections of Icelandic culture in all its myriad shapes and forms, often illustrating a society caught between the traditional and the modern. His movie *Angels Of*

The Universe, a sensitive and idiosyncratic take on the subject of mental illness, was seen by no less than 50 per cent of the entire nation.

Friðrik played a large role in introducing cinema to Iceland in the '70s by importing art-house movies and organising showings for friends and fellow art students. The making of movies didn't properly begin until the '80s due to the huge expense involved in importing the necessary equipment. So Friðrik started his career with cheaper, more experimental art projects. One of them involved strapping a camera to the front of his car and driving around Iceland. More controversial was his short film that showed a copy of *Njal's Saga*, one of Iceland's most cherished cultural documents, being set alight. In the *Saga*, one of the heroes is famously killed when his enemies set fire to his home. Friðrik was adding his own incendiary twist to the tale.

In 1979 Friðrik started the Film Society and, a couple of years later, the Reykjavík Film Festival. The movie that made his name abroad was 1991's *Children Of Nature*, which told the story of an elderly man forced into a Reykjavík retirement home after living in the countryside all his life. The man ends up meeting a childhood sweetheart in the home and they make a run for it back to nature, with which they share an unbreakable bond. The film was nominated for an Oscar as 'Best Foreign-Language Film'.

In the last few years, Friðrik has become involved in a number of collaborations, as a producer and director, with international filmmakers such as Lars von Trier (who worked with Björk on *Dancer In The Dark)*, Hal Hartley and, more recently, Francis Ford Coppola. I had been invited to his offices to watch *Rokk I Reykjavík*, a full-length documentary he made back in the '80s on Iceland's explosive punk scene. It is today a cult movie both inside and outside the country.

The offices of his company, the Iceland Film Corporation, looked suitably film-directorish when I arrived. Promotional films in brown cardboard boxes were stacked along one wall. Tin spools were scattered randomly on tables. Posters of his movies decorated the walls. The main room was large: its dimensions enhanced by two huge windows. When I turned up, Friðrik was sitting in front of these windows, his distinctive moustache and unruly bundle of grey hair streaked with sunlight. His hands were thrust into a large blue winter coat and his feet were swung casually up on a table. If he were any more laid back, Friðrik would have been horizontal.

Friðrik dropped his legs off the table and greeted me. He ushered me into another room, which was littered with more film-spool tins, several editing suites and a couple of workstations. We walked over to one of these stations and, as if on cue, a young man joined us and loaded the VCR. Friðrik motioned for me to take a seat in a chair in front of the screen and he pulled up a chair behind me. I felt like a directorial assistant. As The Disappointments spat out their punk-ish vitriol on the audience, I asked Friðrik why he had decided to make the movie.

'I started the idea with Hilmar Örn Hilmarsson, who has been an old friend of mine since school. I was already involved in the music scene as part of the audience when we had the idea. Hilmar was a kind of creative director with a band called Theyr at the time, and we had been running a magazine called *Black And White,* which covered bands like The Stranglers and Robert Wyatt. We ran a small gallery as well, back in the late '70s, and imported various improvising groups. Through that we met Ásmundur Jonsson, who now runs Bad Taste. Back then, Ásmundur was presenting the only alternative music radio show in Iceland. We became friends with him and some other music people and it all sort of became one movement.

'When we stopped our gallery, the poet Sjon, who was in a surrealist group called Medusa, started to run another one pretty much next door. Peter Schmidt, the guy who did the artwork for Brian Eno, had several exhibitions there. In fact, Brian himself was always supposed to come here. There were flats rented with pianos and things, but he never made it. This era was a good time, the only time in Iceland that there was a movement that covered every field of art.'

Iceland's love of poetry and literature and music and film came together coherently in this period. In the '60s there was a group called SUM who made similar attempts at artistic cohesion, but the '70s were more expressive and proactive.

'The documentary was initially supposed to focus on a singer called Bubbi Morthens,' continued Friðrik, 'who had come onto the scene with all these left-wing ideas and had become a very political figure. No one else was doing anything political at the time, really, although there was a general peace movement going on here that was part of a worldwide anti-nuclear thing. Bubbi's brother, Tolli, had also been involved together in organising some anti-nuclear concerts and things like that, so the time seemed right to make a movie that had a political edge. As we were making it, more and more bands started coming through, and I began to feel that some of them could maybe get into the world market. I thought Theyr, for example, could do that if they got a contract with a good label like Rough Trade. I made the movie to try and reflect how much potential I felt the bands had.'

The cameras flicked to the Keflavík air base: Friðrik was showing the roots of the rock 'n' roll revolution. There was then a short interview with someone about the death of live music in the '70s with the arrival of discothèques in Iceland, and then I got my first glimpse of the movie's intended hero, Bubbi Morthens.

Bubbi, blonde, handsome and muscular, was performing with his band, Ego. He was dressed in a sleeveless top and leather trousers, and throwing out a chorus of *sieg heils* over a fast rock track whilst raising his hand up in an ironic Nazi salute. At least, I hoped it was ironic. The bands kept coming. The look, feel and sound of some of them revealed the influences on the Icelandic scene at that time. The sounds and spirits of Talking Heads, Killing Joke, Siouxsie And The Banshees, Iggy Pop, The Clash and others of the late-'70s/early-'80s global punk/new-wave movement didn't seem very far away. Just like in the '60s, Icelanders were once again taking their cues from the US and the UK.

The live footage in *Rokk I Reyjavík* was continually punctuated with more interviews. Bubbi came back on, reclining in a chair, talking about rock being a political thing and espousing some quasi-Marxist views. In the middle of a concert by The Bodies, the camera panned to a woman calmly knitting as she listened to their gothic proto-grunge. I couldn't restrain a burst of laughter.

'We didn't stage any of this,' smirked Friðrik. 'We just literally turned up at the gigs with cameras. It took around six months to film as we had no financial support from anyone and we needed around eight cameras for each event. Many of the shows were shot at Hótel Borg. Initially we had the idea of focusing more on Borg because at the time all the big shots of the country, all the parliament members etc, would eat there in the morning. Then in the afternoon elderly ladies would come in and drink tea. And then at night time the punks took over. That was pretty interesting, but as it turned out we had to broaden the context a little wider.'

Icelandic riot-grrrrrrl-style band Grylurnar came on screen and gave an insight into the mechanisms of the scene: 'Rent a garage. Get a loan. Buy instruments. Get them in the garage. Connect. Begin. Rehearse, and it works.' It was even more DIY than the '60s.

The next outfit was a band called Sjalfsfroun. Fronted by a kid with a studded leather jacket and a Mohican, they were apoplectically aggressive, despite the fact that the drummer's arms were no thicker than his sticks and the embryonic front 'man' was no older than 14.

After the concert, the baby-faced vocalist sat in a café and talked about his 'stupid government and boring country', before wandering through town with his bandmates. They were all dressed in punk regalia, spitting at each other and pushing their way through shocked and bemused crowds. The film flicked back to the end of their concert, where the singer smashed his guitar up with an axe and threw it into the audience. They threw it back at him – hard, raising their middle fingers in friendly punk salute.

'The film has never been shown in its entirety here in Iceland,' said Friðrik. I wasn't surprised. 'It was banned for children under 14 years old, though we did get away with a lot because cinema was such a new thing here in Iceland. This was only the fifth film ever made or something, and it was put out in 1982. Nineteen thousand people ended up seeing it, but we were thrown out of certain cinemas because they didn't like the audiences, most of whom were punks.'

The provocative parts of the movie didn't end there, either. Bubbi came back to talk about the pluses of smoking grass, decrying alcohol as 'the enemy'. A very young Björk appeared with her band Tappi Tikarrass. She looked deliciously eccentric, dressed up like a doll with rosy-red cheeks and clutching a toy drum and a child's badminton racket. In a film literally crammed with musical misfits, Björk still managed to stand out. Unsurprisingly, Friðrik used her as the cover star for the documentary. And this was a good five years before the outside world knew anything about her.

Her voice already possessed the strength and versatility that would eventually help to propel her to superstar status. In fact, it was with some of the members of the next band in the documentary, Purrkur Pillnikk, that she formed The Sugarcubes a few years later. Purrkur's performance was a cathartic freakout session led by the enigmatic, madcap Einar Örn Benediktsson.

Then, after some live footage of Hilmar Örn Hilmarsson's old musical colleagues, Theyr, came the most disturbing scenes yet from the movie. In a room lit sporadically by a strobe, a woman was being covered in clingfilm and balloons until she resembled some kind of human cocoon. A pre-recorded soundtrack collage of weird sounds and noises built up to sickening levels of intensity while a chopping board was prepared in the middle of the stage. Live chickens were then placed on the board and beheaded. Their severed bodies were thrown at the audience. The strobe gave the performance an even more chaotic, nightmarish effect. I certainly hadn't been expecting this. I looked askance at Friðrik.

'The group were a very controversial and provocative music/art ensemble called Bruni BB,' he said. 'They were named after an Icelandic prime minister who died in a fire in a summerhouse. Everyone thought we had staged this, but it was the same as the other events we filmed. We had nothing to do with the organisation of it. We just went in with the cameras and shot what was happening. The show was broken up halfway through when the police were called in. I think Björk was one of the people who called them in. Yes, look, here she is...'

Friðrik leaned across me and stopped the tape. He rewound it a few frames and then paused it on a still where the police were leaving the venue. Sure enough, off to one side was a harrowed-looking Björk. The next shot showed the group sitting on the floor of the venue with the lights on and the audience gone. One of them was swinging a headless chicken corpse around by its legs. They had a live pig with them. I groaned and closed my eyes. 'No, no, no, it's okay,' said Friðrik hurriedly, 'they don't kill the swine. It was a big thing for the police, though. The next day, they brought me in for questioning and one of the main questions was, "When was the last time you saw the pig?" I had actually seen it the next day, when I went back there to clean up. I went to the toilet and it was in there eating a ham sandwich. I told them this and they thought I was lying and kicked me out.'

Overall, *Rokk I Reykjavík* was one raw documentary. There was no soft lighting, no frills, no make-up. No romance or glamour. Just bands getting up and doing their thing in front of anyone that cared to listen, which was sometimes not that many people. Somehow punk's gritty realism seemed to fit in perfectly with the overall image of Iceland as a cold, occasionally violent, remote and very down-to-earth place. It was the right kind of music in a way for a youth tired of the niceties of rock 'n' roll and wanting to express themselves more vehemently. A generation of guitar-wielding Vikings was ready to protest against living too normal a life on a lonely, isolated rock. The youth was demanding a more inclusive future and had a hunch that music was the way to do it.

Many of the bands involved in the punk movement were made up of more than just musicians. This was a cultural explosion that had built up from a culmination of disparate yet connected ideas, theories and perspectives, which included poetry, surrealism, theatre, the visual arts and all-round avant-gardism. Rock 'n' roll had soundtracked the first youth-culture explosion in the '60s, but punk was now providing the fuel for Iceland's first real counter-culture movement that, in turn, sowed the seeds for the country's still-expanding alternative scene.

After Friðrik had showed me the movie, I wanted to meet Bubbi, whose first band, Utangardsmenn ('The Outsiders' – a punk classic), weren't the first punk group in Iceland but were one of the most popular. They consisted of Bubbi, Magnús Stefansson (who joined

Bubbi later to form Ego), Runar Erlingsson and two brothers from the USA, Daniel and Michael Pollock. They created a highly personal brand of hardcore punk funk, tempered with some Icelandic reggae *à la* The Clash, that rocked Iceland to the bone – perhaps more than any other band before or since. Most of the members are still involved in music today, although they haven't worked together since they split, in 1983. In 2000, the band was named the 'Best Icelandic Rock Group of the 20th Century'.

The esteemed Icelandic music journalist Dr Gunni memorably described Bubbi's arrival on Iceland's static scene as 'finally, a real man, someone who smelled of semen and fish'. An ex-fisherman, boxer, juvenile delinquent and the quintessential cocaine-snorting rock 'n' roll hero, Bubbi has these days kicked the narcos and is ironically one of the best-selling mainstream artists in the country. I saw him performing one evening to an audience that ranged from polite middle-aged people to unruly teenagers. He was playing folk, country and even a couple of frenetic Latin numbers. It was a far cry from his days as a pugilist punk rocker, but his tunes were good, he was handy with a guitar and he still didn't look like the kind of person you'd go out of your way to upset.

'I had a problem youth,' Bubbi admitted casually when I met him in the Hótel Borg. He was pouring himself a coffee as he spoke. Around his thick neck was an ivory pendant in the shape of a polar bear's head. 'I was a criminal kid, always in trouble. Music was my way to escape problems and worries and things like that. When I was a little kid I listened to Edith Piaf and Marlene Dietrich. Then The Beatles came, and I used to clean my brother's shoes before they went to the ballroom just so I could listen to his records.

'I remember the first Beatles LP, as well as The Dave Clarke Five, Petula Clark, The Rolling Stones, Lulu…basically a lot of stuff that came from Britain. We got it all from the military base, and also stations like Radio Luxembourg, which we used to listen to on this massive radio set that gave off an electrical smell.' He chuckled hard at this memory. 'They don't make those any more.'

'When I was around 10 or 11 I heard Woody Guthrie, Bob Dylan and Donovan. These artists had something different from The Beatles and those other groups. I can't describe what it was exactly, just something in the voice and in the music. One voice, one guitar, string sounds, thin guitars, it all just really got me. So I got a guitar and went to the school here to learn classical music, but I didn't like it, it just wasn't my style. I left the school when I was 15 but I was getting into lots of trouble so my brother and my mother contacted the police and made a deal for me to leave Reykjavík for one year. The police agreed that if I stayed out of trouble they wouldn't put me in jail.'

This was sounding like a classic tale. Here was a young man, from an isolated island located roughly in the middle of the north Atlantic, whose disaffection and disillusionment had led to crime and bad behaviour before finally finding an outlet through music. Such is the incredible power of sound. It had often bemused me how something as simple as vibrations travelling through air could turn so many heads, change so many lives, save so many souls. People are conceived to music, live their lives to music and are buried to music. Bubbi was also catching fish to it.

'At 16 I started working as a migrant worker, going from factory to factory, and working as a fisherman on trawlers and small boats on the east and west coasts,' he continued. 'We lived on board the boats and in the factories. I started to write songs about how life was in those days and in those conditions because at the time there were a lot of old jolly sailor sounds that just weren't telling the truth. They were singing about how there were girls waiting in every harbour and how the seagulls were smiling and things like that.'

Most young people I had met in Reykjavík regarded any fish-related work with an undisguised contempt. The jobs at the fish factories seemed to be looked at as the lowest of the low by many. It wasn't so long ago, though, that these jobs were what kept families alive. I was interested to learn what working on the ships had been like 30 years ago. 'The reality was a horror, even then,' grimaced Bubbi. 'In those days, which was around 1973 or 1974, if you worked in a factory you would often work for 40 or 50 hours in a row, then sleep for seven hours and go again.

'When we had free time, we wanted to escape that, so we smoked hash, drank booze...and I started to write songs. At one point I was living on a pub floor on Friday and Saturday nights before we went to the ballrooms. There were always these old-fashioned ballrooms in the villages that had accordion bands playing who were fucking incredible; they were so good at playing these old folk tunes. I started performing by doing concerts in the factories for my workmates. I found out that people liked it. Suddenly someone was singing something they could relate to. I just kept on working, smoking, drinking, fucking and fighting and playing music. I was always a bit of an outsider because I was doing very political songs back then, talking about things that normally you don't talk about in the music business.'

Bubbi was doing what his heroes Dylan, Guthrie and Donovan had done, which was to use music as a mirror to reflect a reality – warts and all – back to society. Like Megas, Bubbi was realising that music could have a purpose above and beyond mindless entertainment. It could be used to smuggle messages through to the public, to make people take a look at themselves and at the people around them, in their own society and in the outside world, too.

'I kept on doing what I felt like doing and not thinking about what the fashions were. I just did them the way I felt like doing them. I realised very early on that it was important to sing in Icelandic. It had nothing to do with nationalism as such, but I felt we had to just be more aware of our culture because the cultures of countries ten times bigger than Iceland have disappeared over time until there is nothing left of them. I kept on touring alone with an acoustic guitar, playing a lot of concerts every year where I would be singing about things such as violence in the home, drugs, fathers abusing their children and things that people didn't really want to think about. Suddenly I found out I was a kind of window for people who wanted to see what life was really about.'

Bubbi realised he could be free of the fishing-boat life if he developed his music. This seemed to be a motivating factor for many musicians in Iceland. The rapper Móri had posited that robots should take care of the tedious work in society so that individuals could be free to create. The reality was, though, that most musicians in Iceland couldn't make enough money to leave their jobs. It seemed more likely that music was simply an escape from the banality of the ubiquitous nine-to-five treadmill.

Bubbi became one of the luckier ones. Having already saved some of his wages from the factories, he took out a loan to supplement it and made his first album called *Eisbar Blues*, named after a famous fish factory in which he had worked. The album was a huge success. In the same year that it was released, punk exploded in Iceland. It knocked Bubbi off his feet, something that many men would physically attempt later in his career but with little success.

'We used to listen to the one alternative radio show we had run by Ásmundur Jonsson. That's where I first heard punk music. I went to England in 1977 and saw The Sex Pistols. I didn't go just to see them but I saw a poster while I was there and thought it was a great name. I had no idea who they were. There were about ten other groups playing at the concert too and it was a scary, scary atmosphere. The people there looked like aliens. I had never seen anything like it. It was very rough and very tough. I saw Generation X there, who I thought were better than the Pistols. I went crazy about it and was like, "That's it! I believe in rock 'n' roll again." I went back to Iceland to do my work in the factories again, but the music stayed in my head.'

The next key influence for Bubbi was Iggy Pop. When he first heard the albums *Raw Power* and *The Idiot*, he flipped. At the same time, he met the two American brothers Daniel and Michael Pollock, who had been listening to similar music. 'We were all listening to a lot of Leadbelly, Iggy Pop, The Ramones,' recalled Bubbi. 'I told them I was going to record an album and asked them to join me. They came with me in the studio. To begin with, things were supposed to be more just playing with guitars, but somehow the whole thing changed. It ended up with one half being acoustic and the other half being rock 'n' roll, very raw rock 'n' roll, powerful like early Iggy or the early Rolling Stones. Stuff with a lot of heart. We lived and breathed it all the way. We literally weren't doing anything else except living in the rehearsal space and doing drugs and making music.'

This music was revolutionary for Icelandic audiences that had been getting used to increasingly sanitised pop. Twenty years on and Utangardsmenn's debut LP is still a thrill ride, a rush of energy, brimming with musical influences and spewing forth attitude like a volcano spews lava. At first the public didn't know how to react to Utangardsmenn. But Utangardsmenn knew how to react to them. 'When people came to watch us we would just shout, "Fuck you!"' explained Bubbi. 'At first there were maybe ten boys and ten girls who thought it was great. There were another 300 who said, "Get the fuck out. We don't want to listen to you." Every town we played in had a bully who would come to the concerts and start fighting.'

Not that this worried Bubbi the human bear too much. He had been in the Icelandic weightlifting team and had also spent some time boxing in Denmark. He was physically very fit. 'And when you mix that with speed and coke, I was a killing machine. These guys would come up to us and try beating up the roadies and the mixing men. I just went up to them and beat them up in return.

'I remember one place on the west coast. They had this enormous reputation for killer guys. We were doing a concert and the atmosphere was not friendly, and while I was performing I saw this guy coming up to us. I saw that this was a hardcore situation. He started to give the mixing man a problem, so I put my hands behind my back in a peaceful gesture and said, "C'mon, man. We're trying to entertain you people. You can't behave like this." Then some guys came in and formed a small circle around us and were chanting, "Beat him!" So I beat this guy up bad. I mean, I really destroyed him. The whole band started to run then, but he chased after us. He came bursting through the doors – he was strong and wild. We ran to the bus and got inside and he was outside ripping the mirrors off. He tried getting onto the bus and we were all kicking him in the arms, the face, the head, but he just wouldn't stop. Someone then saw that we were killing him, so his friends took him away and we said to the driver, "Let's get the fuck out of here!"

'That kind of situation happened many times when we were on tour, maybe because we were just so aggressive on stage, just one, two, three and then "Waaah!" People didn't like it because it was maybe threatening. But we didn't care about being unpopular; we were just on a roll. One time we played a gig in the northeast for a farmer in his house. We played for three hours and then smoked hash and ate sheep with him. That was amazing. But then suddenly things turned. People started to come to our shows and we suddenly became the big thing.

'I became liked by the hard men because the police were busting me for drugs. All of a sudden I was their "man". Then I stopped. I came out and told people, "Drugs fuck you up." I started losing my friends, one by one. The drugs were killing them. I almost ended up in a mental hospital, and you obviously can't go on like that. When I told people I was out of the drugs thing, they began crying, "Judas! Judas!" So I replied, "Fuck you. I'll do what I want." I changed and began to go back to acoustic music, which is what I've been doing now for many years.'

Despite Bubbi's makeover, he still carries some of the political edge that he had when he began. In the tradition of Megas, for whom Bubbi confesses a great admiration, he enjoys criticising the establishment and confronting society with uncomfortable truths about itself. The fact that he hasn't stopped upsetting applecarts can be seen on the cover of his most recent LP, which features a Filipino dressed in traditional Icelandic seaman clothes. The point is being made that immigrant workers now fill traditionally Icelandic job vacancies. This issue has caused split attitudes in Iceland. Some are glad to see what they regard as boring jobs being taken care of by outsiders; others see the sudden influx of immigrants as a threat.

On the album, Bubbi discusses the latter angle, commenting on how Icelanders sometimes have a 'hidden Nazi attitude' towards foreigners. On the video for the song, he went as far as to show images of Mussolini and Hitler. 'People were like, "What the fuck are you doing?" They were shocked and stopped me on the street to say, "How can you do things like that?" People always say you can't mix up politics and music, that that's wrong. From my point of view, you can do it. I mean, the LP didn't do very well, as it got no airplay at all, but you have to do what you feel or there's no point. People just pretend there aren't any political issues, but there are some huge issues that need talking about.

'Look at the fishing companies. There are now ten companies or something that own all the fish in the ocean. The government sold these companies the quotas. Now these guys are zillionaires and meanwhile we've been watching all the villages disappear and collapse, as people can't stay alive there anymore. Three thousand years ago, Plato warned that people should beware of music because it has the power to ruin society. It is the fastest way of getting messages to the youth, who have the power to transform. I still believe that this is true.'

14 Punk International

The music from *Rokk I Reykjavík* and the subsequent recordings I picked up of bands from that era revealed a range of sounds and attitudes that spanned surreal, arty bohemia to dumbed-down garage rock. The influences came from New York's initial wave of punk rockers – Blondie, The Ramones, Television, MC5, Iggy Pop and The Velvet Underground – as well as UK acts like The Sex Pistols, Throbbing Gristle, Cabaret Voltaire and The Cure.

The New York and UK punk scenes arose for very different reasons. The American punks were following on – and reacting to – a tradition of surf and garage rock, with many of them positing deliberately ironic takes on suburban American life. But the Pistols and other English acts were reacting to more political circumstances, namely the economic recession that hit the country in the late '70s.

Since Iceland was more prosperous than ever in the '80s, the scene there was more aligned to America's than England's. It was less about social protest and more about the fight for the right to self-expression and individualism. Icelandic punk was about outrage for outrage's sake, and artists regularly supplemented the virile energy of the music with radical ideas from other artistic realms.

The name Ásmundur 'Ási' Jonsson had been popping up over and over again as I discovered more about the punk scene. I had met Ási briefly in his capacity as label manager for Bad Taste, the label formed by The Sugarcubes back in 1986, when I first came to Iceland. He had loaded me up with CDs to check out, but at that point I had no idea of how influential he had been as a driving force behind Iceland's alternative-music scene. Icelanders on the whole aren't much given to self-promotion. What is there to tell people in a small community that they don't already know?

Ási wasn't going to sit down and brag to me about everything he had been involved in, but when I asked him he was happy to unravel his history for me over the course of a few conversations. His passion for music began in the '60s, when he began to collect rock 'n' roll records and gained employment in record shops across town. His first break came in 1973, when he started a radio show on the national station Rás 1, along with his friend Gudni Rúnar Agnarsson. For the first time, people could tune into local radio and listen to something other than classical music or educational programs, even if it was only for an hour each week. The duo played an eclectic mix of progressive and avant-garde music from the worlds of jazz, rock and pop. The only place you could hear these sounds, aside from Ási's show, was by tuning into stations outside Iceland such as Radio Luxembourg and Radio Caroline. If you had a good reception and the wind was in your favour, Ási told me, you could also pick up John Peel's show on the BBC.

'The first stuff to grab me was popular music like The Beatles,' he said one day as we chatted in the Grey Kat. The café, located opposite Reykjavík's National Theatre, is a hangout for the city's filmmakers, musicians and artists. I saw everyone from Friðrik Thor Friðriksson and Baltasar Kormakur to Biogen and Jakob F Magnússon from Stuðmenn making the most of its charmingly bohemian ambience. I always felt comfortable amongst the rows of books and strange artwork that hung on the walls. I liked the way the smell of the café's famous American-style breakfasts massaged my nose. The Grey Kat is the only place in Reykjavík where you can buy this kind of breakfast, and although the prices are cruelly high, it's the best hangover cure available at the weekend.

'Later on, in the late '60s, I went more into American music and found underground bands like The Grateful Dead and then more experimental bands like The Velvet Underground,' continued Ási. 'I loved this idea of people coming together from classical backgrounds, live backgrounds and film backgrounds. The radio show we started was to try and present some of this music. The people that ran Rás 1 at the time were mainly elderly and enjoyed high rather than popular culture. Many of them were opera singers and composers, so our show became the only "pop" show. We started out playing international music, '70s rock and that kind of thing, but then we started bringing together different cultures and sounds, putting ethnic music together with popular music, classical and jazz.'

Aside from the station, Ási was instrumental in organising concerts, bringing over artists from America and Europe to play in the small galleries run by Friðrik and Sjon. A group of music enthusiasts, Ási included, formed an organisation called Jazz Awakening, which was responsible for introducing Reykjavík to the sounds of Evan Parker, The Feminist Improvising Group, Lindsay Cooper and other celebrated European players who had been inspired by Ornette Coleman and the US Free Jazz movement.

'They were great days,' said Ási, letting slip a nostalgic smile. 'There were bands in the UK and all over Europe that were participating in this movement. They would come here and play very intense sets to 15 people a time, even smashing their instruments up sometimes. At that time I was more into jazz generally, especially the likes of Art Blakey and Dexter Gordon, and tried to bring them over for concerts. We weren't getting many bands playing in Iceland. A lot of this music wasn't getting through here so people didn't know about it and so weren't booking anyone from this more independent field. After jazz we got more into avant-garde rock sounds and then, through Einar Örn, I started hearing the first punk records. That was when we started having more of an international scene.'

Where Bubbi and the Pollocks took a lot of their inspiration from US folk, rock and punk, Einar Örn Benediktsson provided some of the principal links between the Icelandic and UK scenes. Einar's father was based in London during the '70s and Einar spent time visiting him there. He was thus perfectly placed to catch the first ripples of the punk scene as the movement got talked about in music newspapers such as *Sounds*, *Melody Maker* and the *New Musical*

Express. Einar started to spread the word in Iceland and brought records back with him.

Ási at that time had started working in a large record store called Falkinn ('Falcon'). Einar took his new records into the shop and Ási started to play them on his show. These were the tracks that Bubbi had heard, and it was through Utangardsmenn that Einar Örn become more embroiled in the music. At the tender age of 17, he became the band's manager. But his first introduction to punk was through The Sex Pistols.

'When I was about 14 or 15 I remember hearing this horrible news about a band who were spitting at people on aeroplanes and that had green teeth,' Einar told me one day. 'It was an outrage here, but I thought it was very intriguing, so I went out of my way to find out who these guys were. I had heard some music around 1976, and after two months punk-spotting in London and buying records I started to like it more and more. I liked it simply because I found other music very boring. I discovered The Buzzcocks, who I thought were lovely, and then The Stranglers and bands like The Fall. Where most pop bands were singing about love, The Buzzcocks and other bands would sing about being who you wanted to be and doing your own thing. In Iceland, the one thing you need to do is your own thing, so the ethic worked perfectly for me. I made it my life. I started hanging around in record shops and they started importing records knowing I at least would be buying some of them. Out of each shipment, I bought 10 or 12 albums. This music was totally inspiring and had a lasting effect on me which is still strong today.

'When I first saw Utangardsmenn playing in Iceland, I just couldn't believe it,' he continued. 'Their music was a revelation to me because it sounded so much like the music I had been listening to in England. The guitar noises and the tuning made by the Pollocks sounded like The MC5s. It sounded like the real thing and I wanted to be involved. They played a few gigs and asked me through a mutual friend if I wanted to be their manager, so I said yes and started getting them some gigs around the country. Because we had so many gigs, we needed to keep the excitement levels up, so myself and Daniel Pollock kept trying to find new bands to play.'

In 1980, Utangardsmenn played 32 concerts. That meant a lot of support bands to find. Einar and his friends formed their own in March 1981, called Purrkur Pillnikk, who played with Utangardsmenn, but by the time the former started recording their first LP, a year later, Utangardsmenn had split. Purrkur were an electric shock of a band. They kind of took over from The Outsiders, although they were less coherent and slightly more indulgent. Their motto was 'It only matters what you *do*, not what you are capable of doing.' On *Rokk I Reykjavík*, Einar was filmed saying, 'Icelanders have finally realised that you don't have to know how to play an instrument to be in a band. I can't play. Bragi can play very little. Aesgir knows even less and doesn't play the drums at all.'

Purrkur became one of the most influential bands of the punk era. As Utangardsmenn split and Bubbi started to go in more commercial directions, Einar encapsulated more than anyone else the uncompromising ethic of punk. Just a couple of weeks after their first rehearsal, the band recorded their debut outing, a seven-inch ten-track EP called *Tilf*, the shortest song on which lasted ten seconds, the longest 90 seconds. This was the core of punk: short, sharp and to the point. The band followed the EP with the album *Ekki Enn*. They didn't have a label to go to, so in true DIY style Ási, Einar and their friends Björn and Dóra formed Gramm, the first real independent record label in Iceland.

'We recorded the first Purrkur Pillnikk record on the 1 April 1981,' said Ási. 'We made just a few hundred copies, but this approach was very fresh here in Iceland. It was something that hadn't musically been done before. Björk was turned onto this stuff, too, through her band Tappi Tikarrass, and they put out a record through Gramm too. It was all about the attitude of just getting out there and creating music, presenting it in whatever way you wanted to and working in the surroundings you wanted to work in. We could get 50 hours studio time, maximum. If you went over that you had to take a loan out and go to the UK, but somehow we always found a way of just about getting the money to record, even if the record flopped.

'We decided that, if we were going to earn enough money to keep going, we needed more than three or four releases a year, so we started importing, and then a year later, in 1982, we decided to open up a record store. The selections were all associated with the independent scene right from the start. The other labels in Iceland were representing the majors from abroad, so we were left with the alternative stuff that we obviously enjoyed. As an independent, it was always important for us to foster collaborations and links with other bands and artists.

'We were lucky enough to hook up with like-minded people such as The Fall, who came here after they had been on an American tour during which they had almost split up. Mark (E Smith) had argued with his manager or something and she had left the whole band somewhere in Texas to go off with some truck driver she'd met. The rest of the band came here and played with Purrkur. It was an excellent show, which we recorded. The Fall then asked Purrkur to tour with them in the UK, which they did. The next band to come over and hang out were Psychic TV, who made a record here called *Those Who Do Not*, which we released. We sold 6,000 copies of that, which was great for us. While they were here, the main man, Genesis P Orridge, married his wife in a pagan ceremony. Hilmar Örn Hilmarsson ended up recording with them and becoming a kind of honorary member. He even moved to the UK for a while.'

These events were significant. For the first time ever in Icelandic music history, some serious international links were being made with the outside world. Other Iceland bands had tried to involve themselves more with the outside world, but with less success. Most people believe that the '60s and '70s bands were simply too desperate. The relationship between bands and record labels is like any other – if one party shows too much interest, the attraction can fade. The punks at least pretended that they couldn't care less. They treated everyone mean and subsequently kept everyone keen. This attitude would soon pay massive dividends.

In 1983, Ási's radio show came to an end after helping to shape the alternative scene for the last ten years. To celebrate, they organised a live show for the final program – the only show they had ever organised through the radio. Ási and Gudni pulled together people from various bands to form a special one-off Supergroup who called themselves Kukl ('Sorcery'). The people in the band were Einar Örn from Purrkur Pillnikk; Björk from Tappi Tikarrass; Siggtryggur Baldursson, the drummer from Theyr; Einar Melax from poetry outfit Medusa; bassist Gudlaugur Kristinn (also from Theyr); and Birgir Mogenson, once a member of Killing Joke. The event was titled 'We Demand A Future' – a conspicuously political title for Iceland. Alongside Kukl, the organisers also signed up Megas, Stuðmenn and Bubbi Morthens and invited anarcho-punk outfit Crass from the UK. It was the first concert Megas had played for almost a decade. Theyr dressed in Nazi costumes. Crass had never played in front of so many people.

'My idea for Kukl was just to bring all these people out from all these groups and get them to play 20 minutes of special music for the program,' explained Ási. 'It was a long event, about six or seven hours altogether. It was one of the only times there has been any kind of big political statement by musicians in Iceland, even though there wasn't much focus on any one political issue as such. It was just a kind of anarchical statement using punk rock as the driving force. The day after there was an artier, more literary event at the National Theatre which made the statement broader. The whole thing was just about expression and individualism and had nothing to do with any governmental oppression or anything like that as there wasn't anything like that going on in Iceland. We didn't have any real causes, but there was a real sense that we were part of the international community.'

After the concert, the members of Kukl decided to record their first song, 'Söngull'. At this stage all the members still had full-time jobs. Björk was working in a fish-factory, as a background-singer for Megas and was still in Tappi Tikarrass. Einar had been cultivating more links in the UK through his tours with Purrkur and by hanging out with bands like Flux Of Pink Indians and The Fall. Later that year, Einar went to study in London and started to spend time with Crass, whom he had met at the concert.

Einar and others helped Kukl organise some tours around Europe, including Holland and the Roskilde Festival in Denmark. His friendship with Crass grew and culminated in one of the band asking if Kukl would record a small single for their label. Kukl obliged and made six tracks, which became a mini-album called *The Eye*. I listened to this EP with great interest. Kukl, along with Purrkur Pillnikk, were one of the first bands to be taken seriously outside Iceland. Where Purrkur were abrasive and sparky, Kukl made music that was as confused and fragmented as the band's disparate origins would suggest.

The Eye's eldritch brew of howl-at-the-moon strangeness held a mystic appeal assisted by the complementary yin-yang vocals of Einar Örn and Björk. Their contrasting styles – Björk's guttural yells and powerful screams alongside Einar's indulgent yelps and crazy barks – got them known as 'Beauty And The Beast'. Apparently, their live shows were correspondingly bizarre.

The poet and novelist Sjon described some of the Kukl concerts to me one day as we chatted in the Grey Kat. Sjon was in the lauded experimental outfit Fan Houtens Koko and played with Björk and Thor Eldon in a previous band called Rokha Rokha Drum. He was also part of Medusa, one of the instigators of the gallery next to Friðrik Thor's in the '70s and an all-round literary inspiration for many musicians of the era. In the '90s, he began to collaborate with Björk as a lyricist and won an Academy Award for his efforts in the film *Dancer In The Dark*. When I met him, he looked like he had stepped from a film set where he had been playing a '50s European sophisticate. He wore small round glasses and a trilby-style hat, and his clothes were immaculately pressed; he looked like a walking anachronism.

'People went crazy,' he said of the Kukl gigs. 'They were a mix of musicians and poets that had partially sprung from our poetry group, Medusa. We were all seeking inspiration from lots of the same sources, trying to go into dark worlds. Medusa rejected tradition to an extent, even Laxness, although we were influenced by his poetry as he was the first surrealist poet in Iceland. One of the poets in Kukl dressed in his own poetry, in a suit made of pages from his books, and while he recited he drank sheep's blood. Einar Melax played classical pieces but had a balaclava made from meat cutlets. Thor Eldon also used to put meat all over his face and things like that. It was always done with humour: they were just laughing in the slaughterhouse. At the same time, Kukl took themselves quite seriously. They were serious about exploring darkness and things like that. It was in Kukl that Björk came into her own as a poet, I believe.'

In 1984 Kukl toured the UK, with Flux Of Pink Indians, Chumbawamba and D&V in support of the miners' strike. They raised £64 (US $104; €96). They continued to play in Europe, sleeping in their vans and managing to find venues in various countries that could pay them to play. Significantly, they had soon played more gigs abroad than in Iceland.

Inspired by their escapades, in 1986 they recorded another LP, entitled *Holidays In Europe*. The album was still disjointed and discordant and was delivered in their uniquely experimental goth-punk way, but it was brighter and more cohesive than its predecessor. Björk was certainly more to the fore on the LP, while Einar Örn continued to be her perfect foil with his own particular brand of verbal voodoo.

By this stage, Kukl were making impressions all over on audiences and other bands, such as '80s industrial heavyweights Einstürzende Neubauten, who invited them to perform with them. Things were starting to shape up on the international front for an Icelandic band at last. Unfortunately, these were the peak years for Kukl and they disbanded soon after their second album. It was all good practice for the individual musicians, though, especially those who would go on to play together in another group that would form from the ashes of Kukl, called Sykarmolarnir. In English, their name was The Sugarcubes, and they were the first band from Iceland to attain international fame beyond their wildest dreams.

15 On The Music Map

During the second night of Airwaves, I visited Iðnó, one of Iceland's oldest public venues. A few decades ago, the place was used as a theatre, and it was here that the country's first plays were produced. It is now still used for plays and concerts, and it also houses an opulent restaurant upstairs which allegedly gives good views over Tjorn. I had never eaten there; restaurants on the whole in Iceland, whilst usually serving good food (especially fish), are pretty expensive. £20 (US $32; €30) for a main course is not unusual.

For Airwaves, the downstairs of Iðnó had been transformed into a concert hall. The night was a cold one again, although the northern lights were not playing. On my way down to the venue, I had been surprised to see a dishevelled man rifling through a bin. I realised I had never seen a vagrant in Iceland before. I walked over and gave him a couple of kroners, to which he responded with what sounded suspiciously like, 'Merry Christmas.' I didn't pull him up on the fact that it was October.

Inside Iðnó I encountered a large, ornate room with a stage at the far end. A sizeable audience had spread themselves around the room to watch a man tapping out some delicate rhythms on a set of drums and percussion instruments. The beats were tribal and writhed away beneath insouciant waves of ambient sound being made by a man with a laptop beside him. The drummer was Sigtryggur Baldarsson, the rhythmic powerhouse that had been behind Kukl, Theyr and The Sugarcubes. Musically, this was a long way from the output of those bands but backed up the widespread theory that Icelanders find it hard to stop making music once they've started – no matter what levels of stardom they reached.

The next act also included a Sugarcube – Einar Örn Benediktsson. Einar's live performances were legendary with The Sugarcubes, Kukl and Purrkur Pillnikk. He gained a reputation for being a confrontational wildman, taunting crowds as much as pleasing them. When he stepped on stage at Iðnó, he was sipping water from a bottle and looked relaxed. He was flanked by two guitar players, both of whom were wearing headphones. To his left, his ten-year-old son played trumpet – the only musical instrument with which Einar himself has ever been associated. Also on stage was Bibbi Curver, working away behind a mixing desk much larger than the one he had used for his Bad Taste performance the previous night.

Einar strolled up and down the stage as his band began to conjure up a murky mesh of dub, techno and rock. As the music's weird magic began to swirl around the audience like a dark, nebulous cloud, Einar began to prowl like a leopard, contorting his face and muttering short sentences that might have been poetry, comments, rhymes or just nonsensical grunts. People talk a lot about how Sigur Ros invented their own language: Einar Örn was speaking in tongues years ago.

Next to me, a man with a lacerated face was looking smitten by the show. I asked him what Einar was talking about, if anything. He listened hard for a second, grinning with effort as he did so. 'I'm not sure, but I don't think he likes money very much.'

Einar's body twisted around in jerky movements that were in sync with his disjointed ramblings. This wasn't just music; it was performance, too. It confounded expectations, asked questions about what music and entertainment should be, demanded things of the audience. Those that weren't ready to be demanded from began to leave. The rest of us remained, bemused and transfixed as Einar continued his theatrical performance, oblivious to who was, or was not, digging his gig.

A few days later, I met Einar in Apotek, a suave café/restaurant downtown. He was very much back in civilian mode. When I got there, he was launching an uncompromising attack on a slice of chocolate cake. I ordered a coffee and took a seat. I had met Einar several times. It was always a little bit tricky to know what kind of mood he would be in. He had something of the capricious pop star about him. Sometimes he would be cagey and mysterious, other times affable and light-hearted. However, although he was as unpredictable as the weather and largely inscrutable, Einar was consistently helpful and always offered interesting insights.

'I am derogative towards musicians,' he announced when I asked him what he had thought of Airwaves. The statement surprised me. 'There is no reason why musicians should be put on pedestals as prophets. The people I have grown up with and remain friends with are not musicians. They are labourers, painters, writers, but not musicians. I don't mix with them. I come from a musical family, in fact, but they are also involved more in theatre and acting. The history of Iceland is more tied in with that kind of stuff rather than music, which is why there is an inferiority complex here in Iceland that manifests itself at Airwaves. People suddenly lose their cool and run around with press releases and CD-Rs, thinking they should be world famous. But what's to say they should be?'

I was aware that Einar, and the punk scene, were about a lot more than just music, as is the contemporary scene in many respects. Icelanders by their very nature are diverse people. They have to be. There are simply too many things to do and not enough people to do them to allow for refined specialisation of labour.

Musicians are often also filmmakers. Filmmakers sometimes write plays. Photographers cut hair. Hairdressers design websites. Unemployment in Iceland has traditionally been zero, though these days it stands at a 'whopping' two per cent.

But what did that have to do with not liking musicians? Einar's comments seemed harsh and also hypocritical, given that he was a part of the festival and performing with musicians who were, presumably, his friends. Einar never considered himself a musician, which is perhaps where he was coming from. It was the mention of an 'inferiority complex' that held the key to what he meant. It certainly wasn't the first time I had heard the phrase applied to Iceland. From what I could gather, Einar was lambasting the fact that bands were trying so hard to be world famous.

It's a topic he knows something about. In the late '80s and early '90s, he was part of The Sugarcubes, the most famous band to have emerged from Iceland. In fact, they still are one of the biggest known bands, second in sales and popularity only to Björk, who was also with them until she went solo. But the 'Cubes became famous without trying to. Many other bands – Kukl and Purrkur Pillnikk included – tried hard to make a statement abroad. Most of them failed or had limited success. Einar's point was that the line between enthusiasm and desperation is often very thin.

The Sugarcubes weren't the first band from Iceland to gain a UK chart position; jazz-funkers Mezzoforte were, with a song called 'Garden Party' in 1983, but then they disappeared off the global pop radar. When The Sugarcubes came along, they proved that they were much more than one-hit wonders.

The 'Cubes were formed from the ashes of Kukl. When the latter band broke up ('We simply blew a fuse' was the only comment Einar would give), the members returned to their normal lives. They wrote poetry and books, worked in factories, had spells in other bands, studied, hung out, got drunk, lived normally. But it wasn't long before the itch to make music resurfaced again, and the itch simply had to be scratched. 'I was still in London and finished my studies in the spring of 1986,' recalled Einar, angling his fork for a second onslaught on his ample dessert. 'When I got home, I started hanging out with Thor Eldon and Björk at their house. They were married by then. On one of those nights, we started discussing what was good taste and what was bad taste and asked ourselves who dictated such things. Why is a certain drum sound considered good or bad? Who says a £1,000 snare sound is better than anything else? This discussion extended to society and the world as a whole. Thor told me what Picasso once said, that good taste is the killer of creativity, and that it was therefore better to mobilise against it.

'Thor was writing a poetry book called *Take Some Petrol, Darling* and Bragi [the bassist] was also writing poetry, so we decided there was a need to put together some kind of company or organisation of like-minded people and try to form a kind of publishing association. We drew in people from Medusa, from Kukl, from Purrkur Pillnikk, Ási, all these people, and instead of forming a band we formed a kind of creative organisation. But then we also found that we still wanted to do music, so I asked Bragi to take up the bass again and Frikki from Purrkur Pillnikk to take up the guitar, and Siggi Baldursson and Einar Melax came along and we started playing this music, which we regarded as crap, silly pop stuff.'

'Crap, silly pop stuff' seemed like a pretty disparaging description for music that won fans all over America and Europe. But then, this was the point of the band, to play what they deemed shallow – or Bad Taste – music and take it out to the rest of the world for them to judge. It goes without saying that they didn't have much faith in the tastes of the masses. The trouble was, they had all been in bands for so long that no matter what they did they probably would have made it sound good.

Einar and his friends became a worldwide smash, enjoying three chart-hitting albums in the same amount of years and a spate of hit singles to boot. Compared to the intense introspection and mystical explorations of Kukl, though, the music of the 'Cubes must have felt like spiritual therapy. 'Kukl was just a learning process,' shrugged Einar, 'part of a certain era. It was part of the development of us individuals who were in it. The mode of the band was very introvert and heavy, that's just how it evolved, and so in that sense, yes, The Sugarcubes were more light-hearted. But it wasn't a reaction against it, as such. You take time out and remap creatively. If you just stare at the darkness all the time, then it's no good. The time was simply right for us to do something else. We didn't need to be introverted any longer. Also, Kukl hadn't been so successful because it all seemed to happen at the wrong time.'

Is there a wrong time and a right time for good music? The '80s on the whole was a pretty good decade for Iceland in terms of garnering some international attention. Even though there had been a lot of external influences on the country since independence, there hadn't been much cultural traffic the other way. Iceland did hit the international news on several occasions, however, with Laxness winning the Nobel Prize in 1955; the famous Spassky/Fischer chess championship being held in Reykjavík in 1973; Heimaey erupting in 1973; and, of course, there was all the heat around Iceland in the mid '70s, when for the first time in history Iceland was at WAR! Inevitably, it was over fish.

The Cod Wars officially started in the '50s, when Iceland decided to expand her fishing territories after independence. However, the country had for many centuries endured foreign vessels plundering their rich fishing waters. The British, the Dutch, the French, the Germans and even the Basques had all sailed over and helped themselves to the lucrative stocks. The number of fish in the sea around Iceland inevitably began to diminish, a bad thing all round but especially for Iceland, which didn't have many other industries to fall back on.

The imposed zones naturally enough annoyed other nations, who felt they had a right to be there. At one point, the British reacted against the extension of Iceland's fishing zones by putting a ban on the landing of Icelandic fish in England, a bitter irony after the country had helped to feed the Brits during World War II.

In 1972–3 the wars came to a head again when Iceland extended their limit to 80km (50 miles). Britain and Germany refused to accept it. British warships were sent to Iceland and rammed Icelandic boats.

The Icelanders, lacking the military resources for an all-out war, responded with stealth, cutting the fishermen's nets and sabotaging boats. The men involved in these clandestine operations (which normally took place under cover of darkness in small dinghies) were lionised by the nation until they started to reach the type of infamy normally reserved for the old saga heroes. In 1973, Iceland almost went as far as to sever diplomatic relations, but the British Prime Minister Ted Heath and the Icelandic Prime Minister Olafur Johannesson sat down and set an agreement for limited British fishing.

In many ways, the Cod Wars represented a moral victory for Icelanders, as outsiders saw them as something like a series of David and Goliath battles where Iceland was the underdog who fought back against the British bullies – and won.

A decade later, Iceland produced a Goliath of its own. In 1984, the Icelander Jon Pall Sigmarsson won the 'Strongest Man In The World' competition. To prove it wasn't a fluke, he won it again in 1986. If anyone still doubted his abilities, he silenced them once and for all by picking up the title for a third time in 1988.

In 1985, an Icelandic woman, Hofi Karlsdóttir, won the 'Miss World' title. Again, just in case the world wasn't watching, another Icelandic beauty, Linda Petursdóttir, took the title a couple of years later. The '80s were the decade that proved Iceland had not only the strongest men in the world, but also the most beautiful women. Icelanders had always known this – it said so in the sagas – but it was nice to have the rest of the world recognise it too.

Amidst all these bulging muscles and sexy curves, Reagan and Gorbachev opted to hold their peace summit in Reykjavík in 1986, which helped raise the country's political profile. I had heard stories about how unprepared the capital was for the large-scale summit; tourists in Iceland were still something of an anomaly at that time, and there was a distinct lack of facilities. Many Icelanders thus transformed their homes into temporary hotels to accommodate the politicians, their entourage and the attendant media.

If Kukl had happened at the wrong time, The Sugarcubes couldn't have happened at a better time. They appeared at the end of a decade that had been positively rammed with Icelandic prowess, providing some kick-ass music – or 'crap, silly pop stuff', depending on your viewpoint – to soundtrack the new era of achievement. To get the money for their first record, the Bad Taste collective released a postcard of the Reagan–Gorbachev summit, made by Friðrik Erlingsson. It was a bestseller and the proceeds enabled the recording of *One Cube Per Head*, a seven-inch that featured the songs 'Cat' and 'Birthday'. The funds also helped to publish Bragi's first book of poetry, called *Draught*.

'We did our first concert in a tent near the university and just kept on rehearsing,' said Einar, sitting back in his chair and looking sated.

A victorious square of cake remained on the plate. 'I was managing Stuðmenn at that point, and we did a big concert with them. We had been calling our new band Thukl, which means "grope", but for the concert we changed our names to The Sugarcubes. Instead of paying us cash, Stuðmenn paid us in studio time in the recording space they had at the back of Egill's house. I went back out to London with some of these recordings to try and get them remixed, and that was when it all started.'

In 1987 Derek Birkett from the band Flux Of Pink Indians set up his own label, One Little Indian. When Einar came to him with The Sugarcubes' first record, he agreed to put it out. The UK press responded...well, hysterically. The *NME* in particular flipped over 'Birthday', naming it 'Single Of The Week', a strange choice considering the song – a tripped-out slice of weirdo pop featuring Björk unleashing some surreal lyrics about keeping spiders in her pockets – sounded like nothing else out there. The 'Cubes had landed on the pop landscape like aberrant aliens arriving on Earth from Pluto. People loved them.

Later, in 1988, the band released their debut LP, the exceptional *Life's Too Good*, which propelled them to stellar status worldwide. 'Birthday' had sold fewer than 300 copies in Iceland; *Life's Too Good* sold 100,000 copies in the UK and 450,000 in America. A year or so after the release of their first single, The Sugarcubes were touring the world with the likes of Public Enemy, Public Image Ltd and New Order in America, playing to crowds that totalled more than the entire population of their native country. At one time, these young, artistic punks had revered the likes of David Bowie and Iggy Pop; now they were putting them on VIP lists for their gigs.

For a country that was used to being ignored, this must have all come as a shock. How the hell had six musicians from this remote and rocky outcrop suddenly managed to charm the pants off the whole world? 'In a way, it was all quite coincidental,' said Einar, glancing with increasing regularity at the remaining slice of cake. It seemed to be taunting him. 'I knew Derek was setting up a label to put out his own music and I told him we had this new band and had finished demos and artwork and would he like to put it out? It was exactly the same process as with Purrkur Pillnikk, when I went to Ási with a master and finished artwork and formed Gramm to put our music out.

'Our philosophy has always been that if we are content with what we were doing ourselves then we cannot lose. It didn't matter if anyone else was listening to it or not as we were just this self-contained happy unit who were enjoying what we were doing. We were very happy-go-lucky. There was also some luck for us, as when we put out the single there seemed to be a gap in the UK music scene. Nothing was happening at the time. Bands like Depeche Mode and Erasure were not busy, for some reason, and the indie scene was not happening, for some reason. Then suddenly the guy at the *NME* listened to "Birthday" and they just embraced us.' Einar was now chasing the last crumbs around his plate. A man who has survived almost 20 years in the music business in Iceland doesn't let a dessert beat him that easily. 'Why us?' he demanded, throwing his fork down on the table and licking his fingers. 'I still don't know.'

Einar had seemed complacent about the rise of The Sugarcubes. It was widely reported throughout their career that they didn't seem to care so much for all the trappings that usually came with pop stardom. Derek Birkett often complained that the band seemed to spend as much as they earned and that they refused to play the industry game. As a professed anarcho-punk, however, Derek had to try and understand – he would have been compromising his own principles if he didn't – but I wanted a second opinion. Surely someone must have been excited.

I called up Bragi Olafsson, the band's bassist and asked him what was his favourite moment with The Sugarcubes.

He thought for a second. 'Watching John Lydon puke on his hotel bed in front of some family members in Buffalo, and then seeing him going into the bathroom to get a towel to clean up the mess.'

I laughed. That must have been a sight for sore eyes. So was the rise of The Sugarcubes special for him as an Icelander making it big in the outside world?

'There was never any specific moment when it happened,' Bragi said. 'I think we just found it all very funny and thought, "Wow! It's easy to break into this stupid music business." Although we enjoyed being a part of the business, we had a deep contempt for it. When The Sugarcubes started to receive all the attention, I usually sensed a lot of excitement in the journalists that visited us and also our collaborators: they seemed to view us as potentially mad people who consumed a lot of alcohol and tobacco, and we probably did nothing to correct that misunderstanding. It certainly gave us a lot of freedom to say stupid things about our country, as people didn't know very much about it. And of course it felt very good. Björk still says very strange things about Iceland in interviews. Of course we wanted to continue making money and be able to make music and finance Bad Taste, the company, but on the whole I don't think we gave a shit about what you call stardom. And the result is that we are no longer famous.' That, of course, isn't strictly true. Most of the band might no longer be famous, but one of them still is. Very much so.

The 'Cubes' second LP, *Here Today, Tomorrow, Next Week*, wasn't as well received as their debut, but it still got to number 15 in the UK album charts. The band embarked on another hectic tour and press mission and then decided to reconvene in Reykjavík for a while.

During this time, the Bad Taste organisation was in need of some money to keep going. Björk managed to help out by recording a jazz LP with a well-known Icelandic trio. It was called *Gling Glo* and contained several Western and Icelandic jazz and pop standards. It turned out to be a platinum-seller just like the first solo LP she had made at the tender age of ten. Entitled *Björk*, her debut was released in 1977 and was also full of covers, this time of pop hits such as The Beatles' 'The Fool On The Hill', Stevie Wonder's 'Your Kiss Is Sweet' and some poppy versions of old Icelandic children's rhymes, folk songs and even an instrumental track named 'Johannes Kjárval', written by Björk and dedicated to an Icelandic artist.

Björk somehow managed to resist the pull of mainstream stardom, even though her first LP had effectively made her a child star. She gave the pop scene a wide berth before reappearing as a punk. One of her first bands was called Spit and Snot, for which she dyed her hair orange and played drums. Another was Tappi Tikarrass (which means, roughly, 'Cork The Bitch's Ass'), who released the well-received LP *Miranda*.

After this, Björk joined Kukl and then The Sugarcubes. After 20 years of development, the time had finally come for an adult solo effort.

Thor Eldon, the father of Björk's first baby, Sindri, and a successful poet (as well as a founding member of Medusa and the surrealist rock group Fan Houtens Koko), described to me the ending of The Sugarcubes. 'The band stopped as naturally as it started,' he said. 'We just felt like it was a time to move on. Björk wanted to do some music. Bragi wanted to write. I wanted to stay at home and take a break from music. We all had some needs to attend to. The touring was also taking its toll. I guess we were a bit tired of the routine. Maybe it is just called growing up, as banal as that sounds.'

The 'Cubes finally bowed out after three huge-selling LPs and a final tour with U2 – not too shabby an exit for a band who never gave a damn.

As the rest of the musicians set about regaining some normality in their lives after four years of toying with the music industry, Björk started to fulfil her mission to record the songs she had been making in her head for a few years. She was keen to explore the emerging electronic sounds that she had been hearing on her treks across Europe and America.

One of Björk's first forays into the burgeoning dance scene was with 808 State, to whose *Ex:El* album she contributed two tracks. She took her personal vision further with the help of UK beat stalwarts like Graham Massey (from 808 State) and Soul II Soul heavyweight Nellee Hooper. The result, in 1993, was *Debut*. Although it was officially her third LP, Björk perceived the album as being her first real solo project. The LP exceeded everybody's expectations.

For most people, it was daringly different and incredibly diverse. It was lush, romantic, brazen, sideways, heroic, gentle, a kaleidoscopic rollercoaster of emotion which drew on dance music, jazz, classical, folk, ethnic sounds and much more. It was the essence of Björk's musical career distilled into a broad-ranging whole, epic in scope and dynamic in execution. Björk had made something incredibly different sound as if it was meant to be, like a space had been waiting for it all along. She topped it all off with that awesome voice that roared and tumbled and growled and floated as naturally and unpredictably as the Icelandic wind.

The entire music media fell in love with it. So did millions of fans. If The Sugarcubes had been propelled into the big time, Björk was now catapulted into the stratosphere. During an interview for *The Face* magazine, Björk spoke of the new levels of fame her album had brought. Iceland's Foreign Minister had apparently called her at home to personally congratulate her, but before the operator put the call through she passed on her own personal message: 'I'm a big fan of your music. And by the way, would you like me to pass on a message to your grandfather? I see him every day at the swimming pool.'

Since these auspicious beginnings, Björk has gone from strength to strength and now occupies her own special place in the pop firmament. With albums like *Post*, *Homogenic*, *Selmasongs* and *Vespertine*, she has attained a unique balance of accessible songs, honest emotional spirit and cutting-edge experimentation. She is a typical Icelander in the sense that she is an all-round artist who naturally embraces diversity and likes to retain control over all aspects of her work. The clothes she wears, the artwork that adorns her albums, her lyrics and her live shows have all helped create a truly unique talent whose name has these days become an adjective.

They say that Iceland has one of everything. It had taken most of the 20th century to muster up an internationally recognised band. In 1992, Iceland gained their first ever megastar.

16 Pop Stars

The concept of fame raises a paradox in Iceland, as it does in any small community. If everyone already knows everyone else then in a sense everyone is famous. But if everyone is famous, that means that actually no one is famous. Many people in Iceland assured me that everyone in their society gets their Warholian 15 minutes, and often a lot more. Just being someone's great-grandmother is usually a guarantee of some kind of local recognition. Obituaries in Iceland, which are widely read by the populace, usually extend to a page or more per deceased person, so even in death a modicum of celebrity is guaranteed. During my stay there, it was even suggested that I could well be hauled in front of a TV camera or a journalist's microphone, although that never happened.

Being a pop star normally necessitates a degree of distance between performer and audience. From what I had seen, in Iceland that space simply doesn't exist. I saw various 'pop stars' after I interviewed them in such unglamorous locations as supermarkets and post offices. The audiences that most groups played to usually included some of their friends and/or some of their family. If not, they would certainly know their friends and family. How can you have a flamboyant pop-star attitude in front of people you could well be seeing in the supermarket the next day, or who might be cutting your hair or making your dinner when you got home that night?

Yet pop stars exist. The community reveres certain individuals more than others. One guaranteed way of becoming famous in Iceland is by getting famous abroad first. This process underlines a definite hypocrisy amongst music fans, but one by no means limited to Iceland. Many artists around the world complain about being ignored at home until they have been received warmly abroad. In Iceland, bands from the punk era routinely played to tiny crowds, but once they gained the international stamp of approval, were treated like old friends.

Björk was treated like a weirdo and largely ignored at home before The Sugarcubes took off. Now she is by far the biggest pop star in her country. This has perhaps been aided by the fact that she has created distance between herself and her native community by living abroad in places like New York and London. This has made her quite unreachable in a community where normally everyone is accessible.

I had no problem tracking down or talking to any artist I needed to who still lived in Iceland. Most of them were listed in the phone book. But when it came to Björk, normal levels of accessibility were denied. It didn't help that she was having a baby at the time, but even so I suddenly came up against a wall of management, label people, PRs etc. Even her best friends back in Iceland seemed unable to be sure about whether they would be able to contact her. After six months of trying, I finally got a response through her ex-husband, Thor Eldon.

'I spoke to Björk yesterday,' he said, 'and she said that she was far too busy to write anything. She also asked if it was all right for her to skip this one. She said she would be very grateful.' It was the politest turn-down I had ever had from a pop star. Most wouldn't have bothered responding at all. This showed how down-to-earth Björk still is, despite the fact that her fame and success have removed her from her local community and lifestyle to a large extent.

It was while waiting to get my hair cut that I came across a copy of the Icelandic magazine *Seen And Heard*. It intrigued me, since the style was very similar to *Hello!* magazine in the UK, and there seemed to be lots of pictures of what looked to be Icelandic celebrities. It wasn't a contradiction in terms after all. I noticed that Baltasar Kormakur was in there, and I also recognised a few other local bands, though no one from the alternative scene. The hairdresser's was in a trendy clothes store on Laugavegur. I wasn't surprised to learn that the guy cutting my hair was the bass player in a local band, called Fidel, nor that the other hairdresser in the salon was a TV scriptwriter, presenter and filmmaker.

When I left the shop, I contacted Bjarni Brynjölfsson, the editor of *Seen And Heard*, to get some insights into local celebrity. We met in Café List on Laugavegur. 'Bjarni,' I asked, 'how do Icelanders become pop stars in their own country?'

'I really think we created stardom here in Iceland,' he replied. 'We started the magazine in 1996 and instantly became a hit. It seemed to be something that the market here needed. We try to deal with mainstream youth culture. Our concept is just to talk about people with money, success, new four-wheel drives, that kind of thing. We include foreign celebrity stuff, too. We brought a new attitude to Iceland through the magazine which is to recognise people as celebrities, which hadn't been the case really before. We were really shy of calling people stars at first, because it didn't feel that there were any. Recently we've discovered that the public are now categorising people into "knowns" and "unknowns". Traditionally, most Icelanders don't regard people as stars, but the young generation is doing that more.'

This all felt a bit jarring and shallow, given my view of Icelanders as earthy and community based people. What about the fact that everyone already knows everyone else? Why would Icelanders want to read about people in their community in a magazine when they could find out first hand, or through a friend or relative, or just by bumping into them on the street?

'People know everyone to an extent but not really,' explained Bjarni. 'They don't have complete access to everyone's lives, and that's the gap that we fill. People are curious about how other people really live, about who is going out with who, who is dating this model, what pop star is doing what. People really think that when they read the magazine that they know more about people and also about the society they're living in. It's the same elements as anywhere else. A lot of people with ordinary working lives like to read something about the rich and famous. It's entertainment; it's easy. I think Icelanders were curious about these things before the magazine, which explains why we were so popular so quickly.'

There was obviously something in what Bjarni was saying. The magazine manages to sell an incredible 12,000–14,000 copies per month. That would be almost triple-gold for an album – a status very, very few have reached.

'Do you cover music stars in Iceland?'

'We don't cover the alternative scene much,' Bjarni admitted. 'They don't want to be in it, to be honest. They don't really consider themselves pop stars. That terminology is more for the bands that tour Iceland in the summer and play at the Sveitaballs, the gigs in the Icelandic villages. In truth, it's a dangerous situation for us to do this kind of thing in Iceland. If we were to do nasty stuff like the tabloids do, it would ruin us pretty quickly. One family in Iceland might have 200 or 300 members, and if you piss them off they will all talk and then you end up with 4,000 or 5,000 people very against you.'

I pondered the ramifications of Bjarni's last statement. Did this mean that it was impossible for the media to be critical of its subjects? Did the incestuous nature of the community disallow any objective analysis? I couldn't imagine an Icelandic Jeremy Paxman, but how difficult was it to be impartial?

'It's a situation that's apparent with all of the press coverage here in Iceland,' confirmed Bjarni. 'It's difficult to have any real objectivity. There have been big discussions on whether to print names of criminals and that kind of thing because the criminal might be the brother of the biggest company director in Iceland or something. It's not so much hush-hush as people treating things sensitively. It's based on the same curiosity about human life everywhere in the Western world. My dentist had a stack of our magazines in the waiting room. He tells me that people love reading the latest Icelandic sagas.'

The real pop stars, as far as Icelandic music goes, are the mainstream acts that market themselves directly to the local audience. Most of the bands sing in Icelandic and are part of an industry whose infrastructure resembles, in miniature, that of local pop industries everywhere. The majority of the nation's main TV channels and radio stations are in the hands of one big company, Northern Lights Communications. This group was formed a couple of years ago, following a merger between three different companies: Iceland's biggest record label, Skífan; The Icelandic Broadcasting Corporation; and Syn TV. The NLC is the largest integrated media and entertainment group in Iceland and owns four television networks, five radio stations, three retail outlets, two multi-screen movie theatres and two recording studios. In addition, the group distributes music, film video and software. Although a comparison of the American giant Time Warner with a company like NLC might seem absurd, it's worth pointing out that NLC own more of their market share than Time Warner does.

Formed in 1976, Skífan is the longest operating label in Iceland and possesses the lion's share of the local pop-music scene. In the early 1980s, the label began to distribute and license records from major labels like Polygram and EMI/Virgin. In 1998, Skífan merged with Spor, the second-biggest music company in Iceland after Skífan. They brought in the licensing rights for Sony and Warner, and the two labels between them now own a staggering 80 per cent market share of the Icelandic music market.

Skífan has worked with many of Iceland's mainstream pop stars, including Hljómar, Trubrot, Mannakorn, Gunnar Thordason, Bubbi Morthens, Stuðmenn, Megas and Björgvin Halldarson, one of Iceland's first ever pop stars. Björgvin had a cracked tooth and his fame rose to such heights in the '60s that youths cracked their own teeth to be like their hero. Known for his humorous arrogance, he then got his tooth fixed – a luxury many of his young fans couldn't afford.

Björgvin's daughter, Svala, is one of the latest pop sensations to emerge from Skífan. A blonde, slender dreamboat, she is a slight anomaly in that she has been manufactured by the label and her father, not as a local act but as an international hot ticket. They are marketing her as an Icelandic Britney Spears, although her mission has yet to bear any real fruit. Interestingly, Svala's brother is Krummi, the singer in an uncompromising hardcore metal band called Minus, who have been making waves in the UK. Yet another example of Iceland's natural diversity, the whole family respect each other's work and often collaborate behind the scenes, even though they have vastly different backgrounds and audiences.

I met Skífan's head of A&R, Eidur Arnarson, to find out more about the local scene. Eidur seemed laid back and casual for a man who is responsible for all the signings on Iceland's biggest label. This might have something to do with the fact that he is a musician himself, a bassist in the successful experimental pop band Todmobile. I had heard from various members of the underground scene that, if you weren't signed to Skífan, you had problems getting airplay or having your videos played on TV.

'That's totally wrong,' said Eidur when I told him this. He seemed genuinely offended. 'If that was the case, I'd quit the same day. Since we merged, we're more of a business than we used to be, which is the more boring part of the job, but we are still fair. I think that, since the merger, there is less creativity than there used to be. It's more difficult to go to the bean-counters and get them to invest in an album which may actually lose money or that might only make money on the second or third album. That was standard practice in the old days, to build the artist up over a period of time, but the investment approach is more difficult now. Then again, I don't want to downplay the label too much because we also tend to hit the nail on the head and make money right away from the first album, anyway. I've been at both ends of the table, on stage and off, and have seen all kinds of scenarios. I've been head of A&R for just over five years so I think I have a bit of a knack for this. Sometimes you miss, but most of the time you don't. Usually it's based on a feeling and, let's face it, we're working in the safe part of the market, so it can be pretty transparent at times.'

I asked Eidur how he finds out about new bands in a small place like Iceland.

'We don't headhunt as such,' he said. 'It's not really about going to the clubs and listening to bands, as you just kind of know what's around already. It's small but it's interesting, for many reasons. It works very fast, for example. You know right away if a band is going somewhere or not as you can test the water easily through sales, live shows and playing the music on the radio. The reactions here are quick and accurate.'

And what about the bands who aren't lucky enough to get signed to Skífan – or any of the other labels, for that matter?

'The thing is,' said Eidur, 'that, although there isn't much of an infrastructure here, it's easy to release records yourself as an artist. The day a monopoly swallows the whole thing is the day I quit, because it needs to be very open. Bands can get into the charts. They do have a chance of breaking through on their own. If you sell just five records here you can get into the charts at Number 50 or 60. They actually publish the chart from 1 to 30, and to get into the 30 to 50 bracket you need to sell just 20 or so records per week. The top position is well over 150 or 200 records sold within a week, which is actually a success in this type of market, because then you multiply that by eight to ten weeks and you're getting somewhere in terms of sales. If you really want a chart position you can just go and buy 20 copies, but apart from boosting your ego it won't get you very far.

'The radios don't take any notice of this chart, anyway; they play what's going on in the international chart more. Only three of our albums have topped the chart this summer, but each has been for a few weeks. Two of those are more for an older audience and one is a very mainstream compilation of new songs, which is a reflection of the Icelandic market away from the cool alternative side. Material from the alternative market doesn't get much higher than top five in most cases. Bands like Sigur Ros are exceptions to the rule; they stayed at Number One for so long they became an Icelandic Golden Oldie.'

I wondered if pop stardom in Iceland was any different to anywhere else. Did the intimate nature of the community have an effect on the way in which stars behaved?

'The thing is, in the mainstream scene, the man of the moment two years ago is not the man of the moment now,' imparted Eidur. 'Things are fleeting. The role of the media is to put them on the pedestal and then knock them off, just like in other countries. People can't get away with having a pop attitude here, only for that precious 15 minutes. If you try and do that year after year you'll be down the drain, as people here won't want to work with you. Everyone knows everyone, so it's difficult to handle if your friend suddenly starts pretending they are above everybody else. The only time it works is if there is more professionalism involved. Paul Oskar has managed to do well because he's very professional with everything he does. He has kept afloat by changing his style and showing, like Björk, that you can go from being a pop star into being a jazz singer or working with classical people. He is outspokenly gay, too, which I think enables him to be a little more flamboyant and get away with it. His live performances have been some of the best we've had. He can get away with wearing leather trousers with no bottom. A lot of singers just sing, but he goes all the way and entertains.'

I arranged to meet Paul. We chose the location of Reykjavík's City Hall, located right next to the Tjorn. As I crossed the bridge, I noticed that the ducks and birds were not waddling in the water of the lake but walking on top of it. It had frozen over. The doors to the City Hall slid slickly open and I found myself standing in a warm and impressively new reception area. I was alone apart from a receptionist and someone working in the café.

I had got there early, so I decided to check the place out while I waited for Paul to arrive. Perhaps it was a little late in the year for exhibits, as there was disappointingly little to see. In one area I found a series of blown-up photographs which seemed to depict musicians from the turn of the century. The men were holding huge brass instruments outsized only by their gigantic moustaches, which were the size of small stoats.

I walked through to the cafeteria and listened to two elderly ladies chatting quietly to each other. One wall of the café was made entirely from glass and afforded a magnificent view across the lake. I watched the birds on the lake trying to keep their balance on the slippery ice. The combination of the warm sun on my face, the purring warmth of the building's heating system and the gentle rhythms of the lady's conversation sent me off into a reverie that veered dangerously close to unconsciousness. Before I nodded off completely, Paul came bouncing in, dressed in jeans and with blonde streaks running through his hair.

Paul was born into a musical family. His parents were both singers and his older sister, Didda, is a well-known vocalist and classical musician in Iceland. Paul initially didn't want to go into music, preferring the idea of making movies, but after singing in one or two school plays and winning a talent contest he started to take it more seriously. He opened up the first gay cabaret club in Iceland and called it the Moulin Rouge.

'It was a drag club and we provided all the entertainment,' laughed Paul. 'We had cabaret shows every week, and at the weekend we always presented something new. We kept it going for about a year, from '90 to '91. They were great times, a lot of fun, and it also gave the Icelandic public a sense that there was actually a gay scene. It was a focal point. We were very influenced by the New York DJs, who had introduced us to the house and garage sounds, all very disco-influenced.

'The first music I did was very Chic-influenced. I'd been working hard in Reykjavík in the drag scene and I had to take a break, so I went to New York for three months to get some ideas and check the scene. An Icelandic rock band called Ham were on tour in the city at the time, a gig they'd got off the back of The Sugarcubes' success. I'm not a rock 'n' roller at all, but Ham managed to get me. Johann Johansson, the guy who is now in Kitchen Motors, was in Ham at the time as a bass player, and myself, him and Sigurjon, another guy from Ham, started talking about our passion for disco and especially for Chic. That's how the concept for my album was born. Johann was going to be Giorgio Moroder, Sigurjon would be Pete Bellotte and I would be Donna Summer.'

I had watched a video documentary of the band Ham. They were a group of amusing eccentrics who excelled in extraordinary behaviour. They sang in Satanic voices, dressed bizarrely and had no problems with infusing their heavy-metal angst with a spot of Gregorian chanting. They were renowned for sleeping in vans while on tour, falling over drunkenly on stage and urinating in public.

The idea of this band producing a disco album for an ex-drag queen seemed so utterly ridiculous and far-fetched that I had to pinch my leg to remind myself I was in Iceland. Even more remarkably, the album – called *Stuð* ('*Electricity*') – was a complete success, spawning at least three hits and launching Paul into the stratosphere of the local pop scene. Since then, he has managed to get involved in both the mainstream and the alternative scenes in Iceland, playing in Latin pop bands like The Millionaires, presenting documentaries on the alternative music scene like *Pop In Reykjavík*, and putting out several high-profile solo albums and collaborations.

'I have a theory,' he said, lowering his voice to indicate an increased level of confidentiality. 'I think so many people enjoy making music here because we are so few. This means that each and every individual within our society automatically becomes important. Everyone who lives within the village is important – nobody is a nobody. There are a lot of exciting bands and musicians that are actually creating their own sounds here, and there must be a reason. My theory is that growing, living and breathing within this Alcatraz means that, if you happen to be a person with some good ideas in your head, then naturally your ideas become valuable to society. If you happen to be an artist with some good ideas, these ideas will be heard or seen, as there's no way you can remain invisible.

'My native Icelanders are really very honest, too. If I have an idea and I want to make a song, I pick up the phone, call some friends who I know that are good musicians, and the next day we're in the studio doing a demo. A week after that, we're recording it and mixing it. Then I call up the radio stations and tell them I have a song if they want to try it out. Without asking any questions, they do it, as they know me and my material, and the next day I'm walking the streets and I get feedback from people who have heard the song. And they do tell me whether they like it or not. Icelanders will tell you to your face if your album or song is a masterpiece of magic or a masterpiece of shit, and this is so important to any artist, no matter which category or field you're in.

'This feedback is so important to be able to develop artistic skills. If it's a masterpiece of shit then I take myself back to the drawing board. This whole thing happens within two or three months, while you guys in the UK have to wait to get into the studio, wait to get the recording and mixing done, the publishing takes forever, and six months later you get the feedback that we're getting on the streets the next day. I think this is the reason that so many kids like Sigur Ros and Björk have developed their own sound, and the other countless bands at Airwaves.'

I asked Paul if it was difficult to speak out about his homosexuality in a small community like Iceland. It seemed to me that it was a fairly masculine culture. Bar and street fights were not uncommon at weekends, and the whole Viking heritage, although it didn't treat women badly, didn't seem very geared towards ideas of femininity or sensitivity. That said, the early Commonwealth is often held up as a shining example of sexual equality since women were given a lot of rights compared to many societies around the world at the time.

Paul shrugged: 'I decided to come out from day one. The very first interview I gave I told everyone I was gay because I didn't want to be like my fellow musicians around the world, like George Michael or Elton John, and stay in some closet until someone outed me and it had a negative effect on my career. I respected myself enough not to victimise myself in that way, and also I didn't want to make my possible fans in the future feel like they were being duped. For the first two years following that, I only gave interviews to gay magazines, as they were the only people interested. This was in 1991 and the whole concept of an outspoken gay artist was very new.

'In the last ten years, there have been drastic changes towards the gay community, though. This year at our Gay Pride event, there were 30,000 people, probably the only one where the majority happen to be straight. There are many people in Iceland who still aren't comfortable with coming out and who lead double lives, pretending to be married but cruising around the gay areas at night. Some people choose that, and that's their choice. The reason that gay lib has increased so much in such a short time is that Icelanders don't talk in circles; they get to the point. We don't like our politicians to talk in a language that we don't understand, so for me as a pioneer of gay rights it was just a case of giving the right interviews at the right times in a language that people understood.

'The message was very clear and simple: if we simply stop focusing constantly on the things that we don't have in common and start focusing on what we do have in common, this world will be a better place to live in. The campaign was going on for a while before I got involved, but I helped to get the parliament to talk about gay issues. When they did, we got all our rights overnight. As soon as they got round to talking about it and thinking about it, it didn't seem to be a problem. Only one out of 16 politicians had anything against it, so we had marriage rights and everything. This small community has advantages on a creative and a social level, and this is the reason why I like living here, because of my music and because I have more rights here.'

'So how famous is it possible to get in Iceland?' I asked.

'I was so famous at the peak of my career that people didn't leave me alone on the streets,' said Paul with a slight look of horror. 'They were ruthless. I was taken aback as the situations got very scary sometimes. I had everything from teenagers asking for autographs at 2pm in the afternoon to dead-drunk people attacking me on the streets. I didn't feel safe. They attacked me for my homosexuality, because they were fed up with me being constantly on TV...

'The best example I can give are the fans that turn out to be ex-fans. One girl came up to me in a club and showed me her back; she had my name tattooed there. I was very shocked and I asked her, "Do you really think I'm worth this? Did I mean so much to your life?" She expected me maybe to become her best friend, and when I didn't she got very aggressive. After some tequila, she attacked me. What I learned from this is that sometimes the public want to punish you for loving you too much.'

17 Pop In Reykjavík

I dropped down to Sirkus, an offbeat hangout off Laugavegur frequented by people with leftfield leanings. The bar is a great spot to wake yourself up to the kookier aspects of Reykjavík's nightlife amidst a naughtily crackling glow and slightly louche ambience. As usual, there were lots of Pretty Young Things sitting around in scarves and hats, sipping drinks and looking nonchalantly hip. The music was extra loud – so loud I could barely hear myself think. I took a seat at the bar and screamed my order at the barmaid, who seemed to be in a world all of her own, smirking randomly to herself and then looking around to remember whom she had just poured drinks for.

Next to me were the blonde-haired singer and the black-haired bassist from Singapore Sling. I was getting used to seeing musicians around town. Once you spend any time in Reykjavík's bars and clubs, you begin to feel like you're on some kind of movie set, with the same people popping up again and again. It can get to feel a little like *The Truman Show*. Within a week or so of Airwaves, I had seen almost all of the bands in various drinking holes and cafés around town.

I once witnessed Krummi, the lead singer from hardcore metal outfit Minus, decked out in a bright-blue suit, getting down to some steaming funk being spun by Quarashi's guest DJ Magic while Sesar A and the singer from Vinyl looked on from the corner. This was some of the hottest property on Reykjavík's music scene, all in one bar. No one raised an eyebrow.

The music emanating from the speakers in Sirkus was deafening, but there was an underlying feeling of aching melancholy about it that made it bearable and increasingly captivating. The soft acoustic strums, lugubrious bossa-nova beats and slightly cracked vocals slowly became more and more enchanting as I sipped my beer, drank in the vibe of the bar and allowed myself to be pulled in to the music. The hums, crackles and squeaks that had been left in the mix made me imagine I was climbing right inside the machinery like a tiny insect wandering around a maze of circuitry which fired euphonious sounds into my ears. A sense of majestic desolation hung loosely from its fragile structures.

On the bar in front of the Singapore Slingers was a CD case. On it were written the words 'Slow Blow'. I asked the singer if it was some kind of new project.

'No, no,' he said. 'It's his. Dagur's.'

A man lurched unsteadily towards the bar, a curtain of hair hiding his face. He tried to light his cigarette on one of the candles on the bar but kept moving it around the outskirts of the flame. Eventually someone grabbed it from him, lit it with a lighter and passed it back.

I introduced myself and asked if he was part of Slow Blow. 'I am drunk,' he pointed out unnecessarily. He then seemed to snap out of his stupor for a second. He looked up, smiled and pointed at the speakers. 'This is our new album, playing now. It's taken us six years to make it. It's all acoustic. No computers.' He slumped onto a barstool and let his head hang downwards. 'Six years,' he slurred. The Slingers regarded him fondly.

There was no denying that the music was special. I wrote down my details and a few days later enjoyed a more sober conversation with Dagur. He explained that he and his musical partner are not really musicians. Dagur was a filmmaker whose first short had won every award possible in Iceland. His partner, Orri, was a photographer. 'Making music is maybe what we enjoy the most, though,' he said. 'It's like therapy to us, a vacation from our professional careers. We are extremely focused on keeping it fun and not allowing anything into the chemistry that could ruin that. That is one of the reasons why we have never tried to force through record deals or promotion. We believe that the right things will happen when they're supposed to, but most importantly they have to be right.

'In the beginning we enjoyed being as unprofessional as possible, doing all the things you are not supposed to in terms of performance and technique. Today we certainly welcome happy mistakes, but in terms of recording we try to use the best microphones and analogue tapes available. We are very focused on the character of sound, and to us that is just as important as the songs themselves, which is why we collect antique amplifiers and instruments and leave all of the details in the mix.'

I wanted to put to Dagur some questions that had been prompted by Airwaves and my time spent amongst Reykjavík's musicians, questions like, why were there were so many bands in such a small country? Why did so many of them sound so good? Why did none of them sound alike? Why was there so much emphasis on innovation and individuality? How come so many musicians kept popping up in different bands? I didn't expect Dagur, or anyone for that matter to have all the answers, but what in his opinion made the Icelandic scene so unique?

'The fact that the scene is small and concentrated and everybody knows everybody,' he averred. 'The musicians like to hang out together and exchange talent, equipment, contacts and so forth. There is a general feeling of co-operation, instead of competition. The borders are fluid, and the musicians are often members of more than one band, or else they make guest appearances all over the place. There is absolutely no governmental support, and maybe that generates solidarity.'

A few days before my meeting with Dagur, I had been given a documentary to watch called *Pop In Reykjavík*. It was a snapshot of the Icelandic music scene in 1998, directed by Agust Jakobsson. Shot almost 20 years after *Rokk I Reykjavík*, it was obvious that a lot had changed. The bands featured were a lot more diverse, having absorbed more and more global influences, such as electronic music, pop and indie rock. Most of them were more internationally minded, too, some openly admitting to the camera that they saw themselves as global rather than just Icelandic artists. To help me get to the root of some of my questions, I arranged to meet Trabant.

I first met Trabant at the Thule studios, where they were supposed to be working on a self-produced video for their first single, 'Enter Spacebar'. Instead, Vidar 'Viddi' Hakar Gislason, Thorvaldur 'Doddi' Grondal and Ragnar 'Raggi' Kjartansson were all nursing hangovers in the TV room. That night, the band were having a 'concert' at Raggi's house for his birthday. They invited me along.

I had heard Trabant's music on their debut LP, *Moment Of Truth*, which had picked up a great deal of publicity in the UK. A skewed but infectious cocktail of eccentric pop made up of hip-hop beats, funky Hammond, mercurial basslines and irreverent pop chic (with the occasional maraca shake, sitar twang and sprinkle of cosmic fairy-dust), it was a highly innovative and entertaining album. I was looking forward to hearing them live.

I arrived at the house (actually owned by Raggi's father, who also lived there) to find the band dressed up in slick black suits and schmoozing with their friends, who seemed to represent a good cross-section of Reykjavík's artistic élite. There was an atmosphere of gentle but steadily escalating inebriation. Everyone seemed to be in convivial spirits. I struck up a conversation with Toggi, the bassist from Singapore Sling and a man with a voice as deep as a bear's. He was also, as it turned out, one half of a country-and-western duo called Hank And Tank and a successful film and documentary maker. He had been the man behind the extremely funny documentary on Ham.

We sipped beer and ate peanuts for a while in the kitchen, discussing our mutual admiration for '70s Krautrock outfit Can, then slipped into the front room, where the rest of the band were setting up. A robust lady with thick-rimmed spectacles and a penchant for pointing out the merits of wood sculpture kept me occupied for several minutes until the speakers crackled and buzzed loudly into action. The band took their places behind their instruments.

It wasn't a large front room, just about enough for Trabant (whose name was taken from an old East German car that used to be popular in Iceland) and an audience of 20 or so, but the group performed their abbreviated set with aplomb, filling the room with rumbling bass and pounding beats which helped pump the alcohol warmly through our bloodstreams. Raggi's dad, a troubadour himself and a successful theatre director, looked delighted at the muscular music his son and his friends were throwing out. The overall feeling was of a school reunion, only much, much cooler.

I invited the group around to my apartment. When they came around one frosty winter evening, some of them were out of the country, leaving Raggi, Viddi and Doddi to show up on my doorstep. I wanted to talk to Trabant in particular, since they typified to a large extent the promiscuous nature of Reykjavík's music scene. All of the members are in at least one other band, and between them they provide links in some shape or form to a multitude of Iceland's bright young things, including Quarashi, Unun, Apparat Organ Quartet, Slowblow, The Funerals, Kvartett O Jonson Og Grjoni, Kanada and The Leaves. This was more impressive when I realised that hardly any of the band had undergone any kind of formal music or technology training.

When they arrived, Viddi handed me a CD. Viddi looks like the archetypal Icelandic musician. A good-looking young man, he usually wears a slightly ruffled 'slacker' look, complete with thin layer of stubble and incredibly relaxed – bordering on nonchalant – demeanour. That night he wore a baggy, long-sleeved shirt, the cuffs of which were undone and dangled coolly by his side. A lit cigarette hung almost vertically from his lower lip. James Dean would have looked awkward next to Viddi.

'Is it new Trabant material?' I queried, looking at the CD.

'No,' he smiled. 'It's music we have written for a ballet.' Reykjavík's musicians seem to straddle different genres of music and different artistic disciplines as easily and as comfortably as a cowboy straddles a horse. 'A local dance company were putting on a show and for some reason they didn't want an orchestra to do it. They had heard our album and asked us to do it, so we said, "Yes. Why not?"'

The CD artwork was a neat hand-drawing of a leggy lady in a ballet dress sitting on a large keyboard and hugging a smaller one. It had been drawn by Raggi, who doubles up as a visual and conceptual artist. His most recent exhibition in town was a meditation on death, a conspicuously sombre theme for a man so given to grinning.

'It was great,' he grinned, referring to the ballet album. He was perched on the edge of the sofa, decked out in a casual T-shirt, jeans and baseball cap. 'We had to do it fast, and it was pretty difficult, but we learned a lot. We gave them a demo and they just told us to do what we wanted.'

Was it a good source of revenue?

They all shook their heads. 'People don't do these things for the money,' explained Raggi. 'There is no money to be made here. Companies can't invest in any of our artistic product or whatever because they won't get anything back for it. The market is just too small. No one is offering money, which is why bands just carry on and do their thing.'

'For us, music is just like a hobby, you know?' confirmed Doddi, whose extensive frame was slouched across the other end of the sofa from Raggi. He had a hangover. 'It's like…' We all waited to hear what it was like. 'Knitting or something.' Knitting? We all laughed. 'It's true,' he insisted, a wry smile spreading across his face. 'Maybe you only ever make one really big sweater, but you just carry on knitting anyway.'

'It's about having something to do together as friends, I think,' reckoned Viddi, smirking at his friend's outlandish analogy. 'It's something you can do as a group, as a unit, something different to going to the cinema together. You're creating something. If you're writing a book or painting a picture, it's a more isolated thing. Music is more communal.'

Musicians in Reykjavík don't wait around for a record label to offer them a deal. What's the point? They could be waiting forever. Better to just pick up an instrument, join a band, rehearse, play some gigs, join another band, get some more practice, create another sound, raise some money from concerts to hire a studio, record an album, set up your own label, make your own artwork, do your own distribution – and on and on. If you want to, you can then offer a record label a finished album. Better still, your live talents might get discovered in the meantime. Albums are expensive business cards.

'The punk scene here definitely had an influence in that respect,' said Raggi. 'They just threw instruments around. They played violins, guitars, drums – whatever they could get their hands on. It was very artistic and very do-it-yourself, which still characterises the scene here today.' The musical influence of the rock and punk movements on today's scene in Iceland was self-evident. More pervasive, though, as Raggi pointed out, are the attitudes that those scenes have spawned.

The DIY ethic espoused by the bands on *Rokk I Reykjavík* is still fuelling artists 20 years later. Added to this is the fact that many contemporary bands are not just the musical offspring of the rock and punk scenes, but the actual genetic children, too. This, I realised, is an important factor for a burgeoning scene to develop, since a whole generation of budding musicians are getting inspiration and encouragement from their families. Given the artistic heritage in Iceland and the sprawling sizes of many families, most children are likely to have a musician in their immediate family somewhere, or else a sympathetic poet, painter, novelist, etc.

I asked my guests about their own families. I had already met Raggi's father and knew that he was a singer and theatre director. Viddi's parents are also artists and Doddi has many relatives who are involved in music, including some younger ones set to follow his example. 'Our parents really don't preach about music negatively,' he said. 'They don't think music is bad or that that it isn't a decent thing to do. My nephew is 12 years old and has been watching me in music all his life. His parents have been supporting him, and that's the way it goes on. It just gets handed down, like poetry and literature have done.'

Could the next generation in Iceland be even more productive? Would this music boom, introduced just one or two generations ago, grow and grow with each generation until *everyone* in Iceland played some kind of musical instrument? I envisaged, 30 or 60 years from now, an entire nation joining together and forming a giant Icelandic supergroup, which would tour the world performing grandiloquent compositions which incorporated every glittering fragment of music ever discovered, topped off with some ancient chanting. It was a surreal thought, but if any country was going to do it, it would be Iceland.

Raggi disrupted my reverie. 'It helps that if I want to have a career, I don't have to give up music,' he chirped. 'I can do it anytime and still hold down a band. In Iceland, if you want a job, you don't have to have ten interviews with one company, like you do elsewhere; you just call your uncle up or something. We have all had jobs at one time, anyway, because you cannot make money from music, unless you do it a lot, and then you can maybe make a living. Just about.'

'If you really want work, you just go down here, to the fish factory, and you can start tomorrow,' said Viddi, gesturing towards the harbour. I recalled that, two weeks prior to our meeting, he had emailed me to tell me he would be out of Reykjavík for a few days as he was going to pack fish in a village in the North to earn some extra cash. And Viddi is one of the most in-demand producers in town. 'We don't have so much commerce here, but not so much unemployment either. I think that's maybe why so many people make music. We're not making and exporting cars or anything, are we?'

As to the question of why so many bands sound different, Viddi had joked, 'It seems that there are a lot of bands here, but anyone wanting to sign them all up would only need to sign 15 people.' He was exaggerating, but there was a good point being made. The last thing you do if you're in a band is join a band and start making the same music. Since most musicians in Reykjavík are in other bands, this helps fuel the diversity. He also hit the nail on the head when he said, 'In a place like Reykjavík, everyone knows each other – and who wants to sound anything like their friends?'

While Iceland has its fair share of unadventurous epigones, the steady flow of more idiosyncratic acts has ensured its success in the eyes of the world. The band Gus Gus are a good example of how to create a unique blueprint. In typical Reykjavík fashion, they grew out of an incestuous tangle of actors and producers who had been brought together to work on a short film project. Two of the core members of Gus Gus, Biggi and Buckmaster, were initially in a band called T World and were drafted in to help with the music for the film. Some of the actors, Daniel Agust and Emiliana Torrini in particular, were seasoned vocalists and joined the beatmakers to make an album.

The collective took their name from Rainer Werner Fassbinder's film *Fear Eats The Soul*, in which a prostitute makes the best spicy cous-cous in the neighbourhood: she pronounces it 'gus gus'. When Lewis Jamieson from the UK label 4AD heard their LP *Polydistortion*, he liked its savvy mix of pleasant songs and cool club beats so much that he signed the band up immediately for a five-album deal.

Over the years, Gus Gus have steadily shed members and now total just four, including new vocalist Earth. I saw them perform during the last night of Airwaves. For the finale, the promoters had hired a large, impersonal sports stadium just out of town and bookended Apparat Organ Quartet and Gus Gus around international acts like US hip-hop crew Blackalicious, UK superstar DJ Fatboy Slim and Swedish rockers The Hives.

Apparat Organ Quartet opened the show with an organ-fuelled bang. Dressed in suits and wearing an air of austerity, they wrung weird and wonderful rock 'n' roll sounds out of their dilapidated equipment by feeding it through guitar amps and backing the keyboard blast up with crunching drums. The final slot of the night – and the event – was handed over to Gus Gus, who performed tracks from their fourth and most recent LP, *Attention*. In front of a big screen, which played out a stream of funky images, a colourfully clad President Bongo strutted his stuff next to an elaborately attired Earth, while behind a bank of technology Buckmaster (aka Herb Legowitz) helped Biggi Veira generate a grainy, energetic sound that recalled the '80s robotic-funk era.

Gus Gus can often be found in Kaffibarrin. If they're not DJing in the bar, they are often socialising or just hanging out. I met Biggi there one afternoon. His fingernails were covered in purple flaked paint and were twitching at the ends of his long hands as he offered lively, caffeine-fuelled conversation. 'I think we are striving to get the same scene going as in other places,' he explained when I asked him about the motivating factors for his local music community. 'Even though that is obviously restricted, as we only have a certain amount of people. Not a lot of people are making money out of this, but there is space for all these bands to exist so people can go to a lot of concerts all the time here. It's not an industry, but it is a scene.'

I argued that, although there was not much of a local market, I had seen evidence of bands aiming to get some money via international success.

'I think people always have dreams and would like it if something bigger happened abroad,' he admitted, 'but I also think people just like doing this for fun. I think in some ways it's easier to be bigger outside of Iceland than it is to be big in Iceland, certainly on the alternative scene. We have never sold much music in Iceland, although bands like Quarashi have managed to build up a big local fan base before becoming popular abroad. I believe that you can be successful in what you're doing, but that doesn't mean you're necessarily big in terms of sales. People here start out with the attitude that it's fun and then ask things like, "Is there a market for this?"

'Lots of people here just make music and give it out to 50 people, which is fine, but you obviously can't make a living from that. Many people do it here because they love it, and that's why the scene is so different. Most people have other jobs, like hairdressing, working in bars or whatever. I think you always know too when people are trying too hard; there's something missing, usually. With music here, everyone is constantly trying to reinvent the wheel. That is a very Icelandic trait. Anything we do, whether it's building roads or whatever, we seem to need to do it our own way. When you look at the airport, it's different to other airports. We have geothermal heating, hydroelectric power. We just like to try and do things a little bit differently, I think.'

I met Quarashi while in Reykjavík. I was lucky. They are usually touring these days, especially around America, where their popularity seems to know no bounds. The group has a knack of meshing hip-hop and rock into immediate, rump-shaking formulas that would give The Beastie Boys a run for their money. Unlike many of the local hip-hop acts – XXX Rottweiler, Sesar A, Móri, Halldór Laxness Jr, Bent and 7 Berg – Quarashi crew rhyme in English almost all the time. This has undoubtedly helped their crossover appeal and played a large part in landing them a prestigious deal with Sony (in America) in 2001.

The band is made up of Solvi, the band's producer and drummer; Hossi Olafsson, rapper and singer; and MCs Stoney Fjelsted and Omar Swarez. Like many of Reykjavík's bands, the members of the outfit –

formed initially by Stoney and Solvi – were once upon a time involved in rock bands but discovered sampling and the energy of hip-hop and began to experiment with a fusion of the two styles. The group's first efforts were in the shape of a single called 'Switchstance', which sold out of all 500 copies in a week. Their full-length debut CD followed in 1997 and shifted over 6,000 copies, and in the same year they warmed up for guest acts The Fugees and Prodigy. Solvi was then asked to remix the latter's song 'Diesel Power', and in 1999 Quarashi dropped their second LP, *Xeneizes*, which also sold 6,000 copies.

I met the band in Vegemot, a swish café/restaurant in 101 popular with the town's hip-hop/R&B fraternity, as they prepared to launch their third LP, *Jinx*. I asked them whether there was a division between being 'underground' and 'overground' in Iceland.

'We came from the underground,' said Solvi, 'but it's hard to stay underground in Iceland because if you sell five or ten records you register in the charts. The targets are so low here you can achieve quite a lot by doing nothing. Once you get known, everyone hears about you. The only real underground records were in the '80s, when the punk bands used to put out seven-inch records. Today, Icelandic music is much more international and is growing more and more in that direction. People used to not care so much and do it for the fun of it, but now there are more bands starting to try and get an international deal or rep. We have always just done music for the fun of it. We like to get pissed and play concerts in the same way as The Sugarcubes did.'

Lots of bands seemed to be into the more relaxed approach to making and playing music, but the feeling persisted that success was still on the agenda somewhere. I chatted to the band a little more, but they had to go for another meeting. Before they left, I asked if they had any theories as to why the music pouring out of Reykjavík is so different.

'The thing is,' said Omar, 'what would we do with a band who came out sounding like Sigur Ros or Björk? They would never get any respect here, which is why people keep trying to come up with different sounds. You simply have to be different to survive. To earn respect here you have to do that. If you try and just be a pop star it doesn't work because you're seeing your audience in the shop or something the next day. We have just spent a year travelling all around the world, but there's no feeling like coming back here and having the rain and wind shitting in your face and waiting with 200 kroner in your hand to get on the bus.'

18 Thule

I had an overwhelming urge to see some puffins. These colourful and endearingly awkward creatures are in abundance in Iceland, which is fortunate for them since Icelanders tend to regard them as a culinary delicacy. Puffins are not the brightest of animals. They are caught simply by swinging a net around in the air until one flies into it.

I called up a number on a brochure that advertised boat trips to the island of Lundey – 'Puffin Island', as it's otherwise known. The man at the end of the phone happened to be the owner of the boat and explained that the puffin season was finishing. There weren't many of them left, he said, plus the weather was being predictably unpredictable. Why didn't I turn up at the departure point at the scheduled time the next day and see how it was?

The weather was grim the next day, but the Puffin Island departure point was 30 minutes away. Maybe it would be sunnier then. It was pretty much my last chance to try, anyway, so I walked over to the main bus station and waited inside.

The yellow buses that run around Reykjavík are, as one might expect, pretty efficient. They're also quite reasonably priced, which is good because taxis aren't. Long-distance buses are pricey and don't run in winter because the roads are closed.

I trundled through Reykjavík and along the harbour and asked the driver to just drop me off at the Puffin Island ferry. He seemed to know where it was. I was the only one on the bus, so when he pulled up outside what looked like a deserted industrial estate, I knew it was my stop. The driver pointed down a wide curving road that led to the sea. He uttered something mysterious and unintelligible that I had no chance of understanding, but I thanked him anyway and headed off down the road.

Ten minutes later, I was looking balefully through the tiny office window of the captain's hut at the howling rain and driving wind outside. It didn't look like abating anytime soon. There wasn't another soul as far as the eye could see. No one else was going to turn up to take the trip. The captain was next to me, also staring solemnly out of the window. I could almost feel him hoping I wouldn't try to plead with him to go. I looked at him. He looked at me. I shrugged. He brightened and took immediate advantage.

'Would you like a lift back into town?' he said brightly. I sure would. On the way, he gave me some insights into puffins. 'They only lay one egg per year,' he told me. 'They come all the way here just to do that, and then they go off to Canada or somewhere else for their holidays. They are as mad as us Icelanders. They just have a crazy idea and they do it.'

I asked him what he did when he wasn't showing puffins to people.

'I work in a band called Snow White And The Seven Dwarves.'

I asked him what kind of music he played.

'We are musical prostitutes,' he replied. 'We mainly cover songs around the local bars. We play everything from Black Sabbath to Abba. But this week we are going in to record our first record, which we wrote ourselves. It's a protest song about the closure of the strip clubs in town. The government have decided that they are not appropriate and have ordered them to be shut down. I don't see what is wrong if a man wants to go and, y'know...' He glanced at me significantly, wiggled his moustache and slowly uncurled his index finger until it pointed straight ahead.

'Get an erection?' I offered.

'Yes,' he confirmed. 'We have a female singer to do the vocals for it. It should be good.'

A couple of weeks later, as the puffins had all migrated, I signed up for a whale-watching tour. I had been inspired by a markedly sunny day, but since September was segueing fast into October I should have known better. Sure enough, the next day was appalling.

Again, I went along to the harbour anyway, since the whale boats departed from close to my apartment and you could still never be sure what the weather would do.

I had enjoyed many a pleasant walk along this harbour. It's a sedate area with a lack of tourist facilities, and the fresh breeze and pleasing views often make a stroll here feel natural and refreshing. It's a great way of clearing the cobwebs, particularly on a Saturday or Sunday morning.

As I approached the boat, I noticed in the distance four red funnels sticking up amidst the other ship masts. These funnels belong to Iceland's decommissioned whaling fleet. It's a deep irony that Iceland now does a roaring trade in whale watching: a few years ago they were being roared at by the international community for hunting them down. Many of the same fishermen that used to harpoon the creatures are now tour organisers – an inevitability, perhaps, given that they already have the boats and know the seas and the habits of the animals.

As strange as it may sound, many fishermen believe that whale-hunting and whale-watching can co-exist. The key, they say, is balance. If whales are left to breed indiscriminately, they eat the fish and deplete the stocks. This is obviously a bad thing for the fishermen and for the country as a whole, whose exports are still 75–90 per cent based on fishing. If the whales are hunted too vehemently, they become endangered. This is obviously a bad thing, too. As it is, some 100,000 blue whales have been killed over the last few decades.

Humpback whales are also spotted much less these days. For music lovers, especially, humpbacks are wonderful creatures, since they are known for singing the longest and most complex songs in the animal kingdom. They are the only whales that sing, and scientists still don't know why, although the main theories are that they are either attracting mates (the singing is done exclusively by males) or fending off other males. For my money, the former theory sounds more plausible (as well as more romantic) – you'd have to have a pretty bad voice to scare off an unwanted guest by singing at them.

The whales' songs are created by a range of noises, from groans and moan to roars and chirps and trills, and are arranged into simple repeating patterns, usually with two to four different sound types. These short strings of sounds are repeated several times and are known as phrases, which are put together to form a theme. Each song has up to nine themes and generally lasts for between 5 and 15 minutes. Once they've finished, the whales begin to sing them again from the beginning. The males in the whale population sing the same song, using the same sounds arranged in the same pattern, all together. It is a group effort. Each year the pattern changes, but all the singers make the same changes to their songs. It seems that the females must get bored of listening to the same tunes, and so the males change them to keep the sweet-talking going.

The interesting thing is that whalesong is revolutionary as opposed to evolutionary. Before 1972, singing whales were literally unheard of. Perhaps they were seduced by the virile explosion of rock 'n' roll.

Icelanders argue that a lot of the whaling carried out in the country was by foreign fishermen. Icelanders themselves have certainly hunted, but they are very aware of the delicate ecological systems that nature has; they've been working more closely than anyone with them for 1,000 years. The whaling issue continues to be contentious. Many Icelanders I had met were adamant that they knew better than anyone how to hunt whales without destroying the balance of nature. There have been threats to resume scientific whaling (as opposed to commercial whaling) in the near future, though nothing has happened yet.

Although the weather hadn't improved very much, our boat, the good ship *Elding*, rolled determinedly out to sea. I was accompanied on the trip by a mix of American and German tourists. We all sat inside the warm cabin while the boat lurched back and forth sickeningly. There was some literature scattered around which gave facts and figures about the local whale and dolphin populations. Sightings on these trips are pretty much guaranteed, usually of the abundant minke whales and dolphins.

Our hosts on the boat were two young girls on working holidays from Denmark and Germany. They told us all how to spot whales when we got outside. One way, they said, was to look for flocks of birds hovering over the sea. This usually means that there are fish in the water below, and where there are fish there are usually whales and dolphins. You can spot the whales, they said, by their water spouting when they come up for breath. If you don't see it, you can sometimes smell the rotten fish being blown out from the animal's mouths. The idea that I might soon be inhaling whale belch whilst being thrown around on a turbulent sea did nothing for my stomach.

One of the girls climbed up into the crow's nest to assist us in our whale and dolphin spotting as we clambered outside in our waterproofs. She promised to shout if she saw anything, showing positions by way of the clock-as-compass analogy – nine o'clock for directly west, twelve o'clock for north, three o'clock for east, and so on. We didn't really want to go outside, but we wouldn't see much from the cabin. Rain flagellated our faces as we stared out at the endless mass of grey, unwelcoming sea. The boat was rocking violently enough to make us hold onto the handrails most of the time. It was that or fall over.

Several enthusiastic photographers held their cameras under their jackets to protect them from the rain. 'Minke whale, one o'clock!' shouted the girl above us. We all ran to the right of the boat with the grace and speed of children in a sack race. We saw nothing. 'There it is again, nine o'clock!' We all ran left. Cameras whirred, shutters clicked.

'Did you get anything?' I asked a roly-poly gent who was clutching his Nikon tightly with shivering blue hands.

'Nothing,' he sniffed and shuffled solemnly back towards the cabin. He had had enough.

I decided to hold out for a little longer, running back and forth dementedly with the rest of the group only to find myself staring at more empty grey sea. It was nice to see the terns and fulmars sweeping gracefully down, though, delicately wetting the tips of their wings in the water and rising up again.

'Humpback, 12 o'clock!'

Luckily, I was already staring straight ahead and saw a few inches of slick grey flesh emerge above the surface. My heart skipped a beat, but then the whale disappeared back down into the depths of the sea again.

When we landed back in Reykjavík, we were wet and slightly disappointed. We had been out there for three hours and hadn't seen anything remotely resembling the pirouetting mammals depicted in the brochure. We realised, though, that this was more to do with the weather conditions and bad luck than anything else. Them, as they say, are the breaks. At least I had glimpsed a humpback.

I decided to pay a visit to Thule Musik, whose HQ sits just on Aegisgata, near the whaling boats. Thule was the ancient name used for Iceland by some European travellers before the Vikings settled and gave the country its current title. The record label is based on the second floor of a fairly anonymous edifice. Up the stairs and through the main door are a network of offices, studios, editing suites, mastering rooms and recording booths which, on the several occasions that I had visited there previously, had been continually abuzz with producers, musicians, editors, engineers and administrative staff.

Gus Gus used to rent this floor before they realised it was too much space for just one band, yet Thule has grown sufficiently to get maximum use from it. The studios there are the most in demand in Iceland, with everyone from Björk to blues singer KK dropping by for sessions. The vibe in there is usually one of casual creativity, enhanced by a well-used TV/coffee/smoking room which acts as a sanctuary for artists needing a raincheck or a cigarette.

Thule itself is one of the most prominent labels operating in Iceland today. It has been responsible for breaking many acts abroad and is one of the few labels in town that looks directly outside Iceland for the core of its sales and support. In a way, the label can be seen as an electronic counterpart to Bad Taste. Although Thule releases rock acts and Bad Taste releases electronic acts, they are both masters in their respective fields. The majority of Iceland's core dance and electronic scene come to Thule with their demos, especially since the company signed deals with eight distributors in America and set up an office in the States. They now have more international clout than any other label in Iceland.

The label is run by Thorhallur 'Thor' Skulason, whom I found sitting in his office, talking quietly on the telephone. Thor's own musical background is faultlessly cool. His mother, Anna Sigga, was a DJ in clubs and youth centres around Reykjavík between 1975 and 1977. Thor himself won breakdancing and DJ championships and helped to forge Iceland's nascent hip-hop scene before helping to break rave into the country. Most impressive of all is the fact that Thor's grandmother, Kristín J Solvadóttir, was Snow White. I couldn't tell whether Thor, a fairly deadpan character, was joking or not when he told me this. I looked at him with a big question mark on my face.

'My grandmother met one of the artists who worked for Walt Disney when she went to Canada,' he explained as we walked into the TV room. The television was on but the volume was turned down. There was a smell of stale smoke in the room and the coffee machine moiled quietly in the corner. 'They fell in love, and when he was commissioned to create the character for Disney's Snow White he based it on my grandmother. She collected all the drawings and everything that he sent to her, and when she passed away my mother kept it all in our house. We still have it all up on the walls at home. A lot of people didn't believe us for a while, but a few years ago the artist's son came to visit Iceland. He was putting a book together about his father and they wanted to feature my grandmother in it.'

After his adventures with hip-hop (of which he is still a big fan), Thor became one of Iceland's first ravers. I wondered how people accepted it, especially as there was such a bias towards rock music in Iceland.

'Looking back at the scene, which started here around 1989, I think we had the same feeling as maybe the people in the punk movement had. Like them, we felt like rebels for being into this music. We were just a few people fighting against the rest of society to get the music heard and supported. Björk was very interested in the music and used to come to the clubs we played at. I did a remix for The Sugarcubes, in fact, but it never came out. The first electronic compilation appeared in 1991 and was called Ice Rave. It was supposed to be called Ecstasy in Icelandic, but the TV and radio stations didn't like it and so the record label, Skífan, changed it without telling anyone.

'Back then, there were more clubs going on then than today. Now we only have bars, but there used to be a lot of bigger spaces and a lot of raves happening in warehouses and big garages. It was much more of a scene back then, with places like the Moon Club kicking things off in the late '80s.

'One club that kept us going for a long time was Rosenberg. The place never did any advertising. It was just a small underground club for 200 people but managed to stay alive because it had the rock scene and the techno scene all in the same club. The rock scene got drunk at the bar while the ravers were there for the music. The main DJs there were Herb Legowitz, aka Buckmaster, from Gus Gus, and Gretar, a guy who now works in the record shop Thunder. That was the last Icelandic dance-music club that was around simply for the music. You could go there and hear tracks that inspired you. It closed in 1994, but until that point it was always amazing to go and listen to Herb's DJ sets, which would range from deep house to techno. The acid scene was a lot of fun. There were about ten people into the actual dance. We all used line up on the dance floor and make boxes in the air.'

The electronic-music revolution proved as globally penetrative as rock 'n' roll. Perhaps even more so – or at least more rapidly so – given the simultaneous rise of the Internet and dance music's inherent alignment with technology. It seemed to me that the electronic revolution was well suited to Iceland. The nation has inordinately high levels of computer literacy, with the majority of the population hooked up online. The Internet has, of course, had broader communication implications for Iceland than elsewhere since the system's ability to link with the rest of the world has virtually overcome Iceland's isolation.

Where rock 'n' roll caused a generation to reach for their guitars, many young music makers from the '80s onwards have reached for computers and samplers to build a brave new world of futuristic simulacra. House music was memorably described by Mel Cheren of the Paradise Garage in New York as 'disco on a budget' (he was referring to how cheap computer programs had replaced expensive orchestras and live musicians). But it was the rise of disco – and, in particular, discothèques – in Reykjavík that killed off the live scene, according to the documentary *Rokk I Reykjavík*.

Today there is a multitude of DJs and electronic producers hosting clubs and live shows. The only problem, as Herb Legowitz once pointed out to me, is that electronic music has deliquesced into so many different subcategories that Iceland simply doesn't have the infrastructure to support them all. Herb gave up on Iceland when the scene became too stretched, and he started playing abroad more and more. Now he reckons it is more coherent again and he is often found plying groups of shimmying party people with his slinky house and electro sounds.

Thule has managed to absorb many different styles from the local digerati. Their roster boasts an eclectic mix of artists and sounds, including the melodic meanderings of Múm, the disjointed post-techno of Biogen, the muscular but minimal techno of Ozy, the lush downtempo grooves of Ilo and the upbeat fare of stalwarts like Tommi White and Ruxpin. On his newly formed TMT label, Thor has made inroads into less electronic, quirkier pop styles, such as the country-blues sounds of The Funerals, Apparat Organ Quartet and Trabant.

As Thor and I talked in the TV room, a constant stream of people kept popping in to make coffee, hang out or just get some cognitive respite by staring absent-mindedly at the TV. Biogen came in, smoking a cigarette fiercely. He blew the smoke through his nose like a dragon, then left again.

Thor explained how the label began: 'I was living at my grandmother's flat at the time and I had a small studio there in 1983. I was in her living room and the idea to do Thule with the crew of people I knew started there. We bought all the studio equipment together and organised a time schedule so we could sort out who could be in the studio at certain times. Once we got a fax machine, there was no turning back.'

Although Thule is a professionally run label, this is Iceland and there is still a very relaxed feel about its operation. In essence, it is like any good independent imprint in that its primary structure is built by a bunch of friends who like to hang out and make tunes. Thor told me a story about his first official release, which was made in conjunction with a well-known London personality called Goldie. According to Thor and Biogen, they were already working together on tracks when the man with the golden teeth dropped into town. He wasn't the celebrity DJ/producer/actor back then that he is today. In fact, he didn't as yet know his way around a studio.

'Goldie didn't know how to produce, at that stage,' explained Thor. 'He was more into graffiti and MCing. He threw around some ideas and Biogen and I came up with the track. We called ourselves Ajax and got some sponsorship from the local cleaning-fluid company of the same name. Then we gave the track to Goldie to get pressed up. It was called the *Ruffage* EP and we called ourselves The Ruffage Crew, which Goldie kept for himself and still uses. The logo we used was a skull, a version of the one he ended up using as the Metalheadz logo. These experiences helped us learn about production and the music industry.'

In 1994, Thor went to London and met Frankfurt producer Sven Vath and Alex Avary from the Frankfurt-based Electrolux label. He began to send them the material that he and his growing coterie of producers were making and they started to release it. The early material of the Icelandic rave scene was thus released in Germany first. Then in 1995 came the first official Thule release by an artist called, appropriately enough, Cold. Thor and some friends visited England and pressed up the records themselves this time.

'We bought a car in Brighton that was a wreck,' chuckled Thor. 'We had to change the water every half an hour in order to get it to London, and then we distributed the records there by hand. It was a brilliant time. The label didn't really start going until 1998, though, when we got some official distribution. By that time we had a lot of competent producers and still no one had been exporting electronic music from here at all, really, not even Bad Taste, so we stepped in and did it. Our main thing is to export music in other countries, so in fact we act like an export company. It's hard to do this from here, as we're so isolated and dealing with scenes that are far away, but it's getting easier for artists to release abroad generally, which is good for all of us.'

Part of the difficulty in Thule marketing themselves abroad comes from the fact that much of the music on the label, being influenced by the prototypes that arose from Chicago and Detroit in the '80s, is derivative of those sounds. To the listener, they could just as well have been produced in Guernsey or China as in Iceland. Where the rock and punk scenes also borrowed heavily from outside influences, they at least had the opportunity to add Icelandic lyrics or accents to make the music more native-sounding, and hence more unique. Even so, much of Thule's music has been well accepted abroad because, although much of it is instrumental, it still has something definitively Icelandic about it, something in the textured sounds and gelid atmospheres that seems to denote coldness, remoteness and open space.

'I admit that some of our music sounds like music made in the UK or Germany or wherever,' commented Thor, 'but a lot of it definitely has an Icelandic feel. It has a special atmosphere that can only come from here, I think, and the main reason for this is that we have almost no clubs here, only bars. Our artists hence have no knowledge of how the music will sound in clubs, so they simply produce what they hear in their own minds, and that must include what they see and hear around them. We're still very influenced by other places outside of Iceland, but we all try to develop our own unique sound. If we concentrated on just the Icelandic market, we'd probably fail, so our music has to be aware of what's happening around us. I think the most consistent aspect of the electronic music from here is that it is aimed at generating good feelings, you know, very nice emotions.'

19 All You Need Is The Fantasy

Sigridur Nielsdóttir has spent the last 18 months of her life making a series of rudimentary lo-fi albums with a Casio organ, a MIDI stereo, a microphone and a lot of imagination. She has been burning her music from cassettes onto CDs. She draws and colours her own artwork, and then sells her finished products in one or two record shops in town. So far she has made 17 albums; she hopes to record 20 in total.

Sigridur can't read music, and has had no formal training apart from some piano lessons when she was eight years old. The music she is recording simply comes from tunes that have been swimming around in her head for the last 40 or 50 years, maybe longer – she can't remember.

Sigridur is 73 years old. When I met her, she radiated sweetness, and her cheerful confidence belied her advanced years. I had been told about her by Orvar from Múm, who had heard one of her albums and recommended I talk to her. I traced her telephone number and asked if we could meet. The idea seemed to delight her. When she answered the door, she was dressed in a pretty floral blouse and a long skirt. She wore thick-rimmed glasses and a big, bright smile.

She led me into a tiny, immaculate kitchen, which had two unusual features. One was a large Casio organ, which dominated the right-hand side of the room and was neatly covered by a crocheted towel. The other was a dinky single bed pushed between the back wall and the cooker. 'I live here in the kitchen,' she chirped when I asked whom the bed was for. 'I'm buying the apartment, but it's expensive, so I'm renting out my front room for a while.'

I must have looked alarmed. 'Don't worry,' she cooed. 'It's only for the next couple of years, not forever. Then I'll be able to afford the rent.'

Sigridur is not the kind of lady to be written off as a vulnerable septuagenarian. She has plenty of pep, as her musical output shows, and has lived a full and adventurous life with its fair shares of ups and downs. Born in Copenhagen to a Danish father and German mother before moving to Iceland at the age of 19, Sigridur lived in many places around Reykjavík before eventually settling in Eskifjördur, in the remote East, with her Icelandic husband. She found employment at a boarding school there while her husband worked as a fisherman. Sometimes he would be away for months at a time, though Sigridur 'always had something to do…I hated doing nothing'.

Sigridur picked up a CD from her pile under the Casio. The artwork was a photo of an old style Icelandic farmhouse. 'This was our first house,' she said. 'We lived in two very small rooms and a tiny kitchen there. There was myself, my husband and our three daughters. Someone said to us that if we build a house on their land they would rent it to us, so we did, and I got some extra work putting hooks on the lines for the fishing boats. We didn't have any electricity, but it was cosy. We had oil lamps and my husband and I would read books for the children and for each other. There was a man who would wander from place to place and sing songs and tell stories for people in the villages. He was the last of these kinds of people in the East. He stayed at people's houses in return for entertaining them, but when anyone asked him to help out on the farm he moved on swiftly.'

Sigridur is a Seventh Day Adventist. Adventists believe, amongst other things, in the second coming of Jesus Christ. They also believe that we will all be judged by our works and that this judgment of works determines one's salvation.

After living in the Icelandic countryside for many years, Sigridur came back to Reykjavík for a while before moving to Brazil for several years, where she worked voluntarily and made handicrafts to sell or exchange for food and goods on the streets. She told me that she misses this kind of exchange, lamenting the fact that the authorities don't allow it in Iceland. Making music was a way in which Sigridur could continue to use her mind and hands creatively.

While she was growing up, she flirted briefly with the piano and harmonica and constantly wrote music in her head. For the last 30 years she has been recording these songs onto cassette. Her mission is now to get them onto CDs. She passed me a sheet of paper covered in staves and seemingly randomly placed musical notes. 'It's not a real system,' she chuckled. 'It's just what I use to remember the tunes by. If the phone rings or something, it can be very difficult to remember the tunes you were thinking of, so this helps me remember. Some of them just fly completely out of my head...' she pointed out of the window. 'Perhaps they're out there and someone else picked them up.'

I asked Sigridur if all the CDs below her Casio were her own. 'Yes,' she said enthusiastically. 'I started recording them in April last year and I will stop when I have 20. I have one here ready to record, but I need more money.' Her voice dropped to a conspiratorial whisper. 'That's part of the reason I rent my living room out and sleep in here. I'm doing it to buy the apartment, but also because it will help me finish off this music.'

I asked if I could hear some of her music. Given how basic her recording system was – a microphone, MIDI hi-fi and organ – I was expecting the songs to be pretty raw. They were. But they were also very tuneful and, unsurprisingly, had a naive sweetness about them. One or two sounded like jazzed-up hymns. 'Some of them are based on psalms or hymns,' she confirmed. 'The song you are listening to now is called "When Jesus Lived Here As A Man". It started with a tune that I made with some words in the Bible about how Jesus would return and rule all of the world. I tried to recite the text as in the original. Not all of my music is religious, though; the one you saw with the man lying down in the field had a nature-and-relaxation theme, and for that I composed some lullabies and other tunes.'

Sigridur demonstrated her recording procedure. I watched with admiration as she moved with speed and agility around her equipment. 'First I play a melody and record it onto a tape using this,' she said, prodding the hi-fi. She plugged a microphone into its mic socket and rested it on the Casio's loudspeaker. 'Then I put that tape with the melody in the other side of the double tape deck and place another blank tape in. I play the tape I recorded first in the other deck and play another tune over the top of it on the organ and record both tracks onto the second tape. I have to do it in the daytime, when no one is around, so I can be as loud as I like. It needs to be loud to sound right.'

I was sure I had heard some sound effects in some of the songs Sigridur had played me. Was that dogs barking? How did she get those?

'Oh I do those myself,' she giggled, folding her hands in front of her again and regarding me with a sweet smile. 'With my voice, through the microphone. I wrote a song about the sea once and to get the effect of waves I filled a bucket with water and recorded it swishing around. Another time, I recorded some live guinea pigs.' She hands me a cassette. 'I did this for you while you were on your way here,' she smiled. 'It's called "Waiting For Paul".' I was taken aback. I may even have blushed. I took the tape from her. It didn't have a cover but there was a child's sticker on it. It was a little star. I thanked her sincerely. 'That's what I like about music,' she mused. 'All you need is the fantasy and you can do anything you like.'

My conversation with Sigridur was inspiring. After dealing with a music industry that so often focuses on everything except for the actual music, it was refreshing to feel this level of purity, to hear someone taking it back to the basics of hearing a simple tune and finding a way of recording it. Sigridur knew nothing about recording techniques, mixing levels, labels, A&R, licensing, publishing, marketing, PR, remixing or even software. She was simply concerned with making her fantasy a reality.

One of the stores in which Sigridur sells her albums is 12 Tonar. One day I was strolling along Skólavörðustígur, the long road that leads up to Hallgrímskirkja. It's a less busy street than Laugavegur, to which it runs parallel, but it has plenty of good stores and art galleries to browse through. I saw the 12 Tonar blue-and-yellow sign as I walked along and decided to drop in.

From the outside, the building looked typically Reykjavík, with its corrugated-iron exterior. Many houses in Reykjavík have this covering to protect the timber from the rough weather. These are usually painted and are what give 101 its multi-coloured look. Not that there was much iron to paint on 12 Tonar; the wall facing the street was comprised largely of two big, square windows.

Inside, these windows allowed floods of natural light, which reflected off smooth wooden floors and sparsely arranged racks of CDs. There was none of the cramped, higgledy-piggledy feel that many record shops offer. 12 Tonar was almost Lutheran in its generous distribution of space and light. Soft classical music washed over my ears. It felt like an escapist's paradise, a place for aural fantasists looking for a spot where earthly distractions and existential monotony come second place to serious sonic vibrations. No wonder it was a Mecca for Iceland's most adventurous bands, from Sigur Ros and Múm to Björk and Kitchen Motors.

At the counter were two smartly dressed, bespectacled men who looked absorbed in paperwork. Towards the back of the shop was a listening area. There were three or four CD Walkmans with headphones placed on a coffee table along with magazines and books for reference. I sat on a comfortable two-seater sofa, above which hung photographs of the Icelandic presidents, and browsed through some of the reading material. I got lost in an LP entitled *Time and Water* by the Icelandic composer Atli Heimir Sveinsson and felt the stresses of the day dissipate from my body.

I could have done with at least a week of this kind of musical healing. I looked up to find one of the men from behind the counter opening and closing his mouth in front of me. I removed my headphones. 'Would you like some coffee?' he said.

I really had died and gone to heaven. 'Are you the owner?'

He smiled wanly and made an almost imperceptible nodding gesture. 'One of them, yes.' He extended a well-manicured hand towards me. 'I am Larus Johannesson,' he said. 'And this is the other owner, Johannes.' He gestured towards the counter at another bespectacled man clad in casual woolly jumper, black slacks and a slightly disquieting sandal-and-sock combo. The pair looked more like academics than record-store owners.

Johannes looked up and waved. Larus walked back to the till to pour the coffee. Since there was no one around, I wandered over and asked them about the store. 'The idea came in October 1997,' revealed Johannes. 'I had been working at another store, called Japis, which sold hi-fi equipment. Japis started a record label too, but there was always tension between the store and the label, and I felt that the record division didn't get the attention it deserved. Larus was one of my best customers, and in 1997 we had a brainstorm whilst watching Manchester United in a bar.'

Larus placed a small cup of thick black coffee in front of me. He was smiling. 'The only real qualification you need to work here is being a Manchester United fan,' he said.

'We started talking about how things could be done differently,' continued Johannes, 'but with more emphasis on personal service. There were also a lot of labels not being represented that we thought could do well here and so we started off just before Christmas 1997 by importing a CD of coffee-house music, the style of music that was being played in the restaurants in Iceland in the 1930s. The CD had been requested by lots of people while we were in Japis, but they showed no interest in importing any, so we just did it ourselves. It sold really well and enabled us to start up a shop, which we did in April 1998, in a different location to here.'

I took another turn around the store, browsing through the sections of classical, folk, jazz and experimental music. I commented to Johannes that they had a very eclectic and considered choice of music.

'Our fantasy shop would just sell one CD,' he smiled. 'That would be the perfect album and you wouldn't need anything else. We originally envisaged being a classical store. We were enjoying a lot of 12-tone classical music at the time, hence the name of the store. But we soon realised that people are increasingly open to every kind of music.'

This sounded like a continuation of the ethic that Ásmundur Jonsson espoused with his renegade radio show in the '70s.

'In a way, we are, yes,' said Johannes. 'That was the first place in Iceland you could hear every kind of music from modern classical to punk rock. He started to break down the barriers between music genres, and his label, Gramm, backed it up, and now Smekkleysa do the same. The barriers are always continuing to fall these days. We try and provide a space for bands to work. Bands like Múm and Big Band Brutal have played here, amongst others. We give out red wine and let the music take over for the afternoon. In that sense, we are doing what Ásmundur and Sjon did with their galleries in the '70s, providing venues for experimental and freeform music. Icelanders are natural collaborators – as long as there is some booze around, everyone is happy.'

I thought back to the punk scene and its *carpe diem* attitude. The heady days of *Rokk I Reykjavík* were full of bands exploring music and sounds simply because they could. It didn't feel like it was too different these days, with so many interesting artists around finding new ways of making interesting music. 'I think the action is more diverse these days,' agreed Larus. 'But yes, we have an extremely active scene. Lots of people have made comparisons between the Finnish or German experimental scenes and ourselves, although things are more visible there, of course, as they are not so isolated. I think our strong scene is down to our characters. We have a lot of different types of personality here and therefore have the whole spectrum of music, even though it's a very small place. Have you been downstairs yet?'

I hadn't. I descended with him down a spiral staircase and entered into a small basement area. A young man called Eidur with a mop of blonde hair was standing behind a counter. He was nodding along intently to some funky-ass hip-hop that was being thrown out of a small ghetto-blaster. I recognised him as the guitar player from Singapore Sling.

The downstairs section of the store represented the more cutting-edge side of things. There were boxes and crates selling vinyl records, and sections specially marked for reggae, hip-hop, funk and more leftfield sounds.

'People enjoy coming in here,' said Eidur, changing the CD on his boom box. 'It's a social place, really, somewhere for artists to exchange ideas and have a coffee and look for some new tunes. Everyone comes in here at some point. It's like a central meeting point for many people.'

As we talked, it transpired that Larus and Johannes are not academics, but they are both accomplished chess players.

'We have played and taught all around the world,' said Johannes. 'We have had three world-class champions from Iceland over the years, which is a lot for a small country. There used to be a great passion for chess here, like there is with music today. Something to do with the dark winters, I expect. But it's a dying tradition now. There are too many other distractions, like TV and music and Playstations, that have killed it off.'

I noticed a rack dedicated to more avant-garde Icelandic material and another rack full of locally produced demos – CD-Rs that were created by the less visible side of Reykjavík's scene. Amongst these I found a couple of Sigridur's albums. Kira Kira from Kitchen Motors had told me once that she had discovered the demo CD of one Kippi Kaninus here and had arranged his signing to the Kitchen Motors label.

'It was something we just had to do,' said Larus. 'So many people were coming to us with their own music but there were no labels to put it out on. We felt it was important for us to get it out to people, to show people what was happening in bedrooms in Reykjavík. There's probably much more music coming from that scene that no one hears than the main alternative scene. We started a while ago, and now we get bombarded with stuff. We also get shipments coming in from outside of Reykjavík, places like Ísafjörður and Húsavík. The quality varies a lot but there is plenty of good stuff and a lot of diversity.'

This was impressive. Not many labels or shops in our capitalist age go this far in shouting about unknown artists from their local areas. 'If there is no money in it, what's the point?' seems to be the prevalent attitude. Johannes and Larus can see the point: it encourages people to keep going and perhaps to achieve great things. These bedrooms are where the next Björk or Sigur Ros may come from. If nothing else, it keeps people busy in the dark winters and ups the prospects of collaboration. It highlighted to me once again the interdependent and mutually supportive nature of Reykjavík's musical community – the emphasis on friendly, rather than fierce, competition. It seemed like an almost utopian system.

'We have started to build a network that covers this whole side of the scene,' explained Johannes. 'People at the radio station are being very supportive, too. We pass some of the demos onto them and they play them, and the main newspaper, *Morgunbladid*, are also starting to write about them. We also send material to labels and distributors and have had some success, such as with Johann Johansson's *Englaborn* release, which came out just as a CD-R initially. We started playing it in the store and it got a fantastic reaction from people. They would just stop dead in their tracks when they heard it. We pushed Johann to do something with it, and he eventually sent it to Touch Recordings in the UK, who gave it an official release.'

I had heard *Englaborn* and knew Johann. His commission for the album was to write some music for a play by Havar Sigurjonsson. The play's content was extremely turbulent and unsettling, so Johann decided to compose a series of modern classical pieces that conjured up contrasting feelings of contemplative tenderness. Using a string quartet, piano, glockenspiel, harmonium, organ, percussion and subtle electronics, he constructed 16 vignettes of beguiling beauty. The first time I had met him, though, at the Thule studios, he was working on a project of a vastly different nature.

Hunched over the studio's main mixing desk, he was tweaking the EQ on a driving, organ-fuelled song with some serious swing that punched and kicked its way out of the speakers. The song was 'Stereo Rock 'n' Roll', the debut single for Apparat Organ Quartet, a band Johann formed following a dream he'd had of four of his friends playing keyboards together. His dreamtime vision was supplemented by the fantasy of recreating in modern form Steve Reich's minimalist work for four organs. 'I woke up and immediately set about getting my friends together and finding a variety of cheap, discarded organs to perform with,' he said.

Eventually, Apparat added a drummer to the equation to provide some extra rhythmic power. They have recently recorded an LP that has gained gushing reviews in Iceland and across Europe. 'We like to use instruments that have been thrown away,' Johann explained. 'We don't use them for the cheap factor at all, though. People have labelled us one of those bands that enjoy using lounge or cheesy elements, but we're interested in that. We like it when other people do it, but that's not us. We just enjoy the irony that we're making this big, monumental sounding music on such throwaway instruments.'

The thrill of transforming frail junk into robust music must be big. I asked Johann where he got his cast-offs from.

'We literally get them from the garbage heap and the recycling plants. We have a friend there who calls us when he gets something interesting. Our idea is to use elements of mainstream and pop culture, but not in the same way as other people do. We don't want to make the music more accessible. We just think it's interesting and want to push it as it is. I wouldn't say we are fringe artists, either; it's self-defeating to say that. We're just not interested in commercialism. We want to reach as many people as possible, but not at any cost. If we can do it on our own and keep our own perspective intact, then that's fine.'

Johann has been a part of the musical landscape in Iceland for over a decade, in a dizzying number of guises. He was a guitarist in aberrant rock group Ham, has produced for Marc Almond, had brief international success with his electronic band, Lhooq, is a vocalist and keyboard player with Apparat, and also writes soundtracks for theatre, film and TV. One of his principal roles these days, though, is as one-third of avant-garde collective Kitchen Motors.

Kitchen Motors is a trio of individuals dedicated to ensuring Reykjavík's music scene remains vibrant and, above all, interesting and challenging. Alongside Johann are visual artist/sound designer Kristin 'Kira Kira' Kristjansdóttir and progressive-jazz guitarist Hilmar Jensson. KM describe their operation as a 'thinktank' that instigates collaborations, produces strange and charming concerts, puts on exhibitions, puts out records, arranges performances and dabbles in all realms of art from chamber operas to films, books to radio shows. Their fundamental goal is to achieve interesting sonic results based on the ideals of experimentation, improvisation and collaboration.

'There is this fantasy of creating the ideal collaboration,' smiled Johann when I met them all in the Grey Kat. 'If you have a favourite saxophone player and a great drummer and have always wondered what they would sound like together, that's where we come in.' In the four years or so since they began, KM have brought together a wealth of Reykjavík's talent together in formations and locations that wouldn't normally have been considered.

At Thule, Johann gave me three CDs in distinctive plastic wallets, one red, one yellow and one green. These discs contained live recordings of a series of collaborations KM organised entitled *Motorlab*. When I listened to them, I was amazed at the contents. By grouping together musicians from the worlds of jazz, hip-hop, rock, punk, hardcore, classical and pop (as well as other artistic realms) and having them all improvise together, the group really had created some intriguing and challenging musical universes.

When I walked into the café, the group were already there. Johann was dressed in a polite combination of rollneck sweater and sensible shoes. Kristin, in contrast, wore loud yellow stockings and carried a Bart Simpson rucksack. She is the group's loveable wild card, with a penchant for building punishing noisescapes with her groups Big Band Brutal (a collaboration with some of the members of Múm) and Minimum Brutal (when the members of Múm aren't around). She also enjoys creating visual and textual fantasies.

'The interesting thing for me,' she explained, 'is that we're all coming from backgrounds which are unfamiliar to each other. Hilmar is coming from jazz, Johann is coming from cinema and theatre and rock music, and I'm more into noise and visual art. It's very interesting for us to get to know these fields and get to know them through each other. We've learned so much from being able to have these windows into each others worlds and to bring people from all of them together to create a fourth element. It's a very deep social experiment in a way, and it continues to be.'

I asked the three of them how come they decided to embark on this most honourable of artistic missions.

'What initially bought us together was the discovery of all these people in different genres but so many of them listening to the same stuff,' explained Hilmar, a suitably serious jazz cat dressed all in black.

Hilmar's solo work as a progressive guitarist has produced some enigmatic work that has been lauded amongst the international jazz community. Icelandic jazz on the whole has yet to make a mark on the world, but people like Hilmar are taking it into experimental territory where the country's stamp can be firmly seen. 'There's this common pile of music that everyone seems into, even though we all have our own fields that we work in. Everyone likes Morton Feldman, or certain new electronica, rock or improvised music and so on. It seemed like such a shame that everyone was working in their own corners.'

KM have no qualms about putting a classical musician with a rapper, or a jazz player with a laptop producer, or maybe all of them together, plus perhaps a poet and some rock guitarists to add extra colour. Megas had told me that highbrow and lowbrow culture mixed well in Iceland. The results of these collaborations are living proof.

KM have also brought their conceptual art to the masses by playing in public spaces and encouraging interaction. A few months ago they came up with a performance called 'Telefonia', where audience members called a voicemail number displayed on a screen with their mobile phones. They left messages on the machine and a piece of specially designed software collected the messages and mixed them up with the ambient sounds in the room. They performed this at Kringlan, Iceland's biggest shopping mall, much to the chagrin of some of the shop owners, whose goods were bouncing around to the heavy basslines KM added to the mix.

'Established musicians in the classical or jazz fields get to do something deeply different from what they are used to doing,' reckoned Hilmar, who studied and played in the USA with many other respected jazz artists. 'Often they just make a living making music, and they probably get bored in that role and need some refreshment. They get excited about us for that very reason. Then there are the younger people who haven't played so much, who were just excited about collaborating with the more experienced people so that they can learn from them. There's curiosity all round.'

'We felt there were a lot of non-active volcanoes here,' interjected Kristin, 'people that were talented and doing good stuff but not really playing live. You'd meet them on the corner and you'd know they were doing interesting things but not doing it in front of anyone, so part of our mission was to provide a forum for people to be heard, an outlet for them to play live. It all grew from this basic feeling of there being something missing, of there being no place where you could go and see these kinds of artists perform. We got people to perform together out of curiosity as much as anything else. We wanted to know what would happen if people from all these angles came together. People actually love it when they get the call from us. Some people stay around waiting for it. It's a small town and the possibilities are limited, really, so when you do this kind of thing you expand the possibilities and break up the boundaries that have been in people's minds.'

I was surprised at Hilmar's last comment. I'd thought Reykjavík to be a naturally collaborative place and not full of people working in their own corners. I'd thought that the closeness of people acted as an artistic as well as social lubricant, that KM had not introduced the concept of collaboration into the community but had merely formalised it. However, it sounded like they'd done a little more than that. Apathy and shyness were still dangers that had to be overcome.

'Scenes in other countries are more compartmentalised than ours,' admitted Johann. 'In other places, people seem to join up with other people who are doing the same things. Clubs do only this or that type of music; labels only do certain types of music. In Iceland, people are forced to be together. Kitchen Motors doesn't stand for a style, and that's out of necessity more than anything as there aren't enough people to form a real big drum 'n' bass scene or whatever. Hence people just do what they can.'

It seemed like Kitchen Motors were determined to add more creative fuel to Iceland's intimate music scene to help it become even more diverse and dynamic. There was no chance of things becoming stagnant with this trio around to prod people into action. Their mission is assisted by the intimate structure of their community.

Hilmar swigged back the last of his coffee. 'The major TV stations have an obligation to cover everything that goes on, not just specific certain things,' he said. 'The newspapers have to as well. This means that every day we get to read about everything that goes on in our environment, whereas in somewhere like the UK you can subscribe to a paper or TV station that just fits your particular lifestyle and you don't have to look elsewhere. This blinkers you from things you don't want to be looking at, but at the same time those things sometimes help you broaden your mind. In music terms, that means that, if you read the album reviews, you won't just get jazz or pop; you'll get reviews of everything. Every little release is reviewed and will maybe also get an interview. If we have a concert coming up, we know we can get an interview in the papers or get on TV by making a telephone call. It's no big deal. Everyone gets a kind of equal exposure. Everyone gets their space.'

'It's definitely a very artistic community, which makes it easier,' commented Johann. 'I think you can always find some family connection to the arts, if not music then the arts generally. Someone's grandfather's brother or something at least has usually published a book of poetry or something. The Icelandic national identity is very much based in literature and storytelling, and it's a great source of pride for Icelanders, this literary heritage. The tradition has seeped into a lot of music as well, as we're all telling stories but with a guitar or with electronic instruments. Maybe you could look at it as an effect of that.'

'I think it all boils down for a desperate search for something we can call our own,' concluded Hilmar. 'That's why all this literature is so prominent in our schools. One of things we have to do at school is recite poetry by heart. Being so small, being so isolated and so few of us, we have to find something that makes us stand out. We have a strong need for independence that still lingers; it's very strong in our community, and it's blended with this quick transition from being a farming and fishing community to being a modern society. There are still so many links to the past.

'My great-grandmother would sit down and tell us stories about her upbringing that her grandparents told her. The link is pretty direct. It's only recently that we see people losing touch with that heritage. Even though our grandparents are pretty young, they're still old enough to remember the way they were, and they were certainly a lot different to the way they were in neighbouring countries. We were so primitive, really. I think it's fundamental in that so many Icelanders have that drive to prove that they're something more than just a bunch of fishermen and gaining acceptance in other places based on their talent. I think it all stems from an inferiority complex, really.'

Here was the 'inferiority complex as a driving force' notion again. It's not a theory limited to Iceland and it's not anything new; it has been used for many small island nations, from England to New Zealand, by analysts wanting to explain how great achievements came to be made by little countries. But there could be something to it.

On the one hand, Icelanders are proud, independent and self-sufficient. They are usually happy to tell visitors about how terrific their environment is, how beautiful the women are, how strong the men are, how they are highly literate, very artistic and technologically proficient. But the first thing that Icelanders often ask visitors is what they think of their country, revealing an underlying sense of insecurity.

However, this double-sided phenomenon is something of which Icelanders are very much aware. On one of their own TV adverts, a foreign visitor is shown arriving in Iceland by plane for the first time. As he has bags checked, and before he has even reached the outside of the airport terminal, a security guy smiles and asks him, 'And how are you enjoying Iceland so far?'

20 Independent People

Up on a stage in Reykjavík University's cinema, Sigur Ros are playing their first hometown concert for a year. Lead singer Jonsi, thin arms poking through a sleeveless top and distinctive quiff pointing skywards, stands solemnly at the front of the stage. He is bathed in a soft glow of light the same colour as the aurora borealis. Slung across his chest is a guitar, which he scrapes slowly with a violin bow to create otherworldly effects. To his right, Georg Holm dabs at his bass with a drumstick and Orri Pall Dyrason brushes his cymbals to cause seismic susurrations. To his left, Kjartan Sveinsson plots out heartfelt chord sequences on a grand piano while at the back of the stage a seated quartet pluck and saw at their strings, adding a sweeping, dramatic momentum to the band's slow-moving dynamic.

The music unfurls gently, building from low hums into immense crescendos that envelope the entire cinema. It pulls the audience gently but helplessly in, persuading us to relinquish our psychological defences and unshackle our emotional restraints. We are used to modern music that offers short, sharp epiphanies; Sigur Ros offer slow, inexorable revelations that tug at our deepest fears and desires. When Jonsi steps up to the microphone and unleashes a voice so supernaturally pure, so effortlessly angelic that all the hope and all the goodness in the world is conjured up, there is no turning back.

Judging by the stunned and slightly tearful expressions on some of the faces around me, I wasn't alone in experiencing the spellbinding effects of Sigur Ros' music. Most of their songs melted fluently into each other, but in the small pauses that occurred, the silence in the auditorium was profound. The only thing to be heard was the soft shuffling of feet and the odd muffled cough or sniff. There was no talking. No whispering. This enhanced the feeling that we were at some kind of church service and that Sigur Ros weren't playing songs; they were singing hymns.

Their music has secured them the status of being the latest sensation to have emerged from Iceland after Björk. The fact that their lives shows are more akin to religious experiences than conventional rock gigs has helped boost their appeal considerably. When their breakthrough second LP, *Agaetis Byrjun*, came out in 2000, the world's media fell over themselves to find superlatives poignant enough to describe the beauty they were hearing. *The Face* magazine called them 'the last great band of the 20th century'; indeed, it's difficult to imagine any other contemporary band that have had so much emotional and spiritual impact on audiences today.

It wasn't just the press who were falling over themselves, either; in New York last year, five people had to be carried out of a Sigur Ros concert on stretchers after fainting – it was a sit-down event. One Icelandic critic claimed their music was so beautiful it made her vomit, and it's no coincidence that the band's song 'Danarfregnir Og Jardarfarir' is based on the radio jingle that accompanies funeral and death announcements on the national radio.

A few weeks before their Reykjavík concert, I met Sigur Ros in London. They had been touring to support the release of their third LP and hadn't spent much time in Reykjavík. London was the only feasible option if I wanted to talk to them. In general, Sigur Ros do not like certain things about the way in which the music industry works. They do not like giving interviews and do what they can to avoid contamination by the standard practices of greed, shallowness and power that are inherent in the business.

It's an attitude that many bands in Iceland share, in fact. Of course, any self-respecting alternative-music scene in any country will uphold values of independence, community and artistic integrity – that's what makes them alternative – but Iceland in particular has always remained relatively isolated from the devious practices of multinationals and huge record companies who see music and musicians as numbers and commodities rather than creative entities. Icelandic artists tend to develop differently to bands elsewhere. They are sometimes naive when it comes to doing business with the outside world, although they have one trait that enables them to survive: independence.

What makes Björk and The Sugarcubes such fantastic role models for pop musicians in Iceland – and the world over – is the fact that they retained a great deal of control over all aspects of their work. Björk especially has insisted on having a say in all of her creative endeavours. This has enabled her to balance global popularity with cutting-edge credibility while other pop stars have been reduced to facile formulas.

Significantly, Björk still works with the label on which she and The Sugarcubes started, the UK-based imprint One Little Indian, which also epitomises the independent ethic. When I tried to get an interview with OLI head man Derek Birkett, I received an email back from the press department saying, 'Sorry, Derek hates interviews.' There was no more negotiation.

Derek's band, Flux Of Pink Indians, were anarcho-punks who delighted in rebelling against the conventional ebbs and flows of the music bizz. They were doubtless drawn to Kukl, The Sugarcubes and Björk because of a similarity of spirit, a will to defy the regime and to blaze their own trails through to the public realm. But even a moralistic man like Birkett was frustrated by the uncompromising behaviour of The 'Cubes. In Martin Aston's book *Björkography*, he commented, 'I have to say the band are fucking impossible to deal with. I love what they are doing, but they are the only band I've ever worked with for whom the band isn't the priority. That's why they all went off and got jobs after the second album. We operate a profit share, but when they made money they'd blow it in ridiculous ways. Like...when they brought out a poetry book which cost £8 [$13/€12] to buy and £18 [$29/€27] to produce.' He added, 'They were adamant that they would rather sell ten records on their own terms than ten million on any other.'

Icelanders are the world's best when it comes to not compromising. And one thing they don't like compromising on is their art, which they often put before commerce. Centuries of isolation and having had to fend for themselves has created a nation as resilient and self-reliant as any other out there. There is a famous adage of an Icelander, 1,000 years ago, who was told that he had to kiss the feet of a king he was visiting. He didn't have a problem with this. He reached down for the royal foot and pulled it up to his mouth, thus kissing the king's foot and pulling him off his throne at the same time. The point is – and it's the same point made in Laxness's *Independent People* – that, while Icelanders respect others, they will never bow to them.

Many bands in Iceland are independent, but Sigur Ros exemplify the ethic of self-sufficiency more than most of their contemporaries. It's easier to do things your own way if you're making tunes in your bedroom and farming out 50 CDs a time. But the status of Sigur Ros means that the decisions they make have much bigger consequences, not just for them but for their record labels, managers, publishing companies, etc. Still, they insist on 100 per cent control over their own music. They direct their own videos. They design their own artwork and have control over their own merchandise. They have licensed their music to the occasional film or commercial, but they have refused many lucrative offers simply on the grounds that they don't like the ad or movie. Albums in stores these days generally come with stickers containing eulogistic soundbites from the press, which help market the product. On their latest CD, entitled '( )' (try putting that into a soundbite), Sigur Ros insisted that these stickers come with an instruction to be removed after purchase.

The band also refuse to be photographed for their albums. Their first two LPs tellingly have baby/foetal themes on the artwork: an ethic of purity is evident not only in Sigur Ros's music but also in their approach to selling themselves.

'We got a request by the big US talk-show host David Letterman to perform on his show a while ago,' said Georg when I asked him to give me an example of their refusal to play anyone else's game. 'He offered us two minutes to play one of our songs, but the song was six minutes. We didn't mind going there and playing, but we wanted to play the whole song. He said he would make us a compromise and we could play for four minutes. But he obviously didn't understand. Our song is six minutes and that's final. You don't go to an art gallery to buy a painting and say to the artist that you really like his painting but you only want to buy this or that part of it. For us, I think, it's all or nothing. If we want to record a whole album in Icelandic, we would do that and no one would have anything to say about it. We just wouldn't sign the contract if we weren't happy. We need to have full artistic control or it's not worth it.'

When I met the band at their hotel in London's Tottenham Court Road, they didn't look like moody, demanding types. Georg was the first to appear in the lobby, looking slightly dazed and confused but amiable and enthusiastic about our meeting. Jonsi came down next, shy but affable. Kjartan was busy with his girlfriend, as it was her birthday, but Orri also joined us as we walked outside of the hotel to look for a decent place to talk.

As we ambled along the raucous streets of London, the trio didn't say much. I got the impression that the towering buildings and frenetic energy of the city was a little overwhelming for them. 'We don't like big cities,' confirmed Georg. 'Every time we come to London, we have to get out after a couple days. It's so crowded. You just feel like an ant or something.' We turned the corner onto Charing Cross Road and Georg let out a short laugh and pointed: 'Perfect!' I followed the direction of his finger and saw a bar called 101. 'The same number as our postcode.'

Unfortunately the bar was noisy and lacked seating space, so we crossed the road to a quieter coffee shop. As soon as we took a seat, the feeling of interview formality overtook us and I felt the band start to tighten up. There were no expectant looks or signs of preparing for a conversation. Instead, the three of them stared at various objects and remained tight-lipped. The famous Icelandic frost needed thawing.

Sigur Ros have been independent since they formed, back in 1994. Then they were just Jonsi, Georg and former drummer Agúst, a trio of friends who had met at school. Eschewing the usual artistic promiscuity of their environment, they made a pact to stick together and not to join any other bands. Later on, they drafted in guitarist Kjartan Sveinsson and Agúst left to follow a career in graphic design. He was later replaced by Orri.

The band's first LP, *Von*, released in 1997, was very experimental, mainly because it was constructed in a rudimentary studio (which they had to paint because they had no money to pay for it) and they mixed it themselves, as they decided that outside influences would interfere too much with their sound. They had never used a mixing desk before, which didn't put them off, obviously, and also explains why *Von* is drowned in a barrage of strange effects.

'The people that we knew in bands were always swapping around when we formed,' said Georg, by far the most loquacious of the group, 'but musically at that time it wasn't as interesting as it is now. There was more of the same thing over and over again with various rock bands. We didn't really know what we wanted when we got together, but we thought there was something there and we wanted to keep it, which is why we made the pact.'

'When we started making music together, we didn't really have any aims or goals,' interjected Jonsï, cupping his hands comfortingly around a cup of calming herbal tea. 'We were and still are just writing something because it kind of connects us. We want to make something, which makes us feel good, and hopefully it will also make some other people feel good, too. If it's successful, then it's a bonus. We have a strong vision of what we want, of what sounds right, of what kind of soundscapes we want and how a song should sound. It's not easy and it maybe takes a long time to get there, but it's about not giving up along the way.

'We have learned that making a record is really hard. We want to concentrate on the vibes and the atmosphere we can create, but the industry is all about money and being successful and making big songs instead of just the music you want. Being from Iceland helps as it keeps us a little bit away from this crap. Iceland seems so far away that people tend to leave us alone.

'At the end of the day, you have to have faith in yourself. We would never compromise our own musical vision and I actually think that's a very Icelandic thing. In Iceland it's almost impossible to be a big pop star because the scene is so small, so it kind of keeps you on the go and keeps everything in perspective.'

The lack of financial motivation, I felt, was one of the driving forces behind the vibrancy and diversity of Iceland's scene. What makes other music scenes become stale and unoriginal is the fact that, as soon as a sound or a style becomes popular, it becomes a valuable commodity and is invested into by larger companies. The big companies use their promotional power to push their music to potentially vast audiences and tend to milk something until it has generated large amounts of cash and the public are sick of it. In Iceland, 'vast' is the last word you'd use to describe the local audience, potentially or realistically, which is why big businesses stay away and perhaps why a sense of purity and innocence pervades much of the island's music.

I asked Jonsi about his lyrics, or rather his lack of them. I had noticed at the concert that his words, like the abstract images on the screen behind him, were unrecognisable yet familiar. The band started out singing in Icelandic. In 1999, they signed to the UK label Fat Cat, but instead of switching to English, like most internationally minded bands, Sigur Ros opted to keep with Icelandic. This was something that even The Sugarcubes conceded, although Björk sings in Icelandic when she performs at home. This is a tad strange when you consider that her Icelandic fans know the lyrics in English only. When asked about this, Björk explained that singing in English to Icelanders would be like talking to her grandmother in a foreign language.

Icelandic lyrics didn't seem to concern Sigur Ros, but they have since found their own way around that issue without compromising. Jonsi sings not in English or Icelandic any more but in another language entirely, a kind of semi-invented tongue that the band and the media have dubbed 'Hopelandish'. Where Megas wanted to bring out the fullest in his glorious, ancient and flexible mother tongue, Sigur Ros have smelted it down and removed its structural complexities to leave just hues, tones and colours.

When I put the question of lyrics and language to Jonsi, there was a long, awkward pause. He kept his head down, avoided eye contact and fiddled with his cup. For a few seconds I was afraid he wasn't going to answer me at all – it wouldn't have been the first time he had refused to answer questions from an interviewer – but a moment or two later he looked up coyly. 'I don't know where they come from,' he said. 'They have just always been there. When we write songs, I also put down vocal lines. Maybe Orri will do a drum beat and I play a guitar line or something and then I just put in the vocal lines without words. I've always written like that. Even when I used to play guitar on my own I would play the vocal melody and the guitar melody together.

'These two elements always go together for me when I'm writing songs, not one or the other afterwards. I was in a band before where we used to write the songs and then add the lyrics afterwards, but then we started to feel that we were just adding lyrics out of tradition, just because everyone else did it. Now it just feels right to work as we do now. We don't want to add anything else just for the sake of it. When we released *Agaetis Byrjun*, it was all in Icelandic except one song and it was nice to see people's reaction all around the world. They seemed to understand or at least get some meaning without understanding Icelandic. I think it's nicer that way.'

So where did the term 'Hopelandish' come from? 'The tag came about because we were joking around amongst ourselves on the first album. The title of the first album means "Hope", and there was a song on it with the same name, which I sang without any lyrics. That's when we called them "Hopelandish". Then some journalist found out and it went from there. I thought the lyrics we did write were quite passionate, actually, when we did them. There were a lot of word games, too, because every word in Icelandic has two or three meanings, so one sentence can mean a hell of a lot. This makes it really hard to translate, on the other hand. I don't miss the lyric writing though.' He shoots me a wry grin. 'I'm not really good with words. They are so hard to use as they're so easily misunderstood, whereas music is just so honest and straight to the point. I'm easy to be misunderstood, and this is why we don't do many interviews. We prefer to let the music speak for itself.'

The job of trying to protect music in an industry driven to disposability is not an easy one. I wondered how a label managed to market a band that abhors the idea of marketing. During our interview, Sigur Ros had spoken highly of the boss of Fat Cat, Dave Cawley, who told me that the band had signed to them – and MCA in America – simply because they had offered them the most artistic freedom. According to Georg, they all sat on his bed one day, smoking cigarettes and drinking beer, while they worked out a deal.

'We all fell in love with Dave and we still think he's a brilliant man,' said Georg. 'He loves music, and that's it; he doesn't care about business at all, really. He doesn't even like to talk to us about it as he just gets frustrated about these things, like we do. Fat Cat understands that without our independence we can't do anything, and they understand that what we do artistically is very much our thing. If someone else starts messing it and changing it, it stops being our thing. Even now, if we're having a bad day or something's happened, we have a little chat with Dave and it's sorted.'

Fat Cat seems a likely choice of label for Sigur Ros. It too is known for being stubbornly resistant to industry forces and has also had links to Iceland for some time. The label grew out of a record shop of the same name in Covent Garden that specialised in leftfield and experimental music. In the early '90s, the store was a favourite haunt of Björk and The Sugarcubes, and when the shop's founders, Dave Cawley and Alex Knight, decided to start a label, they went to One Little Indian and set themselves up as a subsidiary.

Fat Cat Records left OLI a few years ago to go fully independent. Although the company has had a relatively short life as a label, it has championed a flood of brave new sounds, from the avant-garde/brutalism of Japanese noise assassin Merzbow to the adventurous meanderings of US multi-instrumentalists Mice Parade. They have also done what very few labels do these days: put out compilations of demo tracks they've been sent.

I contacted Dave in his hometown of Brighton to find out more about their relationship with Iceland and their mission to retain artistic integrity in an increasingly dehumanised corporate environment.

'I first went to Iceland when Kiddi, the owner of the shop Hljómalind, bought me and a friend out to DJ,' recalled Dave. 'He used to buy records from the old Fat Cat store for his shop, and we had a mutual love of underground music and championing new, unheard sounds. We played some good parties out there, including a youth club disco. It was hilarious to watch kids chase each other around to the sounds of Carl Craig. We got thrown off the decks at the Moon Club because I don't think we were cutting it for the Saturday-night drunks.

'I first heard Sigur Ros when they were playing on the same bill as Gus Gus and Grindverk [another Fat Cat project] at the first Airwaves. Alex [Knight] and myself were DJing that night and we were both blown away by how good we thought they were. Alex made an effort to go and see them over the next few days, and it just went from there.'

I asked Dave whether he had felt particularly inspired or impressed by Sigur Ros's independent streak.

'I think we connect on many things,' he said. 'I just know how talented they all are and get excited about the thought of helping them find new ways to be creative and express themselves. We want as many people as possible to hear and see their art without them feeling compromised in any way. This of course is a really hard path to walk, being that money and record-industry bullshit is always involved, but I feel you at least have to try. We try not to just follow the same well-worn path and take our own course on things. It's hard when you're working with other people who are used to things happening a certain way, but you just have to break those barriers and old formulas down.

'It's not an easy task, and sometimes we slip up, but we try our best. On one level, musically, we put out exactly what we want and don't pander to fashion or trying to have "hits" and big sellers; we just follow our heart and our ears and try to champion music we all love and talk about music that needs to have a voice. Iceland has its fair share of industry clichés, just like anywhere else; it's just that the outside world is not subjected to them. But Icelanders do like to do things their own way and can seem to be pretty stubborn about taking advice, which is fair enough. You have to learn by your mistakes and victories, otherwise you're not being yourself.'

The English, too, are well known for being stubborn and self-reliant when they want to be. Obviously this was one of the bonding factors between Sigur Ros and Fat Cat. Although the UK has one of the largest commercial music scenes in the world – and is also a global leader in dishing out vapid hyperbole – Fat Cat are part of a network of underground resistors who try to elevate music to its rightful place as a respected art form rather than a commodity.

After Sigur Ros signed with Fat Cat, Jonsi handed Dave a tape of his own favourite Icelandic band, Múm. 'It was a tape with some demos of the tracks they were making for their first album, and we fell instantly in love with their sound,' recalled Dave. 'The other thing that hit me about them was the beautiful packaging the tape had.' Dave signed them immediately.

The band, comprising twin sisters Gyda and Kristin Anna Valtysdóttir (both of whom are classically trained), Orvar Smarason (Kristin's boyfriend) and Gunnar Örn Tynes, throw themselves into many areas of art, from music to theatre, film and literature. In 2001 they composed a soundtrack to Eisenstein's cult silent film *The Battleship Potemkin*. Both of their full LP releases to date, *Yesterday Was Dramatic, Today Is Ok* on Thule in 2000 and *Finally We Are No One* through Smekkleysa in Iceland and Fat Cat in the UK in 2002, defy categorisation.

Where Sigur Ros create expansive universes that swirl with earthy spirituality, Múm construct coruscating micro-worlds from insect-click nanobeats, intricate live instrumentation and melodious warmth, topped off with the awkward beauty and childlike innocence of the girls' voices. Their live shows are as transfixing as Sigur Ros's, but in a different way.

The four of them are constantly on the move, jumping from instrument to instrument, tinkering with computers, cellos, glockenspiels, accordions, melodicas, harmonicas, kazoos, trumpets, bass guitars and anything else they can blow, scrape, tap, press, pluck and tinker with to add more colour and depth to their fairytale music. The slight builds of the pretty twins doesn't prevent them heaving accordions or bass guitars up onto their shoulders.

Múm don't like interviews, either, commenting, 'You should just get a CD with the articles on us so that people can hear the music for themselves.' Although they have done them in the past, they agreed to meet me only because I didn't represent a magazine or newspaper. 'It's a waste of time,' grumbled Gunnar. 'They often don't have any interest in your music and ask the same questions all the time. They don't enjoy it and we don't, so what's the point?'

I promised that I wouldn't ask them about elves, the effects of nature on their music or any of the other questions that they find irritating or pointless. Still, only three members of the band arrived at Café Mokka at the appointed hour: Gyda was not there. No explanation was given and I didn't ask for one. Gunni waltzed in first, kitted out casually in slightly billowing jeans, sneakers and baseball cap. Next was Orvar, a handsome blonde beanpole with ruffled hair set above his head like a sail. Then Kristin and her little brother. We squashed around a table as the smell of waffles and jam wafted over us.

Orvar and Gunnar, who had previously been in a Pixies-influenced guitar band called Andheri, formed Múm in 1998. The duo had put out a limited edition ten-inch single as Múm, but when they were invited to help write the theatre music for a play called *The Nature Opera* they teamed up with Gyda and Kristin, who happened to be in the theatre band.

It wasn't until 1999 that the band performed for the first time as a quartet, and their first single release carried the snappy title 'Assholes In Apesuits'. They followed this with their debut LP, released in Iceland on Christmas Day 1999. Following more theatre and film-score commissions, the band then put out a remix LP called *Please Smile My Nose Bleed* on Morr Music and eventually signed to Fat Cat, through whom they released their second LP, *Finally We Are No One*. Two of the songs from the album were created to be listened to underwater, taken from a set of tunes the band recorded for a one-off concert in a swimming pool, where they played the music through a special underwater speaker. The rest of the album was recorded in a remote lighthouse in the Westfjords.

'When I listen to the last album, I am reminded of the place where we recorded it,' said Orvar, focusing his large eyes on me. 'It was a very barren place. We were in the lightkeeper's cottage rather than the actual lighthouse. They're selling land in the country for really cheap now, as no one wants to live there, especially in the Westfjords. In the daytime we made music, listened to the national radio, walked, read, looked at birds. It was very simple and nice and it made a difference to our music.

'I think the new album is different; it's freer, less sweaty. Foreign people would like to hear something mystical, of course, but what kind of influence our environment has had on us, we can't say. It made a change from the first one, that's all I know. For the first one we had been promised a good studio, but they were literally building it around us, so we ended up working in a dark, sweaty room with just a computer and a microphone. We had to leave every couple of hours.'

I told them that their live performance reminded me of some kind of theatre performance due to the non-stop motion.

'It doesn't feel theatrical when we're on stage,' said Orvar quietly. 'We didn't interact with the audience a lot; we just did our thing. We've done other gigs where everyone was closer, but everything seemed very far away at the theatre. We're not used to that. We're used to more closeness and intimacy. We tend to just play and fit everything in wherever we can. When we rehearse, we just walk around the room trying these different things out on various instruments and toys we have around, and that's pretty much what we do on stage, too. We end up playing most of the instruments ourselves on the recordings, but now and again we get someone to come in and play for us on the more complicated ones.'

Delving headfirst into a world of strange instruments without being tutored in playing them seemed particularly Icelandic, although the girls' classical training would obviously have helped. 'You only need to understand each instrument slightly to tap into the process of writing music,' explained Gunnar, exhaling smoke coolly from the side of his mouth. 'Playing what you write yourself is much easier than playing someone else's music. We play what we know and express ourselves on the instrument we are comfortable with. We don't just say, "Oh, let's play this or that." It's more about connecting yourself to the instrument or the music. We gradually become a little bit better each time, as if we were learning, but it's just not done in a traditional way, that's all.'

'We play them in a very simple way,' assured Kristin, who had until then been quietly drawing on some paper with her brother. 'Sometimes we [girls] play the bass without really being able to. We just kind of make it up. Playing a really simple line on another instrument can be really challenging in that sense, but it shows that you don't have to know how to play an instrument to be able to play music. It's like when the singer sounds out of tune; it's something she shouldn't be doing, technically, but if it sounds good, it's okay by us.

'I was dragged into this attitude. Playing a melodica wasn't really what I expected to be doing when I was getting classically trained on piano. It can make you freak out when you're doing your own thing because you're brainwashed by music school not to just make things up like that. I realised I had been in a cage and that we hadn't had too many options at classical school. I liked playing piano but we couldn't play what we wanted, so this was my alternative. I realised that starting a band can be fun, and that's the best way. If you have that attitude, often the good things come afterwards. We don't have a lot of musical pressure here, so people are not scared of trying new things out. There isn't such a barrier between genres here. People will happily mess around and do whatever they want to.'

I asked the band what their primary influences were for their music.

'Sometime you feel influences from music, but really influences can come from everything,' said Orvar. 'They can come from things you see and things you appreciate. Sometimes they are incredibly subtle, something just like this…' He stirred his latte slowly with a spoon. We were all hypnotised for a few moments by the swirling, milky universe he had created. 'After a while, you just get this special feeling. It can be just seeing something outside on the street. That's the thing that people get from our music sometimes, the unexplained things. It's beyond words, which is probably why we choose music as an art form and why we don't like talking about it. Sometime in the future we will make an impact with our music, but I don't think we have yet.'

'I remember watching this art exhibition about masturbation,' smirked Gunnar. 'I went with my school and it was in this tiny room in a gallery. It was just a TV screen showing some guy sitting there, masturbating. The vision was really shocking. It was so personal. I didn't get angry, exactly, but I was really shocked. Then we realised this man was a genius because his work had had so much impact on us. There was lots of other art at the exhibition, but only his left an impression. In the end, it didn't matter what he was doing; I just remember the effect he had on my day, and I realised how good it was.

'People don't get our music in the same way, sometimes. They think it's just some fairy stuff with nothing behind it. I don't really know the point of what we do, myself. Sometimes I feel like there's some storytelling, but then there's no point pretending if you don't know. I know our music is simple, but it has a lot of detail. When we make songs, it's more like sculpting or painting. We build layers and then spend time scraping bits off. People say that it's just nice sounds, but it's not. We have some contrast and contradictions, and that's what makes things move somehow. It's all about releasing feelings or energy.'

Feelings. Energy. Movement. These are the things that fuel Iceland's music scene. And these are the things that individuals making music in Iceland are reluctant to compromise. There had to be a correlation between the non-compromising standards of Iceland and the fact that it produced music that was consistently original. What would happen, I wondered, if money were introduced into the music scene in Iceland? Would that mess everything up? Would it then be a scene just like any other? As it happened, this was a question that many people were starting to ask themselves as the issue of funding began to leak onto the agenda.

21 The Future

On their website, Sigur Ros make this statement: 'We want to change music forever.' It's not a casual statement, by any means. When I met up with them in London, I asked them what they meant by it.

'When I wrote that, I meant we wanted to change the way people look at music,' Georg told me, 'and the way that the record industry thinks about it. The whole attitude towards music these days is that it's not an art, that it's just part of popular culture. But it doesn't have to be just pop culture. Going to modern gigs can be just as important as going to a classical concert.

'In Iceland, they are two different things. The government and the city of Reykjavík give symphony orchestras and classical musicians a lot of funding and venues to play in. Musicians like us don't get anything. Nothing at all. The only thing we get is a "Go away". We need in Iceland a 2,000-capacity venue with a good sound system in which anyone can play. They keep building sports stadiums that are always empty, even though music concerts in Iceland are always full. They're wasting money on the wrong things, and I think we are going to campaign against it.'

It is difficult to say how many people come to Iceland because of its music. I managed to get hold of the tourist statistics for the last 30 years and they yielded some interesting results. For ten years, between 1972 and 1983, there was a steady influx of around 65,000–75,000 tourists per year. From 1984, around the time that Iceland's alternative music scene was beginning to get some international exposure, the stasis finally began to break.

By 1986, when Kukl were at the peak of their popularity, the figures doubled to around 120,000. Then, in 1989–90, when The Sugarcubes were busy knocking the world sideways, there were almost 150,000 visitors to Iceland.

The latest figures show that the country now pulls in around 300,000 tourists per year and those statistics are still continually increasing.

It would be folly to suggest that music has been the biggest reason for people coming to Iceland. Tourists obviously come for a variety of reasons: for its incredible nature, its remoteness, its refreshing lack of commerce, its friendly and hospitable people, its naturally heated pools, its infamous nightlife, its endless summer sun and the potential to have a decent snowball fight. But it would be equally dumb to say that music hasn't played a major role. If nothing else, the countless interviews with Björk, The Sugarcubes, Sigur Ros, Gus Gus, Trabant, Múm, Kitchen Motors, Minus and other bands have given an insight into Iceland's other myriad charms. It's no coincidence that the official Icelandic Tourist Board website has a whole section reserved especially for Björk – for many people, Björk is still the only thing that springs to mind when the country's name is brought up.

Some people come specifically for the music, as is the case with Airwaves. A few days after the event, I dropped in to meet the main organiser, Thorsteinn Stephensen, a red-haired man with the kind of motivated and professional demeanour that is rare amongst Iceland's casual music scene. Thorsteinn has been one of the main promoters in Iceland for many years, putting on a host of one-off club nights and events through his company, Mr Destiny. Airwaves is his biggest project.

Thorsteinn showed me briefly around his busy production office, located in 101, and then led me into a waiting area with sofa, chairs and a coffee table. 'All the things we do here at Mr Destiny revolve around the appeal of Reykjavík,' he explained, taking a seat and gesturing for me to do the same. 'If we were to compete on a price level with the promoters from other countries that are throwing in offers for the bands that come over here, we wouldn't stand a chance with a single one of them, so we try to keep good contacts with the people that have been here at previous editions, and they help us to get the bands we want. We work with people who want to come here.'

Airwaves is set up with an emphasis on local acts to draw in people from abroad. Most other music festivals across the world do the opposite – draw in local crowds by bringing in foreign talent. But then, not many other cities have such a dynamic music scene. Out of the 70 or so bands that played Airwaves this year, only around nine were from overseas. What did the local crowds feel about that?

'The bands at Airwaves do play in Reykjavík and around Iceland a lot,' admitted Thorsteinn. 'If you like Trabant, for example, and you're from Reykjavík, the chances are that you've probably seen them three times this year already. But people come because they like the overall concept. They get to see some foreign bands and also they get to be a part of the party. It's not every day that an event like this happens in Iceland. It's the same thing for the bands – when they play Airwaves, it's slightly different to when they play elsewhere. The atmosphere is very different.'

Although it's a relatively young event, Airwaves has had its fair share of success stories. Sigur Ros and Fat Cat hooked up through the festival (although Einar Örn had already been cultivating links between the two parties). Quarashi got signed after playing the event. Thule ended up with some distribution deals. Bands like The Funerals and Apparat Organ Quartet got the chance to carry on the buzz that their albums had already created with some kicking live shows. But Thorsteinn warns the bands that play Airwaves that the festival is by no means an easy road to success.

'It's a long process,' he explained. 'You meet someone that likes you and your band, then you start talking and maybe a year or two later something is happening. It's not an overnight thing. The big problem we face is that there is no follow-up procedure after Airwaves. Industry people come and, if they see someone they like, there isn't anyone they can talk to other than the band members because the band are not signed and usually don't have managers except themselves. If they are signed to any of the labels here, they generally don't know how to deal with international deals, as they're only used to selling records on the local market. There is no support system. There's a lot more music than outlets.

'We try to give them good advice, of course. A lot of them get in touch with me and I try and give them contacts and maybe act as a go-between now and again. But they need some kind of manager if they're going to do anything like that. They need someone to guide them through the process more carefully, to do their demos, their videos, arrange tours and meetings. After the festival, it's always the same thing – the guys come and sit in here and say, "Okay, we met this guy from a record label and what are we gonna do now?" But there's no one to do the work for them or help them out.'

Although Icelandic bands are usually hip to most of the music game, they can be naive to some aspects of it. Their local scene is slightly removed from the processes that power the global pop machine, and it can often come as a shock for some to discover how things work in other countries. Several bands I spoke to had been horrified at their experiences of the outside industry and had shirked away from it completely.

The local bands who play Airwaves do so for free, but Thorsteinn and his team promote them in various ways. They produce, for example, a comprehensive (and amusing) festival brochure for visitors, a promotional CD, which is given out to industry people, and a website that has information and contact details for all the acts. I had noticed on the artist profiles that the 'management contact' was usually one of the band's cellphone numbers.

'Thorsteinn,' I asked, leaning forward on the sofa, 'what do the Airwaves organisers get out of this?'

'For the first three years of the event, we lost money,' he replied. 'This year we'll be lucky to break even. But it opens up the door to the whole industry for us. All the booking agencies know about it now, so if I want to get the Red Hot Chili Peppers or someone to Iceland, I have a much better chance, being the promoter of Airwaves. This year

I think we will break even. We can't really expand because Reykjavík is too small and we just don't have the infrastructure to cope with more people over a weekend. So we just keep going and keep the opportunities coming for the bands. We need to do this, or in the end everyone is going to lose interest. It's important for us to have a very small success story after each event.

'I'm noticing this year that people are talking about Airwaves now. People feel they want to be on top form and are very excited about it. It's raising people's games. People are now realising that they have a possibility of going somewhere outside of Iceland. Even if you get a distribution deal in Germany or something, it can make a whole lot of difference for you. Selling an extra 3,000 records can make or break you because everyone is losing money being a musician in Iceland.'

It seemed quite simple, the way that Thorsteinn was putting it, and I was sure that most artists in Iceland realised that they could do well if they just pushed themselves a little. But many of them just didn't seem overly bothered, or didn't really know how to go about it. Thorsteinn would probably make a good manager, but, like everyone else, he's too busy to do it. But don't Icelandic musicians have a fantastic role model in Björk? Only a decade ago, she proved that a combination of musical talent, an open-minded perspective on the world and a spot of self-promotion could achieve great things.

'Björk's story has influenced a lot of people, both in a good way and in a bad way,' said Thorsteinn. 'In a good way in the sense that people try and go along their own road instead of someone else's, but in a bad way because people don't realise that Björk is a stand-alone phenomenon. It's not only that she's a phenomenon in the world of Icelandic musicians, but she is a phenomenon in the world of pop music. There's hardly anyone who has the same kind of general respect all over and sells millions of records and is a pop idol. A lot of people don't realise that they may have to compromise somewhere along the way. They think they can do it the same way. They only have a small part of the picture and, to be fair, most of them only have a small part of the talent that she has.'

Part of Björk's success certainly came from her cultivating connections outside Iceland. Most of the people she has worked with since the break up of The Sugarcubes have been non-Icelanders. The lesson here perhaps is that these external links help to provide the relevant international exposure. But how can artists make those connections in the first place without any money? They can't earn much at home, and the labels in Iceland don't have the budgets to help with marketing abroad. Airwaves has done a grand job of bringing the international market to the bands, but what other options are there?

Edda Publishing Ltd is a relatively new company which was formed from the merger of the two leading book publishers in Iceland, Mal Og Menning and Vaka-Helgafell. Where Skífan hold the monopoly on the music industry, Edda is by far the biggest book-publishing company in Iceland. In 2000, Edda established a music department that today runs three record-label imprints: Ómi for jazz and classical music, FD for adult pop and world music and Hitt for alternative, rock, metal, hip-hop and electronic. The main goal of the company is to publish quality music by Icelandic artists and boost Icelandic music internationally – a goal that has been attempted before by many and managed by few.

To date, Edda's appearance on the market looks promising. Hitt have already signed Úlpa, Singapore Sling, Fídel, Ensími, and Klink among others – all great, very individual, high-calibre acts. I dropped into their plush offices on the outskirts of town to meet the music director and A&R chief, Skúli Helgason.

Skúli used to have his own show on the national radio and seems to have an instinctive passion for music. 'We have a project called Futurity,' he explained. 'It's a platform that I raised last year as a reaction to the state of the music business in Iceland now. The revenues for music generally are diminishing all over the world. There is a 15–20 per cent decrease in sales globally, due in part to the effect of the Internet. What this means in a tiny market like Iceland's is that companies become more wary of signing new bands that have no history of selling thousands of copies. This in turn means that the momentum we've been having for the last few years in terms of producing interesting bands could die if we're not careful.

'In a reaction to this, I decided to produce this Futurity project, which invests in unsigned bands that haven't released any records and gives them their first break. We've been getting support from sponsors, which has given us the chance to put a little more money into recordings and PR for these very promising bands. The scene here now is better than it was even ten years ago, in terms of international exposure. We have Airwaves now every October, which is an important platform and shows we have something here that we can focus on and work with.'

To enable Futurity, Edda have teamed up with Músiktilraunir, the local 'Battle Of The Bands' competition, which has been running in Reykjavík for a few years. The tournament is funded by an agency run by the local city government and judged by music critics and a representative from each of the major record labels in Iceland. The winner of each competition has traditionally been awarded studio time to record a demo, but then has still had to find a deal. Smekkleysa have often provided the winners with a contract but have never guaranteed anything.

Edda have put their money where their mouth is and have offered the winners record deals regardless of the nature of the bands that win. The most recent winner was Búdrýgindi, a group of 15-year-old punk rockers. Edda kept their word and signed them. Búdrýgindi accordingly received a nomination for the Icelandic Music Awards in 2002 as the brightest hope of the year, along with rap act Afkvaemi Gudanna, another band who are part of Futurity.

'We're taking quite a risk, of course, as you never know beforehand what happens, but that is necessary if we want to build up new talents in the industry,' said Skúli. 'Our motto to begin with was to put out anything other than mainstream pop, as that's what Skífan have been focusing on. Our Hitt label is the main focus internationally at the moment, as it has the biggest potential in terms of getting licensing or distribution deals abroad and probably has the most concise catalogue so far. But our categories are never so clear-cut. This is Iceland, so it's always a little vague, which admittedly doesn't help in trying to market material. People want nice easy genres to put everything in, but a lot of the music from here crosses these genres and falls between the cracks of different styles, which is why it's more original.'

I asked Skúli what he thought needed to happen over the next few years for the scene to keep churning out renegade sounds.

'We have a very strange situation here at the moment,' he said. 'Everyone agrees that music has been the essential factor of putting Iceland on the map internationally, but we are still working with minimum support from the government. We don't have any concise efforts to export Icelandic music. The government just hasn't seen the light. They put the occasional grant into some tours for Icelandic bands, but the support is both sporadic and unfocused.

'I am expecting, though, that we will have some success with the government in the coming years. The music business has been lobbying the Icelandic government for a special export fund that might help artists and their publishers fund marketing projects, tours, etc, in foreign markets. That would eventually bring more revenues to the government in terms of taxes and tourism and will function in the same way as the Icelandic Film Fund, whose annual budget has increased fivefold due to a recent agreement with the Ministry of Culture and Education. It means that they can produce two or three times the amount of Icelandic films per year. We are only asking for the same governmental support for the music industry first and foremost to be able to assist artists that have potential in foreign markets.'

I felt ambivalent towards the idea of funding for Icelandic bands. On the one hand, I felt that the bands needed all the support they could get, but on the other that the Icelandic music scene was much more interesting and produced good results at least partly because money wasn't an incentive. If cash were introduced into the equation, wouldn't it affect the artistic output of the bands?

Just before I was set to leave Iceland, Bibbi Curver sent me an email telling me he was in New York doing some production work. He mentioned that his friend Hanna Björk Valsdóttir was preparing an academic thesis on the Icelandic music scene at New York University and had been researching issues of funding.

I contacted her and she told me that in 1996 the Ministry of Industry and Commerce in Iceland put together a group of people to research the possibilities of creating a music industry that would export Icelandic music 'in the same way that, say, fish or lamb is exported'. Apparently, the Minister of Industry and Commerce was interested, but the Ministry of Culture intervened to get the issue passed to their department, as it was a cultural issue. Since then nothing has happened.

Getting Icelandic music some attention abroad was one thing. Exporting it like fish or lamb was quite another. The image was horrendous. I couldn't see many Icelandic bands wanting to perceive their work as an export product or wanting to be treated like commodities. Would this mean that the only bands that would apply for funding would be the types who didn't care about compromising their work? Then what kind of Icelandic music would the rest of the world be subjected to? Obviously the funding issue needed some serious thought and discussion.

When I spoke to Einar Örn, he was against the idea of a music fund because he felt it could create rivalry and fights in a scene that currently enjoys a lot of cohesion. He believed that it was probably best that bands like Sigur Ros or Múm were left alone to make their music and develop their sound; then there was something interesting to put on the international market. Smekkleysa (which is still today run by The Sugarcubes and Ási) believe more in focusing on their local scene first, then pushing for international exposure if it feels right. Their low budget means they are reliant on their vast network of friends and similarly minded *Independent People*.

It's certainly true that money can corrupt, but perhaps with the correct set-up a fund could distribute finances fairly. The bands were more than capable of making first-class music already; they just wanted a bit of a push rather than a hefty cash injection. But how can people tell who is more deserving for any available funds?

'I think bands that have received good reviews abroad or been invited to play at shows or festivals outside Iceland should receive funding to do so,' said Hanna Björk. 'They should be given the opportunity to follow up on any interest abroad. All other arts are funded in Iceland, so it is easy to argue that so should music (other than classical, which already receives funding). But they also have to realise that more funding does not necessarily mean better music or more opportunities to export bands. I'm more afraid of what will happen if they will start exporting crappy Icelandic music. Possibly the international scene will lose interest in it and the reputation of Icelandic music could be damaged. The hype will fade. And then what?'

I certainly couldn't imagine many bands accepting funding if they had to compromise in any way. Hannah also mentioned that the hardcore/metal/punk scene in Iceland was planning a mini-festival called 'Fuck Airwaves – This Is Hardcore', 'not because they have anything against Airwaves, just because they think it is too commercial and they don't want to be part of that. That is a very Icelandic attitude that will not change.'

Funding or no funding, the scene has showed no signs of slowing down over the last couple of years, with more bands than ever ready to conquer the world. Music, after all, is a form of communication, a way of connecting with the rest of the world, of being a part of the game instead of feeling left out. Icelanders don't have a huge musical legacy, but they have excelled in the last two decades at sending good vibrations around the globe.

After centuries of not having the means to make music, Icelanders have been making up for it big-time. This is just the beginning for them. They are bringing a freshness and innocence to music-making that many other countries have lost, which is what makes many of them sound so exciting. Icelanders will continue to create good music whether people give them money to do so or not, of that much I was sure.

Back in the Airwaves office, Thorsteinn concluded our conversation with these words: 'It doesn't matter what kind of management or organisation people try to put in place over here. It will always be chaos.' He was smiling as he said it. And so he should. Chaos has never sounded so good.

Appendix 1

Sounds, Tastes, Places

TEN VENUES FOR THE SOUND OF ICELAND

ASTRO
Austurstræti 22
Reykjavík
552-9222
A swish bar with 'proper' club nights and DJs from abroad.

CLUB 22
Laugavegur 22
Reykjavík
551-5522
Hip and popular with a particularly grungy vibe in the upstairs section
at the weekend.

GAUKUR Á STÖNG
22 Tryggvagata
Reykjavík
551-1556
A premier live venue with something different every night of the week.

KAFFIBARRIN
Bergstadastræti 1
Reykjavík
551-1588
Packed at the weekends, this is Reykjavík's hippest bar/café.

LEIKHÚKJALLARINN
Hverfisgata 19
Reykjavík
551-9636
Located on the ground floor of the National Theatre. A popular club which is regularly updated in décor and often features good live music.

PRIKID
Bankistræti 12
Reykjavík
551-3366
Very popular with hip-hop crowds at the weekend.

REX BAR
Austurstræti 9
Reykjavík
551-9111
A trendy bar in the heart of the city serving copious amounts of house, funk, jazz and soul.

SIRKUS
Klapparstíg 31
Reykjavík
511-8022
Quirky, late-night bar popular with artists and trendies. A real leftfield venue.

SKUGGABARRIN
Pósthússtræti 11
Reykjavík
551-1440
Next to Hótel Borg, this club is popular with young people and offers the latest dance sounds.

SÓLON
Bankistræti 7a
Reykjavík
562-3232
A café/restaurant by day; the bar and dance floor upstairs is quite commercial but great fun at the weekends.

TEN VENUES FOR THE TASTE OF ICELAND

ASKUR
Sudurlan∂sbraut 4
Reykjavík
553-8550
In addition to the soup-and-salad bar, Askur specialises in fish and lamb and puts on a hearty all-you-can-eat Sunday steak buffet.

HÓTEL GEYSIR
Haukadalur
486-8915
The menu at the hotel's restaurant includes various Icelandic specialities, such as rye bread baked in the heat of geothermal springs, and *skyr* (a delicious yoghurt-like food made from skimmed milk) with cream.

LÆKJARBREKKA
Bankastræti 2
Reykjavík
551-4430
Excellent international cuisine and a quiet, cosy atmosphere.

KAFFI DUUS
Duusgata 10
Keflavík
421-7080
Situated in the heart of Keflavík with beautiful views over the harbour
and up to the mountains, and a menu that has something for everyone.

KAFFI LIST
Laugavegur 20a
Reykjavík
562-5059
A Spanish-style bar serving tapas and Mediterranean meals.

KAFFI MOKKA
Skólavörðustígur 3a
Reykjavík
552-1174
The oldest coffee house in Reykjavík, great for jam and waffles.

KAFFI MÚLA
Hallarmúli
Reykjavík
553-7737
Quality home-cooked Icelandic cuisine.

NÆSTU GRÖSUM
Laugavegur 20b
Reykjavík
552-8410
A 'One-Woman Vegetarian Restaurant' serving substantial vegetarian
meals at reasonable prices.

SKÓLABRÚ
Reykjavík
562-4455
Situated just off Austurvöllur, Skólabrú is famous for its fish specialities.

VALHÖLL
Thingvellir National Park
Thingvellir
482-2622
The restaurant at this hotel serves fresh trout from Thingvellir Lake, smoked or broiled, and delicious *pönnukökur* (crêpes filled with whipped cream and jam).

TEN VENUES FOR THE ICELAND EXPERIENCE

AKUREYRI
The capital of the north and Iceland's second biggest city, with 15,000 inhabitants. While managing to retain its small town appeal, Akureyri boasts all a large town has to offer and lies within easy reach of a host of interesting places, including Goðafoss, Dettifoss, Hrísey and Grímsey, an island bisecting the Arctic Circle

THE ÁRNI MAGNÚSSON INSTITUTE
Arnagardur
V/Sudurgata
Reykjavík
525-4010
Contains the Icelandic manuscripts that were returned to the people of Iceland between 1971 and 1997, after being kept for centuries in Denmark.

THE CULTURE HOUSE
Hverfisgata 15
Reykjavík
545-1400

Houses fascinating cultural and historical exhibitions detailing Iceland's rich heritage. Particular attention is paid to the Settlement and discoveries of the Vikings, and their lasting influence on Iceland today.

GEYSIR
The area surrounding Geysir is a great place to visit while travelling around the southern part of Iceland. The place has various kinds of services and entertainment to offer, simply adding to the attraction's natural beauty.

GULLFOSS
The 'Golden Waterfall' is Iceland's most famous waterfall, and one of the natural wonders of the world. It is located in the mighty glacial River Hvita ('White River'), just a few kilometres from the world-famous Geysir. The enormous white glacial cascade drops 32m (35 yards) into a narrow canyon, which is 70m (76 yards) deep and 2.5km (1½ miles) long. Its spectacular two-tiered cataract hangs in the air like fine drizzle, forming a rainbow in the sunlight.

HALLGRÍMUR'S CHURCH (HALLGRÍMSKIRKJA)
Skólavörðustígur
Reykjavík
551-0745
The inspiration for Hallgrímskirkja, a rocket-shaped church in Reykjavík, came from a stair-step effect, which occurs when water seeps into and separates porous rocks.

VOLCANO SHOW
The Red Rock Cinema
Hellusund 6a
Reykjavík
This two-hour programme shown at the Red Rock Cinema is a fascinating visual demonstration featuring a collection of stunning videos made by Villi Knudsen.

REYKJAVÍK ART MUSEUM – HAFNARHUS
Tryggvagata 17
Reykjavík
590-1200
The six halls house exhibitions from the museum's general collections, as well as from the Erró Collection, which is one of the prides of the Hafnarhus. In addition, other Icelandic and international art exhibitions are a regular feature of the museum's programme.

THINGVELLIR
The meeting-place of Iceland's ancient parliament (the Althing) was called Thingvellir ('Parliament Plains'), where representatives journeyed once a year to elect leaders, argue cases and settle disputes. Today, Thingvellir National Park remains the ultimate symbol of Iceland's independence and unity, a landscape inseparable from the national soul.

WESTFJORDS
A majestic landscape with fjord after fjord, towering above shore and sea, the Westfjords are an ideal place for hikers and all nature lovers, in summer and winter alike. But for all the intensity and variety of the landscape, perhaps the most enchanting attraction is the peace, quiet and endless calm.

Appendix 2

Hotels, Getting There, Getting Around

SOME HOTELS IN ICELAND

GISTIHEIMILIð BORGARTÚN
Borgartún 34
Reykjavík
511-1500
A popular Reykjavík guesthouse. Rooms are comfortable and breakfast included.

GAMLA GISTIHÚSð
Mánagata 5
Ísafjörður
456-4146
Situated in the Westfjords and close to the town centre, this is an historic and picturesque hotel with extremely reasonable rates.

GISTIHEIMILIð SVALA
Skólavörðustígur 30
Reykjavík
562-3650
Another centrally located hotel situated in quiet, attractive surroundings.

GISTIHEIMILIð 10
Laugavegur 101
Reykjavík
562-6101
Centrally located and within easy reach of the city's plentiful attractions.

HÓTEL ESJA
Suðurlandsbruat 2
Reykjavík
505-0900
An eight-minute bus ride away from downtown Reykjavík, the hotel boasts stunning views of Mount Esja.

HÓTEL FRÓN
Klapparstíg 35a
Reykjavík
511-4666
Located in the heart of Reykjavík, this new hotel is only a few minutes' walk from the National Theatre and a host of cafés, restaurants, art galleries and museums.

HÓTEL KEFLAVÍK
Vatnsnesvegi 12
Keflavík
420-7000
A first-class hotel in the heart of Keflavík town and only a five-minute drive from Keflavík International Airport.

HÓTEL VIK
Vik 870
Klettsvegur
487-1230
An attractive hotel, beautifully situated beneath the Vikurhamrar cliffs.

GETTING THERE

BY AIR

Icelandair (505-0700) flies between Keflavík International Airport (the airport for Reykjavík) and Glasgow, London, Paris, Frankfurt, Hamburg, Berlin, Amsterdam, Milan, Zürich, Barcelona, Madrid, Copenhagen, Stockholm and Oslo. In the summer season, Icelandair also flies daily between Keflavík and New York JFK, Washington, Boston and Minneapolis.

BY SEA

It is possible to travel between Scotland and Iceland by ferry. This takes more time, but offers the possibility of bringing your own vehicle. For more information contact P&O Scottish Ferries (01224 572615).

GETTING AROUND

BUS

Long-distance buses use the BSÍ terminal (552-2300) at Vatnsmýrarvegur 10. There are daily services in the summer months, or connections between Reykjavík and Akureyri, Mývatn, Skaftafell, Höfn, Akranes, Borgarnes, Reykholt and Reykjanes.

Reykjavík has an excellent bus system (551-2700), which operates from 7am (10am on Sunday) until midnight. On weekdays, they run at 20-minute intervals until 7pm; on weekends and evenings, buses run every half-hour.

TAXI

The best of Reykjavík is all within walking distance. Given the relatively high cost of local taxis (around £50/$90/€83 for a 40-minute ride from the airport), they are best used only when cheaper and efficient bus services are not available.

BICYCLE

As Reykjavík is such a spacious city, sightseeing by bicycle is popular. Good cycle paths are clearly marked on city maps but are not signposted. Bicycles may be hired from Borgarhjól (551-5653).

Bibliography

ASTON, Martin: *Björkography* (Simon & Schuster, 1996)

DAVIES, Norman: *Europe: A History* (Oxford University Press, 1996)

JÓNSSON, Darrell, HJALMARSSON, Gunnar and WAYMAN, Robert: *A Complete History Of Icelandic Music: Ancient And Punk* (22nd-Century Totems Publication, 1992)

KARLSSON, Gunnar and KRISTJANSSON, Jonas: *Iceland And Its Manuscripts* (Stofnun Árna Magnússonar, 1989)

KERSHAW, Ian: *Hitler: 1936–1945: Nemesis* (WW Norton & Company, 2000)

LAXNESS, Halldór: *Independent People* (Vintage, 1997)

NIELSEN, Svend: *Stability In Musical Improvisation: A Repertoire Of Icelandic Epic Songs* (Forlaget Kragen Kobenhavn, 1982)

ROSENBLAD, Esbjörn and SIGURDARDÓTTIR-ROSENBLAD, Rakel: *Iceland From Past To Present* (Mal Og Menning, 1993)

SIGURDSON, Gisli and JOHANSSON, Sigurjon: *Vikings And The New World* (The Culture House, 2000)

STURLUSON, Snorri (translated by Anthony Faulkes): *Edda* (Everyman Paperback Classics, 1987)

YATES, Anna: *Viking Discovery Of America* (Iceland Review, 2000)

Index

A Bleikum Nattkjolum (album) 163
Act of Union, 1918 132
Afkvaemi Gudanna 274
Agust, Daniel 222
Agust (former drummer, Sigur Ros) 257–8
Airwaves Festival 8–24, 134, 191, 193, 212, 262, 269–72, 273, 277
  origin of 11
  signings resulting from 270–1
Aki (bassist, Men In Black) 149, 152–4, 156
Akranes 143, 152
Akureyri 40, 46, 150
Albarn, Damon 21
alcohol, regulation 19–20
aliens 117
alliteration 76
Almond, Marc 247
alphabet 16
Althing 57, 69, 72, 97, 132, 133
aluminium 151

America, Viking discovery 65, 66, 69–70
Andersen, Steindór 72–9, 82, 84, 110
Andheri 264
Angels Of The Universe (film) 145, 168–9
animal husbandry 42
L'Anse aux Meadows 70
Aphex Twin 17
Apparat Organ Quartet 11, 219, 223, 235, 246–7, 270
Arason, Jon 27
archaeology, Viking site in North America 69–70
Ari The Learned's Book of Icelanders 65, 97
Arnarson, Eidur 208–10
Arnason, Ingolfur 56, 57
Árni Magnússon Institute 28, 64–5
art, Norse myths in 98–9
Asatru 72, 83, 88, 94, 97, 101, 102–8, 112
Aston, Martin 255

aurora borealis 7–8, 120
Austurvöllur (Reykjavík) 131–2, 134–5
Avary, Alex 236

Bad Taste (see *Smekkleysa*)
Baldursson, Siggtryggur 188, 191, 195
Barrelhouse Blackie 136
'Battle of the Bands' 80, 274
The Battleship Potemkin (film) 263
Beatles, The 136, 140
Beatmakers, The 222
Beatniks, The 136
beer 20
Beinteinsson, Sveinbjörn 72–3, 74–6, 97, 168
Benediktsson, Einar Örn 14, 173, 184–6, 188–90, 192–9, 270, 276
Big Band Brutal 244, 248
Biogen 17–18, 235–6
Birkett, Derek 198–9, 255

Björk 19, 23, 91, 146, 162, 173–4, 186, 188–90, 232
Dancer In The Dark 169, 189
early career 200
fame 11, 204
influence of *rimur* on 29
as national symbol 269
and nature 121, 122
and rave music 233
as role model 255, 272–3
singing in Icelandic 259
solo career 201–2
with The Sugarcubes 173, 194, 198
bjorliki 20
Black And White (magazine) 170
Blackalicious 223
Blackwell, Otis 164
Blazroca (see *Eyvindarson, Erpur*)
Blondous 150, 152
blot (pagan ritual) 104–8
Blue Lagoon 125
Bodies, The 171
books, publishing 62
Borg, Hotel (Reykjavík) 135, 172, 175
Brain Police 140–1
Breiðholt 30–1, 90
Britain
Cod Wars 196–7
influence on Icelandic music 136, 171, 175, 178, 184

invasion of Iceland 1940 133
Norse influence 55–6
Bruni BB 173
Brynjölfsson, Bjarni 205–6
Buckmaster (Gus Gus) 222, 223, 234, 235
Budardal 139
Búdrygindi 274
buses 227
Buzzcocks, The 185

Canada 69
cannabis 90–2
Carnegie Arts Awards 82
Celtic roots 155–6
chanting, *rimur* 72–4, 78–9
chart, record 209
Cheren, Mel 234
chess 244–5
Chesterton, GK 101
Chic 211
Children Of Nature (film) 169
Christianity 27, 61, 79, 94, 97, 102–3, 114
Christmas children 79
cinema 169
City Hall (Reykjavík) 210
clairvoyants 113
climate 9
17th- and 18th-century changes in 27
Cod Wars 196–7
Coldplay 134

Coleman, Ornette 184
Columbus, Christopher 66, 69
Cooper, Lindsay 184
Coppola, Francis Ford 169
country music 51–3
cowboys 51, 54
Crass 188–9
Crawley, Dave 261–3
creation myth 94–6, 102
crime rate 8, 88
culture, traditional 49–50
Curver, Bibbi 14–15, 192, 275

Dagur 216–17
Dancer In The Dark (film) 169, 189
dancing, historic ban on 38
Datar 156
dating 23
Davidsson, Olafur 77
Debut (Björk) 201
Delphi 90
demos, locally produced 245–7
Denmark, rule in Iceland 27, 131–2
Didda 168, 210
Diddi Fiddla 29–38, 57
Disappointments, The (see *Vonbrigdi*)
discothèques 235
Disney, Walt 233

Dome Church 26
Domkirkja (Reykjavík) 135
Draught (Bragi's poems) 197
dreams 113–14, 117–18
drugs 90–2
drunkenness 148, 154, 158
Dublin 56
dwarves 95, 109, 111, 115
Dylan, Bob 159, 160, 163, 165
Dyrason, Orri Pall 253

Earth (Gus Gus vocalist) 223
Edda Publishing Ltd 273–4
Eddas 61, 71, 75, 96, 99, 101–2
Eden 59
Egertsson, Thorsteinn (Stenni) 136–9, 156–7, 160
Egill's Saga 72
Egilsstadir 149, 152, 158
Ego 171, 175
Eidur (12 Tonar) 244
808 State 201
Einar (manager, Men In Black) 149–53
Einoma 17
Eirik the Red, King 65, 69
Eiríksson, Eyvindur P 85–8

Eiríksson, Leifur 66, 68–9
Eiríksson, Magnús 139–40, 142–4, 160
Eldon, Thor 19, 189, 190, 194, 201, 204
electronic music 234–5
Elf School 117
elves 58–9, 68, 95, 109–15, 117–19
energy, natural generation of 120–1
Eno, Brian 170
Ensími 273
Epaves Bay, Newfoundland 69–70
Erlingsson, Friðrik 197
Erlingsson, Runar 175
Esja (mountain) 41, 43
export, of music 276–7
The Eye (Kukl) 189
Eyvindarson, Erpur 82–7
Eyvindarson, Eyjolfur (see *Sesar A*)

fairy stories 111
Falkinn (record store) 185
The Fall 185, 187, 188
fame 203–6, 209–10, 214
famine 27
Fan Houtens Koko 189, 201
Faroe Islands 56
Fassbinder, Rainer Werner 222
Fat Cat (label) 259, 261–4, 270

Fatboy Slim 223
Feminist Improvising Group 184
festivals
    Airwaves 8–24, 134, 191, 193, 212, 262, 269–72, 273
    country music 51, 53
Reykjavík Arts Festival 75
Reykjavík Film Festival 169
fiddla 26, 29, 36–7
Fídel 205, 273
fifth song 29
fights 153–4
Film Society 169
fimmundar söngur 29, 37
fishing industry 176, 181, 196–7
Fjelsted, Stoney 224–5
fjords 40
Flateyjarbok (Book Of The Island Of Flatey) 65
Flowers 138–9
Flux Of Pink Indians 188, 190, 255
folk music 28, 36–8, 39, 79, 135
folk tales 99
food 59, 106, 191
football 155
fortune-tellers 113, 116
Friðriksson, Friðrik Thor 51, 74, 117, 168–74, 184, 189
Frikki (guitarist, Purrkur Pillnikk/Sugarcubes) 195

funding, of music 276–7
Funerals, The 11, 18, 134, 219, 235, 270
Futurity project 273–4

Gaelic settlers 56, 155–6
Gaukur Á Stöng 62
gay scene 211, 213–14
Generation X 178
Georg (Sigur Ros) 256–8, 261, 268
Germany
    occupation of Denmark, World War II 132
    plans to occupy Iceland, World War II 132–3
Gerrekson, Jon 27
Geysir 58, 59
geysirs 35, 58, 59
ghosts, belief in 112–15, 117
Gísladóttir, Ragnhildur 145
Gislason, Vidar 'Viddi' Hakon 159, 218–22
Gling Glo (Björk) 200
gnomes 111
gods, Norse 56, 88, 94–7, 99, 100, 102–4, 107–8
Golden Circle tour 58–60
Goldie 236
Gorbachev, Mikhail 197
Götterdammerung (opera) 100
government support for music industry 275

Gramm (record label) 186, 198, 243
Grand Rokk 12–15, 18, 89
Greenland
    discovery of 69
    Viking settlement 65
    Vikings disappear from 9
    wife-swapping 23
Grey Kat (café) 183, 189, 247
Grimm, the Brothers 99
Grindverk 262
Grondal, Thorvaldur 'Doddi' 218–22
Grylurnar 172
Gudmundsdóttir, Gudrun 25–6, 28–9, 39
Guitar Islancio 137
Gullfoss (waterfall) 58, 59–60, 151
Gunnarsson, Runar 156
Gunnell, Terry 62, 68, 113
Gus Gus 11, 24, 222–3, 232, 262

Haddi G Haralds 136
Hafnarfjördur 73, 110
Hakonarson, King of Norway 72
Halfdan the Wide-Reaching 55
Halldarson, Björgvin 207
Hallgrímskirkja (Reykjavík) 15, 65–6, 241

Hallgrímsson, Jónas 160
Ham 211, 218, 247
Harold Fairhair, King of Norway 8, 55
Hartley, Hal 169
Hauksdóttir, Hildur 151
Heath, Edward 196
Heida 14
Heimaey 33–5
Heimskringla (saga) 72
Helgarsson, Jon 165
Helgason, Skúli 273–5
Here Today, Tomorrow, Next Week (The Sugarcubes) 200
hidden people 109–19
Hilmarsson, Hilmar Örn 74–9, 81–3, 86, 88, 109–10, 122, 161–2, 170, 173, 187
Himmler, Heinrich 100
hip-hop 80, 82–3, 85, 87, 91, 224, 225, 233
history 26–8
Hitler, Adolf 100, 166, 180
Hitt (record label) 273–4
The Hives 223
Hjartason, Hallbjörn 51–4
Hjlorleifur 56
Hljómar 136–9, 154, 207
Holm, George 253
Hólmavík 41, 45
Homegenic (Björk) 121
homosexuality 210, 211, 213–14

Hooper, Nellee 201
'Hopelandish' 259–60
horses 42
hot pools 125
hot springs 35, 58
house music 234
Hrafnkell (see *Kelli*)
humpback whales 229,
231–2
Húsavík 245
Hvita, River 60

Ice T 81, 85
Iceland
    economy 12
    history 26–8
    origin of name 8
    population 12
    tourism 268–9, 275
    in World War II 132–3,
    135
Iceland Tourist Board 269
Icelandic Broadcasting
    Corporation 207
Icelandic Cowboys (film)
51
Iðnó 191–2
Iggy Pop 178
Ilo 122, 235
independence
    declaration of 57–8
    movement for 131–2
Independent People 47–8,
256
inferiority complex,
    national 193, 252

Ingi, Jormundur 97–8,
    101–4, 107, 112–14
Internet 234
Írafár 149
Ireland, Viking raids 56
Ísafjörður 40, 110, 245
Ivor the Boneless 55
Izzard, Eddie 93–4

Jakobsson, Agust 217
James, Richard D 17
Jamieson, Lewis 223
Japis (hi-fi store) 243
Jazz Awakening 184
Jensson, Hilmar 247,
    248–52
Johannes (12 Tonar) 242–6
Johannesson, Olafur 196
Johannesson, Larus 242–5
Johansson, Johann 211,
    246–51
John, Elton 213
Jonsi (lead singer, Men In
    Black) 149, 153–6
Jonsi (lead singer, Sigur
    Ros) 75, 253, 257–60,
    263
Jonsson, Ásmundur 170,
    178, 182–8, 195, 198,
    243–4, 276
Jonsson, Sigurdur (see
    Diddi Fiddla)
*Journey To The Centre Of
    The Earth* (J Verne) 143
Julie (friend) 40, 44–5
Kaffibarrin 21–2, 223

Kanada 219
Kaninus, Kippi 74, 245
Karlsdóttir, Hofi 197
Keflvík air base 52, 122,
    133–4, 136, 140, 160,
    171
Kelli (guitarist, Men In
    Black) 149, 150, 153,
    155–7
kennings 78, 96
Ketilsdóttir, Asa 40,
    45–50, 74, 79, 151
Killing Joke 188
Kinks, The 140
Kira Kira 30, 245, 247–50
Kitchen Motors 30, 211,
    245, 247–50
Kjartansson, Ragnar
    ('Raggi') 218–22
KK 232
Klink 14, 273
Knight, Alex 261–2
Kókóstré Og Hvítir Mávar
    (film) 147
Kormakur, Baltasar 21–4,
    204
Kringlan (shopping mall)
    249
Kristinn, Gudlaugur 188
Kristjansdóttir, Kristin (see
    Kira Kira)
Krummi (lead singer,
    Minus) 215
Kukl 72, 188–90, 191–2,
    194–5, 197, 200, 255,
    269

Kvartett O Jonson Og
   Gronji 219
kvöldvaka tradition 78

Landmannalaugur 122–4
landwights 109, 112–13,
   119
langspil 26, 29, 36–8
language 16, 80, 87, 165,
   259
Laugavegur (Reykjavík)
   12–13
Laugavegur trail 122–30
Law Rock 57, 60
Law Speakers 57, 60, 72, 97
Laxness, Halldór 47–8,
   62–3, 86, 159, 163–5,
   189, 196, 256
Laxness, Halldór Jr 62–3,
   224
Leaves, The 11, 134, 219
Led Zeppelin 138
Legowitz, Herb (see
   Buckmaster)
Letterman, David 256
Lhooq 11, 247
life after death 119
Life's Too Good (The
   Sugarcubes) 198
Lindisfarne 55
literature 49, 60–2, 251
Lord Of The Rings
   (Tolkien) 101
Lundey 227
Radio Luxembourg 175,
   183

Lydon, John 199

McCartney, Paul 139
MacDonald, George 101
McDonald's 13
MacLaren, Malcolm 146
Magnússon, Árni 64–5,
   132
Magnússon, Finnur 98
Magnússon, Jakob F
   145–7
Mal Og Menning
   (bookstore) 25
Manchester United 243
Mannakorn 140, 207
Marshal Plan 135
Massey, Graham 201
Maus 14, 134
Með allt á hreinu (film)
   147
media 206, 246
Medusa 170, 188, 189,
   195, 201
Megas 74, 81, 134,
   159–67, 177, 180, 188,
   207, 249, 259
Melax, Einar 188, 190,
   195
Men In Black 149, 152–8
Merzbow 261
metaphors 78
Mezzoforte 194
Mice Parade 261
Michael, George 213
Millionaires, The 212
Minimum Brutal 248

Ministry of Culture and
   Education 275–6
Ministry of Industry and
   Commerce 276
minke whales 230–1
Minus 14, 122, 134, 207,
   215
Miss World competition
   197
Mist Famine 27
Mogenson, Birgir 188
Mokka Café (Reykjavík)
   18, 264
Moon Club (Reykjavík)
   234, 262
Móri 89–92, 177–8, 224
Morthens, Bubbi 134,
   137, 149, 155, 171,
   172–81, 184–6, 188,
   207
Morthens, Haukur 137
Morthens, Tolli 171
Mr Destiny 269
Múm 11, 122, 235, 238,
   244, 248, 263–7, 276
music, Icelandic
   British influence on
   136, 171, 175, 178,
   184
   business 14–15, 144,
   273–4
   export of 276–7
   government support
   275
   influence of nature on
   121–2

international reputation of 193–202
in Reykjavík 215–26
as tourist attraction 268–9
US influence on 135–7, 147, 171, 184
(see also under type)
musical instruments 26, 29, 36–8
Iceland's historical lack of 25–6
music revolution 131, 134–47
Músiktilraunir 80, 274
Mussolini, Benito 180
mythology, Norse 61, 78, 94–7, 101, 121
in art 98–9
hidden people in 111–12
and Nazi Party 100–1

names 22
NASA (nightclub) 134
NASA, practise for moon landings 122
National Library of Iceland 28, 97
National Museum 36–7
National Theatre 36, 145, 183, 188
nationalism 131
NATO 133
Nattura 35, 144, 166
nature, Icelanders'

relationship with 119, 120–1
Nazi Party 100–1, 132
Neubauten, Einstürzende 190
Newfoundland 70
Nibelungenlied (German saga) 96, 99
Nielsdóttir, Sigridur 238–41, 245
nightlife 19–21, 215
Njal's Saga 60–1, 77, 169
Nobel Prize 47, 62, 63, 196
northern lights (see aurora borealis)
Northern Lights Communications 206–7
Norway, rule in Iceland 26–7, 132

obituaries 203
'Odin's Raven Magic' (concert) 75
Olafsson, Bragi (bassist, The Sugarcubes/poet) 194–5, 197, 199–200, 201
Olafsson, Egill 145–7, 198
Olafsson, Hossi 224
Older Edda 75, 96, 99, 101–2
One Cube Per Head (The Sugarcubes) 197
One Little Indian (record label) 255, 261
organs 26

Orishas 89
Orri (drummer, Sigur Ros) 257, 260
Orridge, Genesis P 187
Orvar (Múm) 238
Oskar, Paul 209–14
outlawry 60
Ozy 235

pagan society (see Asatru)
paganism 86, 88, 94, 97, 98, 102–8, 113
Palli (drummer, Men In Black) 149
Papar 149
Parker, Evan 184
parliament, first democratic 57, 69
Parliament House (Reykjavík) 64, 132
Peel, John 183
penises, museum of 66–9
Perlan (revolving restaurant, Reykjavík) 65–6
permissive society 23
Petursdóttir, Linda 197
Petursson, Hallgrím 65
Phallological Museum (Reykjavík) 66–9
Picasso, Pablo 194
Pink Floyd 32
poetry 49, 62
Eddic 61, 71, 75, 96, 99, 101
rimur 72–9
skaldik 71–2, 96

Pollock, Michael and Daniel 175, 178, 184, 185–6
pollution 120–1
Ponik 140
Pop In Reykjavík (documentary) 217
pop stars 203–14
Presley, Elvis 163
press 206
prohibition 20
Prose Edda (see *Snorri's Edda*)
Psychic TV 187
Puffin Island (see *Lundey*)
puffins 227–8
punk music 72, 74, 134, 146, 159, 162, 168–81, 184–90, 220–1
American 182, 184
British 182, 184
Purrkur Pillnikk 72, 173, 186–9, 191, 194–5, 198

Quarashi 11, 215, 219, 224, 270

Raddir (album) 39–40
radio stations 150, 154, 206–7, 246
BBC 183
country music 51, 53
Radio Caroline 183
Radio Luxembourg 175, 183

Rás 1 183, 184
Radiohead 134
rap music 80–92
rave music 233–4, 236
Reagan, Ronald 197
rebel music 159
record shops, Reykjavík 140–1, 141–6
recording studios 138, 146
Reformation, the 27
restaurants 191
rettir (animal round-up) 42
Reykholt 72
101 Reykjavík 21–4
Reykjavík
architecture 241–2
Arts Festival 75
crime rate 8
101 District 9, 142, 143
Film Festival 169
growth of 64
mellow atmosphere 12
music in 215–26
origin of name 57
peace summit 1986 197
population 13
rough side to 90
rhyme
battles 87
structures 75–6
rimur 29, 37, 46, 72–9, 168
links with rap 81–4
society 77
Rin (music store) 140–3

Der Ring Des Nibelungen (opera cycle) 99–100
rock 'n' roll revolution 131, 134–47, 171, 174
rockers 136
Rokha Rokha 189
Rokk I Reykjavík (film) 146, 169–74, 182, 186, 217, 221, 235, 244
Rolling Stones, The 134
Romanticism 99, 131–2
Rosenberg (club) 234
Royal Academy of Fine Arts, Copenhagen 98–9
Ruffage Crew 236
Runar (bassist, Hljomar) 138
Russia, Reykjavík peace summit 1986 197
Ruxpin 235

Sacred Ash 93–4, 96, 105
sagas 60–2, 71–2
and discovery of America 69
versified by poets 78
Saian Supa Crew 89
Salin Hans Jons Mins 149
Samuelson, Gudjon 66
Schmidt, Peter 170
Seen And Heard (magazine) 204–6
self-expression in Icelandic punk music 182

service stations 50
Sesar A 82–7, 84–9, 134,
    215, 224
Sex Pistols, The 146, 178,
    185
sexuality 23
sheep 42
Sigga, Anna 233
Siggi Johnnie 136
Sigmarsson, Jon Pall 197
Sigur Ros 11, 75, 122,
    192, 209, 253–63, 268,
    270, 276
    influence of *rimur* on
    29, 72–3
Sigurdsson, Jon 131–2
Sigurdsson, Njal 37
Sigurjon (Ham) 211
Sigurjonsson, Havar 246
Sindri (Björk's son) 19,
    121, 201
Singapore Sling 14, 134,
    215–16, 218, 273
singing 26
Sirkus (Reykjavík) 215–16
Sjalfsfroun 172
Sjon (poet) 170, 184, 189,
    244
Skagaströnd 50–3
skalds 71, 96
Skarphedinsson, Magnús
    116–19
Skífan (record label) 162,
    207–8, 233, 273, 274
Skólavörðustígur
    (Reykjavík) 241

Skulason, Thorhallur
    'Thor' 232–7
Slow Blow 216, 219
Smarason, Orvar 263–6
Smekkleysa (record label)
    14, 39, 170, 182, 192,
    197, 200, 232, 236,
    243, 263, 274, 276
Smith, Mark E 187
Snafu 10–11
Snorri's Edda 71, 75, 96,
    101–2
Snow White And The
    Seven Dwarves 228
Solvadóttir, Kristín J 233
Solvi (Quarashi) 224–5
songs, Old Icelandic 26,
    28–9, 37, 46, 49, 79
Spassky/Fischer chess
    championship 196
Spilverk Thjodanna 163
spirits, belief in 112–13, 116
Spiritual Society 116–18
Spor (record label) 207
Spotlight 16–17
SS, runic symbol 100
Stalin, Josef 166
Starr, Ringo 147
Stefansdóttir, Erla 109–12,
    114–16, 119
Stefansson, Magnús 174–5
Stephensen, Magnús 79
Stephensen, Thorsteinn
    269–72, 277–8
*The Storm In The Wake Of
    The Calm* (Sesar A) 85

strip clubs 228
Strokkur 59
'Strongest Man In The
    World' competition 197
Stuð (Ham) 211
Studio Stemma 36
Stuðmenn 144–7, 154,
    163, 188, 198, 207
Sturlungsaga 83
Sturluson, Snorri 71–2, 75
Sugarcubes, The 11, 14,
    72–3, 146, 173, 182,
    191–2, 225, 255, 269
    formation of 194–5,
    197–200
    end of 201
SUM 170
Sumbel (pagan ritual) 107
supermarkets 30–1
supernatural, the 116–19
Surtsey 35, 96
Svala 207
Sveinsson, Atli Heimir 242
Sveinsson, Kjartan 253,
    257–8
Sveitaball concerts 82,
    148–50, 153–8, 206
Swarez, Omar 224–5
Sykarmolarnir (see
    Sugarcubes, The)
Syn TV 207

T World 222
Tacitus 71
Tappi Tikarrass 173, 186,
    188, 200

taxis 227
tectonic plates 57–8
television 206–7, 250–1
Theyr 72, 74, 170, 171, 173, 188, 191
Thingvellir 57, 60, 132
Thordarson, Gunnar 136–40, 148, 207
Thordur (Asa's son) 41, 45–7
Thor's hammers 101–2
Thorsmork 122, 129
Thorsteinsson, Bjarni 28–9, 36–7, 39
Thukl 198
Thule Musik 17, 218, 232–7, 246, 248, 270
Thule's (long poems) 46
Tjorn 191, 210
Todmobile 208
Toggi (bassist, Singapore Sling) 218
Tolkien, JRR 101
Torrini, Emiliana 222
tourism 268–9, 275
Trabant 11, 217–22, 235, 270
trekking 122–30
Trier, Lars von 169
trolls 68, 95, 109
Trubrot 136, 139, 144, 166, 207
12 Tonar 241–2
Tynes, Gunnar Örn 263–7

Ubbi 55
UFOs 117
Úlpa 273
United States
  influence on Icelandic music 135–7, 147, 171, 184
  Reykjavík peace summit 1986 197
  troops in Iceland 133
unknown artists 245
Utangardsmenn 174–5, 185–6
Unun 219
US Free Jazz movement 184

vagrants 191
Valsdóttir, Hanna Björk 275–7
Valtysdóttir, Gyda 263, 264
Valtysdóttir, Kristin 263–4, 266
Vath, Sven 236
Vatnsendahverfi 29
Veira, Biggi (Gus Gus) 222, 223–4
Velvet Underground, The 134, 183
Verne, Jules 143
Vidalin 9, 12, 18
Videy 143
Vikings
  discovery of America 65, 66, 69–70

gods 56, 88, 94–7, 99, 100, 107–8
  history recorded in sagas 61–2
  language 16
  raids 55–6
  settle in Iceland 8–9, 55–7
Vinland 69, 70
Vinyl 134, 215
Vivid Brain 83
volcanic erruptions 120
  1784-5 27
  Heimaey 33–5
Völsunga Saga 99
Völuspá (see creation myth)
Vonbrigdi 168, 170

Wagner, Richard 99–100
Westfjords 40, 42, 87, 151, 264–5
Westman Islands 33–5, 57, 96
whale-watching 228–32
whaling 230
White, Tommi 235
Wilde, Oscar 70
Wiligut, Karl Maria 100
World War II 132, 135

XXX Rottweiler 80–2, 85, 224

York 55